Evidence for Bible Wisdom

Sam Kneller

Published by Sam Kneller, 2021.

Also by Sam Kneller

The Explanation
Inventory of the Universe
Audit of the Universe
Audit of Humankind
Origin of the Universe
Origin of Humankind
Origin of Woman
Agony of Humankind and the Antidote

Standalone
Evidence for Bible Wisdom

Watch for more at https://www.TheExplanation.com.

Table of Contents

This book is dedicated to seekers with open minds.

The only position I can take is to admit with humility that "I don't know." What I express regarding beliefs is only my opinion according to my spiritual connection with God, but I may be interpreting things wrong. I'm always open to new interpretations. I love learning.

A wise man once said, "Teach me that which I see not"

Proprietorship

EVIDENCE FOR BIBLE WISDOM

First edition. July 30, 2021.

Written by Sam Kneller.

Website: TheExplanation.com[2]

Join The Explanation Newsletter[3]

1. https://theexplanation.com/
2. https://theexplanation.com
3. https://theexplanation.com/subscribe/

Biblical Hebrew

Think about this:

Can you fully understand a document in a translated language?

If you haven't experienced the pleasure or hassle of learning and speaking a second language, you might not be able to do justice to the answer to that question.

My native language is English. I've now lived in France for the better part of my life, the last 40 years, since 1978. My French is pretty good, but I would in no way say I'm a French speaker. When it comes to colloquialisms, jokes, plays-on-words, and slang, leave me out. I don't know when to laugh, and I don't know what to answer. The simple evidence is I don't understand what people are saying. Yes, I speak French, but to say I master the language like a French person would be a gross exaggeration.

There's a lot of Bible-arguing going on based on one's native language. It's like fighting over bricks and forgetting about the house of which each one is a part.

Let me give you one example here. The original Biblical Hebrew word *commandment*, as in the *Ten Commandments,* is translated with over 50 (that's right, fifty) different English words by the translators of the King James Bible version. Amazing when you think about it. In Hebrew, this word *commandment* has only three letters: dbr. How can you get 50 different English translations from that?

I won't get into a detailed explanation here of why this is so, but it should make you stop and think: How can this be?

If you start learning the Hebrew alphabet and vocabulary today, it'll take you forever to learn how to read and study the original language, and you'll still never be able to grasp the nuances of all those 50 shades of *commandment.*

That's why the **Annex** is devoted to *Unlock Bible Meaning with 7 Keys to Master Biblical Hebrew.* There you'll find a summary of the free, acclaimed online course, including all the freely accessible online Bible tools at UnlockBibleMeaning.com[1] for your study–even if you don't possess a Bible.

Let me say openly. You've never seen a method like this that will help you unlock Bible meaning so quickly and easily.

Hundreds of students have followed this course. Here are just a few reviews:

> The instructor was precise in his delivery and how to check the meaning. It was really helpful to learn the power of the Hebrew behind the words. Phyllis C.
>
> It's a SHAME! after many Bible translations, most people still have a blurred "understanding" of what Sam Kneller so elegantly clarifies in this course. See it for yourself. This is a MUST TAKE COURSE for everyone, no matter their beliefs (or non-beliefs) are. Hey!, if you can't really comprehend the CLIMAX in 'the first story'... forget PhDs. Thanks! Jesse C.
>
> He explains in a very slow and concise manner. Allowing a student to keep up with the lesson. JoAnne J.

1. https://unlockbiblemeaning.com

An excellent lesson on word meanings and how to study them. It is not always what we think or what we have been taught. We need to understand what the authors meant when they wrote this, knowing that the entire was inspired by God for teaching us, correcting us, etc. (2 Timothy 3:16-17). Marcel R.

I think it is well organized and very informative. I thought the instructor could be a little more enthusiastic but I think that might just be because everyone who teaches now acts as they have just won the lottery. Overall, I think it was great. Myrna P.

For someone so old willing to take his time to share his knowledge with the world, he deserves 5 stars. If the video you find it too long, doesn't matter, pay attention to the materials he has to share. In fact, the aim of this course is for him to enable you to self-learn independently. Shung J.

C'est concis, bien documenté, bien présenté verbalement. C'est vraiment superbe à tout points de vue. Bravo Viviane L.

I found this course to give a clear and useful example of using the website and tools mentioned. Need to be open-minded and willing to explore the Bible, rather than dogmatic, to get the most from this course. Thanks, Sam, for introducing me to these tools. I look forward to further explorations. Robin S.

This book uses this Bible study method to give you additional understanding of the Bible and its instruction.

Housekeeping Issues

Because of the nature and especially the extent of this subject, it is impossible to include every aspect and every answer to each point. For this reason, links are peppered throughout this work. They lead to freely available articles at TheExplanation.com. They form the heart of The Explanation series of books expounding God's plan for humankind.

Hence the need for an internet connection as you read. That said, the subject is understandable without navigating to those links. All links were correct at the time of publication. If you find an issue, let me know at sam@theexplanation.com Thanks in advance.

You will find all the Bible tools to follow along with this e-book at https://UnlockBibleMeaning.com

- The entire King James Bible online. Search by book, chapter, verse, or word or phrase.

- The Interlinear Bible with Biblical Hebrew, English, phonetics, Strong's numbers and link to his annotation and list of KJV translations

- Strong's Bible Concordance for each Hebrew and Greek word with its annotation and list of KJV translations

- The Hebrew-Greek Concordance. Also called Englishman's concordance. It gathers together all the Bible verses with the same original Biblical Hebrew and Greek words so you can study the various usages of each word in context.

At the end of some chapters of this book, there are ideas for *Further Study*. I suggest these exercises for your enrichment to dig for Bible Study gems to enhance your understanding. You can skip these and move on or simply peruse the content. Some comments complement the information in the chapter.

Please note that for ease of reading I have modified some of the old English presentation. As an example, *do* and *does* replace do*est*, and *thee, thy* become *you, your*. There is absolutely no modification of any vocabulary in the King James quotations throughout this book. Even the English spelling is maintained.

If you've come across this book for the first time, then please know it is part of a much larger work: *The Explanation* series. See all the books[1].

www.TheExplanation.com/books

Join The Explanation Newsletter[2] no spam, total privacy. Receive Sam's latest blog post notifications and information about *The Explanation.*

---

1. https://theexplanation.com/books
2. https://theexplanation.com/subscribe/

Preface

God's Word, Biggest Dilemma & Challenge of Your Life. Why? To believe or not... the basis of your thinking and convictions is at stake.

The opening statement of God's Word poses a preposterous predicament. "In the beginning God created the heaven and the earth" Is it foolish? Outrageous? Nonsensical? Or not? John, the Apostle, links this statement directly to Jesus Christ, "In the beginning was the Word, and the Word was with God, and the Word was God. The same was in the beginning with God. All things were made by him; and without him was not any thing made that was made. In him was life; and the life was the light of men" (John 1:1-4). God's Word relates Christ to Creation. Can you believe in one and not the other? Is there wiggle room for interpretation of God's Word?

Theology

I follow several theological and Bible-oriented groups on the Internet. One of the main punching balls of Bible commentators, whether pro or con, is taking down the Genesis Creation account. There are many ways used to deform God's Word and His actions. Here's one, "Myths ... may not be factually true, but they're far more *truthful* and influential than facts." If I read that correctly it says myths carry more truth than facts. I don't believe that's the case, at all. This article basically demolished the veracity of God's Word about the Creation narrative and all the public comments agreed with the analysis. I do not wish to dwell on this aspect of the subject.

Evidence for Bible Wisdom was never supposed to be written. I was about to start the *Unlock Bible Meaning with 7 Keys to Master Biblical Hebrew* course (now finished), and the eighth volume of

The Explanation series with the working title *World Wanders*. That's not a typo, the world is wandering around in search of solutions; this volume explains we're wandering up the garden path. It uses Biblical Hebrew[1] similar to the prior books in the series. Anyway, *Evidence* started in September 2020, during the pandemic, with a blog post about Covid-19 and Quarantine. The reason was the lack of literature referring to God's Word about this subject. When it was the case, how Covid-19 is a curse from God, which is not the case.

I immediately found myself writing on various controversial, difficult-to-explain subjects in God's Word readers trip over in their quest for understanding. This book is a beginning effort to help seekers of understanding find some solid evidence in favor of God and the Bible. Bible wisdom is God's wisdom in God's Word. Most readers consider humans to be authors of the Bible; the surmisings, or as we saw above, cultural myths handed down and put to paper, or parchment, by some old folks. Consider this.

> If God is an All-Powerful Being, then He can inspire His Words, preserve and transmit those same Words down through time to reach us today.

I think most people have difficulty with that statement, which reveals the state of faith in God's Word today. That's the reason I wrote this book. We cannot understand if we do not approach God's Word with the correct frame of mind: There is a God, and the Bible is His Word. Without respecting God's Word, it becomes data for human analysis, and unfortunately, a lot of theology has descended to that basement level. We need to take the elevator and rise toward a higher vision, a clearer sky where we can receive a Godview of His plan for humankind. That's the reason for this book.

---

1. https://unlockbiblemeaning.com/

This volume is not about religion, doctrine, Church orientation, or specific beliefs you must have to be in some faith. It is evidence there is wisdom in the Bible. Wisdom in God's Word, far beyond what the human mind can conceive. Wisdom pertinent and relevant to living in the 21st century. Rules, principles, and guidance to make you a better individual and to establish a more cohesive community.

The motivation for writing this book is double

- First, to show the Bible is not just a 'Book of spiritual guidance for an exclusive group of Jesus believers.' That is indeed a primary role, particularly what we call the New Testament. But a primary almost unknown role is equally *God's Word addressed to ALL nations, worldwide*, via the Old Testament nation of Israel. (Don't confound it with the nation of Israel in the Middle East. They relate but are NOT the same.)

Just as the New Testament addresses all people in all nations to come to Christ, using the Apostles from Israel. Similarly, the Old Testament is a message addressed to the entire world. God's Word gives the rules for an individually fulfilling life and united, harmonious humanity. All humans are ONE race, one blood, one body, one mind... one set of rules applies to one set of people.

There are cultural and technical differences between peoples and epochs. But practical Bible wisdom has nothing to do with such cultural, scientific, and informational aspects related to nations and times, be they 1000, 3000, or 6000 years ago. Men, women, and children at all times in the history of humankind were identical to the 21st century. Yes, they lived longer or shorter life spans, yes; they were healthier or sicker than us. Yes, they had less technology, toys, and tools than us, Yes, they had and have different education, culture, and traditions but... we are all ONE PEOPLE spanning our thousands of years of existence.

- Second, detractors focus on the irrationality, cruelty, bigamy, controversy of God's Word. Most people, including Christians, do not understand the grandeur of God, thinking He is a respecter of persons, choosing a minority people to the exclusion of the majority. Nothing could be further from the truth. Yes, God chose a minority of people, just like there can only be one chief of state, family, school, company, association... with a committee, government, parents... to manage the ensemble. But God is present for the ensemble and has provided clear guidelines and benefits for ALL His creation, not just a minority.

Critics, be they secular or even theologian, latch onto all this mystification, they focus on details out of context of God's overall plan. They misunderstand and throw out imaginations that further confound already confused minds.

You can take a quote out of any speech, book and make it say whatever you want... but you're distorting it from the context in which it was stated. It would be better to question a discrepancy rather than criticize it in your ignorance. *Evidence* addresses many *apparent* incongruities in God's Word. I say apparent because they are not incongruous at all; they are puzzle pieces assembling perfectly in God's plan. *Evidence for Bible Wisdom* reveals God's plan and how these supposedly vagrant parts add substance to the whole.

Tough subjects

We will broach some touchy and rough Bible subjects. The Explanation is not here to skirt issues but give you answers to the big question in life. You'll learn How to Govern a Country Responsibly[2] and Leaders and Followers, Proper Organization.[3] As I wrote the theme, Bible Wisdom became clearer. Evidence followed in the title Conclusive Evidence for God? Prove Undeniable Existence.[4] I also began editing a future book about the Mind and rewrote a chapter about Nefesh Chaya Meaning. The Most Butchered Bible Term[5]. That chapter explains clearly what a human being is.

The one recurrent observation that detractors make concerns the light on the first day while the Creation narrative refers to the sun and moon on the fourth day. Two chapters straighten out this piece of the puzzle: Meaning of the Sabbath Day. God Rested & We Rest. That's It?[6] And Biblical Feast Days. Amazing Meaning for You in the 21st Century[7].

The principal theme of this book is the relevance of the Bible in the 21st century. Older People in 21st Century Society. Practical Bible Wisdom[8], and Agriculture—Practical Bible Wisdom for the 21st century[9] I heard an interviewer ask a Priest why a good God allows so much suffering? A very important question which he sidestepped; this chapter gives a straightforward answer, Fig Leaves or Clothing? Tinker or Build? Practical Bible Wisdom[10]. The conflict of

2. https://theexplanation.com/wp-admin/post.php?post=3239&action=edit

3. https://theexplanation.com/wp-admin/post.php?post=3263&action=edit

4. https://theexplanation.com/wp-admin/post.php?post=4240&action=edit

5. https://theexplanation.com/wp-admin/post.php?post=4889&action=edit

6. https://theexplanation.com/wp-admin/post.php?post=5569&action=edit

7. https://theexplanation.com/wp-admin/post.php?post=5733&action=edit

8. https://theexplanation.com/wp-admin/post.php?post=3316&action=edit

9. https://theexplanation.com/wp-admin/post.php?post=3533&action=edit

individual and community rights[11] in a liberal society... These are practical questions akin to God's concern for an exclusive group or all of humankind.

Many think God is dumb and cruel. The Bible is fairytales, myths, and the writings of some illuminated authors. Believers don't know what to make of Genesis. As for the book of Revelation, some focus on prophecy to drown the real Bible teaching. The in-between writings are looked on as the surmisings or written to bolster a small nation in dire circumstances. Or the story of a supposed God-man (Jesus) rejected by a world He came to save.

Evidence tackles some of the most common enigmas that baffle Christians and are a heyday for detractors: God condones slavery, God orders the wholesale killing of entire nations, even the entire world during Noah's flood. Even believers doubt God's Word is a valid solution in the 21st century. Many reduce it to a historical novel while shouting Jesus saves us. They've extracted an ethereal spiritual message; God saves, but they do not know why God is saving them, and certainly not what God is doing on Earth.

Most religion is an exclusive practice related to their group, be they a handful or a third of the world population. They are the *one*, while God condemns the rest of His Creation to some limbo.

The goal of *Evidence for Bible Wisdom* is to show how the Bible transcends what we humans consider groups, separations, boxes, piecemeal. It assembles the overall puzzle of the entire Bible story. Not to be picky, but to transcend these individual points for a global view, what The Explanation calls a Godview. How does God see

---

10. https://theexplanation.com/wp-admin/post.php?post=3359&action=edit

11. https://theexplanation.com/individual-rights-vs-collective-rights-the-bible-balance/

the complete kit and caboodle? That is true theology, looking at it through God's eyes.

Questions and doubts are a normal part of learning. The more material you add to the mixture, the more you can become jumbled. Evidence for Bible Wisdom helps you come out of twilight and darkness into the light of day. You're a seeker of truth, and this book will put you on the right track.

1. Big Picture

Why is humankind on Earth? Since we're here, why do we suffer? Surely, if there's a supernatural power watching over us, they wouldn't let this happen? We can speculate all day long, here's evidence there's a coherent, complete master plan of which we are an incredible part.

Can You Build True Worldview on Opinions?

Is it possible to have a solid worldview based on statements like; in my view, my opinion, my feelings, and experiences tell me... What is the basis of a coherent worldview?

In constructing a worldview, how much does your opinion count? How much is your opinion worth? Compared to mine? Your neighbors? A scientist? A philosopher? A religionist? The foundation is everything.

The Explanation, unabashedly, claims to help you build your worldview. Why do I make that promise? After all, it's a rather presumptuous proposal. Especially, why would my worldview be any better than yours?

Here are seven questions from a book, The Universe Next Door[1], by James Sire The answers form the foundation of any worldview. Test yourself.

1. What is prime reality? The really real?
2. What is the nature of external reality, the world around us?
3. What is a human being?
4. What happens to a person at death?
5. Why is it possible to know anything at all?
6. How do we know what is right and wrong?
7. What is the meaning of human history?

Difficult, right?! Let me ask you a question. Can you answer any of these based on your opinion, your feelings, or your experiences? If so, how do you know you're right and those with different opinions, wrong?

Why are we broaching this subject? This book covers some controversial social subjects like slavery and gender relations. Justice, family, mind... There is much conflict on such issues, with everyone having their opinion and view.

Personalview

Your view has no more, nor no less value than my view, or that of the next, or the next person. Depending on the viewpoint of the person telling the story, put ten people in the room and you'll have eleven opinions. Talk about confusion. Let's illustrate why we have so many points of view. We could refer to this as *personalview.* It could be someone with little education or reading knowledge. It could be a highly educated individual who considers their discipline as the base of all knowledge. Or someone who has thrown reason to the wind

1. http://guweb2.gonzaga.edu/faculty/calhoun/courses/201s/201world.html

and is in personal pursuit of answers. This is the most focused view, not to say, shuttered, blindfolded, like a horse with blinders on view.

We all fit into this category to one degree or another. Here is a list of hundreds of issues subject to controversy[2]. Look and see where your personalview stands. Here's a shortlist.

Personalview. Creating a worldview from an issue in which an individual is highly involved.

The number of issues is baffling. Consider this, since Gutenberg's printing press in 1440, estimates put the number of books published at about 130,000,000[3]. The classification systems must consider the myriad subjects, the points from which author worldviews depart. Look at the variety of topics in the Dewey Decimal Library system[4] and the BISAC book categories[5]. Personalviews are plethoric.

Four bases of worldview

In *Audit of Humankind*[6], I wrote a section on *How Humans Reason*[7]. It broke the process down into four major areas:

2. https://en.wikipedia.org/wiki/Wikipedia:List_of_controversial_issue

3. https://www.mentalfloss.com/article/85305/how-many-books-have-ever-been-published

4. https://en.wikipedia.org/wiki/List_of_Dewey_Decimal_classes

5. https://bisg.org/page/BISACEdition

6. *https://theexplanation.com/read-all-the-content-of-audit-of-humankind-online/*

7. *https://theexplanation.com/read-all-the-content-of-audit-of-humankind-online/*

1. Observation[8] including opinions, feelings, experiences, what some would call instinct.
2. Philosophy[9], scholarly answers to the big questions in life (like the 7 above).
3. Science[10], proving with the measurable.
4. Religion [11]focused on the spiritual, non-measurable.

Depending on our *mind environment,* the instruction both from others (parents, community, Church, school teachers, coaches, mentors...). Coupled with personal study (reading, meditation, travel, personal experiences...), we develop our worldview. This is the influence of nurture.

Our personal worldview, and I daresay each one is different, is based on the fact no two humans are in total agreement about everything. But each personalview emerges from our approach to the four cornerstone foundation.

All of our personal knowledge and ideas fit into one, or maybe overlap into a plurality of those four categories.

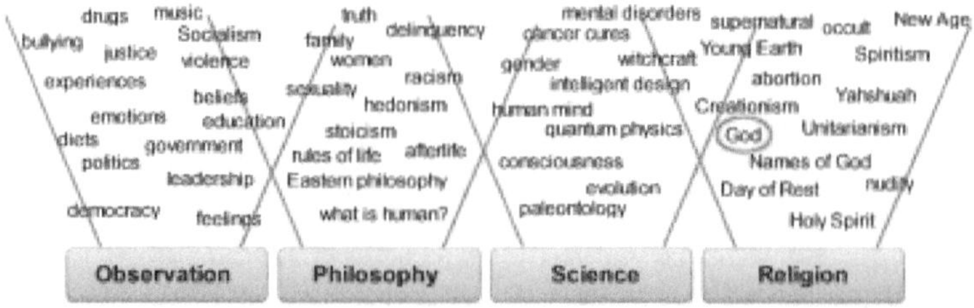

8. https://theexplanation.com/observation-first-way-human-reasoning/

9. https://theexplanation.com/philosophy-love-wisdom-whose-wisdom/

10. https://theexplanation.com/science-world-savior-human-reasoning/

11. https://theexplanation.com/religion-solution-world-peace/

Worldview. Based on the four foundations of reasoning. God is a part of religion.

Departure point of reasoning

When you're in a conversation with someone, or reading a book, do you consider the departure point of your interlocutor? Usually, you can pick it up in the first few minutes. For a book, in the preface or the first chapter. It's going to be from one of those four principal areas, and more likely from a more downstream point of view, more detailed branches or twigs. This is important because it means everything prior to the bigger and parallel branches is minimized or simply omitted.

This is the problem with paleontology. We construct a genealogy tracing human history through prehistoric creatures. Then we dig up something new and need to reconstruct the entire chart. Who knows what the schema will look like tomorrow?

Apes

I was reading Jane Goodall's life experience[12]; what she has accomplished is truly remarkable. As a child, she dreamed of Africa and animals. She saved money until she could go to Tanganyika (now Tanzania) and realized she wanted to stay there. She needed a way and money to follow her dream of befriending and working with chimpanzees. A friend suggested she contact the Kenyan paleontologist and archaeologist Louis Leakey, who hired her for a particular reason. He believed a study of great apes could provide indications of the behavior of early hominids.

---

12. https://en.wikipedia.org/wiki/Jane_Goodall

Over the many years and countless experiences, she found similarities between humans and chimpanzees in the areas of emotion, intelligence, and social relationships. She was the first person to witness apes shaping stick tools to poke into termite mounds and extract them for a gastronomic meal. Apes have a sense of reasoning and inventiveness. This observation was in line with the established ancestry link between apes and the human species.

Goodall also noted dissimilarities. The violence of dominant female apes in killing the offspring of their rivals, even stooping to cannibalism. Along with regular forays to kill and eat smaller monkeys.

I cannot say to what extent Goodall's research fortified the scientific stance humans descend from apes, through hominids. But it certainly comforted and reinforced their beliefs. On the other hand, no one can explain their violence or the total absence of other *tools* beyond those for eating. Science has picked the facts it wants and swept under the rug those experiences it can't explain.

Inventory of the Universe

The first book in *The Explanation* series is *Inventory of the Universe.* A journey from the vastness of outer space to the minuteness of the quark. From the physics of elementary particles to the psychology of the human mind. A portrayal of our known universal environment.

A 4* review of the book remarked. "This is like an updated and longer, *View from a height*[13] by Isaac Asimov. An overview of the world and science from physics to biology..." I admit it's nice to be compared to Isaac Asimov. His book covered 17 essays dealing with biology/chemistry/physics. However, the reviewer missed the essential, or I wasn't clear enough in the book.

---

13. https://en.wikipedia.org/wiki/View_from_a_Height

Here's the point I emphasized frequently.

Human life: "To speak in terms such as function and to refer to sheer numbers is inadequate to describe the processes performing like a battalion of flying trapeze artists in total sync in our bodies, in human life, in flora, in fauna, and in the universe. The full gamut I'm doing my best to help us understand."

Human body: "Hundreds, thousands, and millions of timely processes are taking place night and day. This is the ultimate in chronobiology: the notion of very complex biological procedures and the clock being in the right place at just the right split second. It's so much more than simply mixing a few chemical elements together. Timing, the instantaneous coordination of umpteen intricate systems, is a decisive ingredient we cannot omit."

Epilogue: "All the processes of each aspect of our environment fit together. For examples, see the nitrogen cycle, the water cycle, and butterflies, wasps, and bees pollinating flowers and plants.

These processes impact, intermingle, and create an interface so other processes can express themselves. We live in a fully integrated, interdependent environment with no missing or redundant parts."

Later, in *Origin of the Universe*, I coined the phrase coherent completeness[14] to express the concept of a worldview taking into consideration every single aspect of our Universe. One that explains the controversies and the violence of apes.

Consciousness

Another major scientific field where there's no consensus and lots of questions is the nature of consciousness. I exchanged with a friend who has done extensive studies in this area. I asked, "Is consciousness

14. https://theexplanation.com/coherent-completeness-is-the-logical-reasoning-of-the-ssource/

part of the brain, or external from the brain?" Here are the key points she answered.

- The brain facilitates communication with consciousness.
- Whatever that is.
- Consciousness doesn't reside in the body.
- It gives us the ability to receive awareness.
- This contradicts the fact, consciousness outlives your body.
- Near-death and channeling experiences corroborate the existence of something conscious beyond the physical body.

Here's my reply, "You put it very well also when you said, 'there are so many opinions and it depends on the authors.'" This brings us to another question I asked...

Why are there so many opinions?!

That quick question "Why so many opinions?" and her response, "Yes why?" got me thinking. *The Explanation* revolves around *worldview*.

A worldview is taking into consideration *every* aspect of life and death, etc. In *The Explanation* series, I classify the millions of pieces in these categories: Space, Atmosphere, Water, Earth, Flora, Fauna, Humans, Body, Brain, Mind. In other words, everything in the known universe. A full worldview should be able to explain *all* those elements and details in *one* coherent, complete picture! *The Explanation* sets that goal.

Why so many opinions? Simply because of what my friend said, "it depends on the writer." Each person is answering from their point of view. A point of view is a fractional point somewhere between *space* and *mind*. Science only considers the physical. Religion places the spiritual first and rejects some science. Each person is trying to establish a worldview departing from their basic knowledge and know-how. They are expanding from one point in a million. Another person will depart from a second point in the million. A million people departing from a million different points. Impossible to assemble a coherent picture.

The only way to understand a *point* is with*in* the millions of other points. You need to understand how the million points assemble before you can say, *this is the place one point occupies.*

Put another way, people are assembling the overall puzzle from their expertise, which only represents one piece of the million pieces of the puzzle. Impossible. That's why we have so many opinions and the resultant confusion.

You've got to first have the million pieces assembled before you can see how your piece fits in the whole.

The question is. Where is the entire worldview? How do you find that worldview?

Well, can a human create such a worldview? I mean, if you look at all the pieces from Space to the Mind, the entire Universe, it seems organized and coherent. How did it *get organized*? Is it pure chance?

Is a human, or humanity, responsible for its *existence* and *organization*?

If it's not humanity, then who is it?

God and the Bible

Wow, yes, I'm making a gigantic jump from humanity to God. In *The Explanation* series, I take a few chapters from How Humans Reason[15] at the end of *Audit of Humankind* and the beginning of

Origin of the Universe[16] to make that transition. Please visit those links. Here, I have to jump right in.

As much as people say they believe in God, He rarely enters the discussion concerning why there are controversies, even among those who believe in Him. Or He enters from the religion base with minor consideration for the other three, observation, philosophy, and science bases. Ideas are twisted and we have 100 million books of differing opinions about ape nature, violence, the human body, brain, human nature, consciousness, awareness, mind, and the other million pieces.

If God is the Creator, somewhere, all these elements involve Him.

The confusion comes when you don't involve God Who is the Creator. You cannot sort out the pieces of the puzzle.

God is responsible for worldview. Did He tell us about it... among other things, about human nature, consciousness, awareness, mind, near-death, and channeling experiences? Each is one point among the million points. Certain pieces, like the mind, are important, but they are still just points *in* the overall puzzle.

God tells us about these pieces. Where are *all* the points? In the Bible, so that's where *The Explanation* has to go. To the Author of the million-piece puzzle.

Proverbs 9:10

The fear of the LORD is the beginning of wisdom: and the knowledge of the holy is understanding.

---

15. https://theexplanation.com/read-all-the-content-of-audit-of-humankind-online/

16. https://theexplanation.com/read-content-origin-universe-online/

It starts with God and moves on to practical Bible wisdom. It's the knowledge of God's Word that gives understanding *and* not a worldview, but *Godview.*

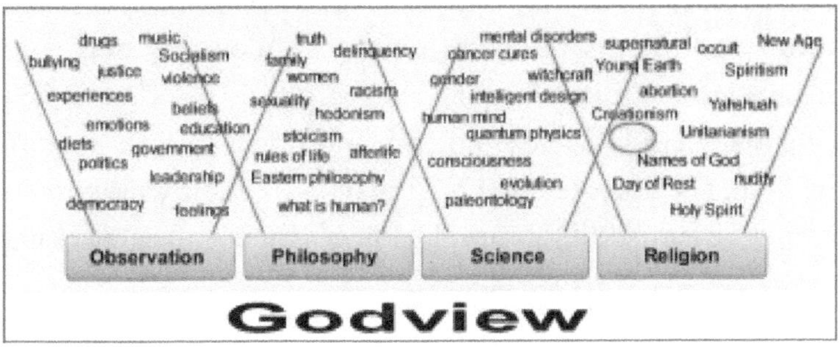

Godview assembles all the pieces of worldview with God as the foundation. He is no longer IN religion,

God is the base of religion.

The Bible talks about human construction of their multiple differing worldviews.

Isaiah 45:9, 29:15-16

9 Woe to him that strives with his Maker! Let the potsherd strive with the potsherds of the earth. Shall the clay say to him that fashions it, What make you? or your work, *He has no hands?*

29:15 Woe to them that seek deep to hide their counsel from the LORD, and their *works are in the dark*, and they say, Who sees us? and who knows us?

16 Surely your *turning of things upside down* shall be esteemed as the potter's clay: for shall the work say of him

> that made it, He made me not? or shall the thing framed
> say of him that framed it, He had no understanding?

Read those verses closely. Isa. 45:9 says let the potsherd strive with the potsherds of the earth. It's describing human potsherds' bickering debates in politics, government, science, philosophy, and religion. Each person or author thinking they're right, "be admonished: of making many books there is no end; and much study is a weariness of the flesh, (Ecclesiastes 12:12)." Isaiah says, "their works are in the dark, they've turned things upside down." There's no agreement.

Many talk about and refer to God, but the bottom line is, they've removed all trace of God from the very foundation of Godview. In worldview, God is just another one of those million pieces, maybe a little more important than other pieces, but certainly not the foundation. That's the meaning of *He has no hands.* We humans think we're here and no Creator formed humankind, He's absent! We don't think there's a Godview.

If someone put a computer in front of you and said it happened by chance, you'd call for a psychiatrist and a straightjacket. You know a computer doesn't just happen out of thin air. But you apply that principle to the existence of the Universe, humankind, the mind, and the millions of interconnected systems in the perfectly arranged picture that is our Universe. It just happened.

Come to your senses. In Isaiah 29:16, we must realize 100%, God has understanding, He is the foundation. Worldview emanates from God. God, from His foundation, builds up and establishes the million pieces in their specific slots.

That's Godview.

Can you prove that?

Undeniable Evidence for Existence of God?

I'll show you seven proofs God exists. That statement started me on the quest for evidence for God. Fifty-five years ago an agnostic boy became a believing man. Here's the story.

I spent hours pouring over literature and books, long before the internet came along, studying evidence for God. I'd never opened a Bible to study it until then. Some proofs in the booklet, like answered prayer, made little sense to someone who had never prayed. Others, like the need for a Creator to launch the Universe, sounded logical, but how can you prove that?

One proof or evidence for God motivated me into deeper study, fulfilled prophecy. Events foretold hundreds, even thousands, of years in advance. Of course, you could make hundreds of predictions and one or two could conceivably come to pass. But to do so consistently, is it evidence for God? Well, that supposition had the merit of seriously plunging me into Bible study.

What does the Bible say? Who wrote this book anyway? What were their credentials? How do we know we have the original writings from thousands of years ago? So many questions having nothing to do with evidence for God. Or do they?

Yes, they do, as I was going to find out in due time. I didn't know what I was looking for, but reading the Bible was an education in itself. At the time, I lived in Belgium, in a small room, boarding with a widow. Other than my work, my chief entertainment was bowling. I had plenty of time to read and study. There were no computers, and I didn't know what a concordance was.

I was unaware of verses like the following.

> **1 Corinthians 1:20-22**
>
> 20 Where is the wise? where is the scribe? where is the disputer of this world? has not God made foolish the wisdom of this world?
>
> 21 For after that in the wisdom of God the world by wisdom knew not God, it pleased God by the foolishness of preaching to save them that believe.
>
> 22 For the Jews require a sign, and the Greeks seek after wisdom:

I'd heard no preaching, and I wasn't looking for signs and miracles I didn't believe in, or Greek wisdom. I just wanted to read and understand.

I'm writing this chapter 55 years later. After studying theology and exercising the Christian Ministry for some 25 years. Each person follows their path as God calls and works with them. Nobody can put evidence for God or proofs in front of you to convince you of God's existence. Your personal quest reveals the answers. I offer you my path simply as an example.

Here are a few points I've garnered over the years I'd like to share with you. They'll help you evaluate whether evidence for God makes sense. People think God exists because they have an experience like a vision or a dream or a feeling of warmth or healing. It can be the emotion of singing or being caught up in the euphoria of an ecstatic crowd. I don't deny the personal impact such events can play. But the reality and evidence for God are not in acts, emotions, or feelings.

The Physical World Around Us

I don't like the word *prove* for God. He is not some scientific experiment or math formula. However, should natural events around us, in our reading, documentaries we watch, and news accounts, awaken in us deeper questions? I hope so and the Apostle Paul agrees.

> **Romans 1:19-20**
>
> 19 Because that which may be known of God is manifest in them (Sam: people in general); for God has shown it to them.
>
> 20 For the invisible things of him from the creation of the world are clearly seen, being understood by the things that are made, even his eternal power and Godhead; so that they are without excuse:

Fifty-five years ago, I didn't know about this verse either. If there's one way to seek evidence for God, this is it. The *things that are made*, the physical world around us, *reveal the invisible and eternal power of God*. This might surprise you, but there's nothing spiritual in this verse. It says anyone, by simply surveying their surroundings, can conclude there's evidence for a higher power. Just watch and think.

Here's just one example I heard about recently. It's so flagrant I kicked myself for not realizing it years ago. Don't be put off by this next subtitle, it hides evidence for God.

Geochemical to biochemical processes

This is one of those fundamental queries few talk about with evolution and the origin of life. It means, how do we turn a rock into a living creature. It has nothing to do with living creatures developing into higher beings like apes to humans. This is the transformation of a mineral into a living cell. The inorganic matter like sand, water, and sun into even the smallest form of life like a one-celled amoeba. There is absolutely no evidence. There is no known process. There are no skeletons or archaeological artifacts. Nothing, nada.

There are only maybes, could bes, suppositions, and *I think*. This absence of evidence is not proof of God. But it should prick your mind. This is a visible fact manifested to us by science that should tick a box, be a clue to the possibility there's something invisible out there.

It's impossible to develop such a subject here. Read this for a scientific search of transforming minerals into life[1]. Always note the number of *could have* (3), may have (2), plausible (2), possible (1)

---

1. http://elementsmagazine.org/past-issues/origins-of-life-transition-from-geochemistry-to-biogeochemistry/

in such articles like *myriad possible combinations of environmental conditions to find those that could start life.*

True, the above *proves* nothing. That's where we need extreme caution because of the info-gap. We know we don't have all the knowledge, but we could discover it in the future. The widespread mythological idea, also spread by religion, Earth is the center of the Universe[2], is one example. Until science proved otherwise. Science is very useful, but it has its limits that science should recognize. As an aside, in Matthew 3:9 Christ said, "God is able of these stones to raise up children to Abraham." God can transform the geochemical into biochemical. See the contrast?

There are many other visible testimonies for the evidence of power, intelligence, and design. The first book of *The Explanation* series, *Inventory of the Universe*[3], is devoted to just this subject. You can read accounts of chronobiology[4] (synchronization of biological processes like just-in-time arrival of hundreds of amino acids to form a protein), apoptosis[5] (the programmed death of cells to form a baby's hand or brain), stem cells[6] (one type of cell transforms into the myriad types of body cells), protein folding[7] (split-second folding of long protein strands to form *motors* powering your body).

Inventory of the Universe does not mention God, not even once. But it *makes the invisible things of him from the creation of the world*

2. https://en.wikipedia.org/wiki/History_of_the_center_of_the_Universe

3. *https://theexplanation.com/inventory/read-all-the-content-of-inventory-of-the-universe-online/*

4. https://theexplanation.com/pollination-chronobiology-flora-how-it-works/

5. https://theexplanation.com/apoptosis-programmed-cell-death-even-before-birth/

6. https://theexplanation.com/stem-cells-differentiation-core-of-your-body-s-regeneration-process/

7. https://theexplanation.com/protein-folding-machines-continual-movement-keep-body-running-smoothly/

clearly seen. From the Big Bang to the human mind there are wonders after wonders, amazement after amazement, impossibilities after impossibilities.

The why questions dumbfound scientists themselves. Individually none of these unanswerable questions or these natural and biological scientific phenomena prove anything. But, combine them and think, how many clues do you need? How much evidence is necessary for you to cross the line of *un*belief to belief in the realization there's an invisible something much bigger than the human hand, coincidence or hazard?

Many have opened their minds to these facts. This is reality. What are you waiting for?

> **Psalm 19:1**
>
> The heavens declare the glory of God; and the firmament shews his handywork.

Watch a video and hear the famous astrophysicist Stephen Hawking talking about the Big Bang[8]. He refers to incredible universal events as, "thankfully it was imperfect," and "lucky for us," etc. We needed many improbable detailed events for the Universe and humankind to exist. These are the *invisible things, clearly seen*, he and so many other scientists simply refuse to see.

Two Separate Worlds: Physical and Spiritual

This is belief, this is the beginning of your personal evidence for God. Yes, I say the beginning, because it wavers and disappears or grows and flourishes. It can be turned up or down, come and go. It depends on your hearing and the preaching. It will be tried and tested, it's not

8. https://theexplanation.com/science-and-theology-agreement-on-real-evidence-for-big-bang/

a constant, but it should become your underlying motivation and purpose.

The Bible talks about the origin of this physical knowledge possessed by all human beings, the beginning of evidence for God.

> **1 Corinthians 2:11**
>
> For what man knows the things of a man, save the spirit of man which is in him?

Only humans can understand this evidence for God because they have a mind, *the spirit of man in him*[9]. I watched a TV program, *Le Monde de Jamy* (Jamy's World, a science lesson) where they displayed animal intelligence. Amazing. How a monkey retrieves a peanut from the bottom of a long vertical tube. I knew how, because I'd seen it before. It pours water in and the peanut floats to the top. They find this solution faster than humans! They even have a solution when there's no water available. They urinate in the tube. Astonishing, I hadn't thought of that one. Yes, they are intelligent.

But do you think a monkey could write about its exploit as I did in the preceding paragraph? Not in a light year of light-years. If you're reading this, be assured you're more intelligent than a urinating monkey!

Why?

Because you have the *spirit of man*. Please read about the spirit as related to the mind for more details[10]. Humans grasp science, philosophy, religion and we express ourselves regarding our observations. The human mind allows us to intelligently (hopefully)

---

9. *https://theexplanation.com/two-spirits-gods-spirit-spirit-in-humans/*

10. https://theexplanation.com/human-mind-mind-power-neshama-ruach/

analyze our world and come to conclusions. Like realizing there's something bigger than us, an invisible power.

Second phase in Evidence for God

But to *know* that power—God—is a different matter. You need an additional ingredient coupled with your mind as well as proper guidance and teaching. It has nothing to do with feeling or emotion. Show me where that is involved, if you believe it does. You must have God's Holy Spirit.

God's Holy Spirit

This is the second ingredient to understand the evidence for God.

> **1 Cor. 2:9-13**
>
> 9 But as it is written, Eye has not seen, nor ear heard, neither have entered into the heart of man, the things which God has prepared for them that love him.
>
> 10 But God has revealed them to us by his Spirit: for the Spirit searches all things, yea, the deep things of God.
>
> 11 For what man knows the things of a man, save the spirit of man which is in him? even so the things of God knows no man, but the Spirit of God.
>
> 12 Now we have received, not the spirit of the world, but the spirit which is of God; that we might know the things that are freely given to us of God.
>
> 13 Which things also we speak, not in the words which man's wisdom teaches, but which the Holy Ghost teaches; comparing spiritual things with spiritual.

The evidence for God, of the invisible things clearly seen by those desiring to see such phenomena, tells them about His Power. But they do not tell you about God and Who He is, nor His plan. The above Biblical context explains humans need the Spirit (with a capital S) of God, a spiritual connection with God, to move forward. You can read more about God's Holy Spirit and how it works with humans here[11]. Whereas the human spirit opens our mind to understanding the physical world and the evidence of the need for *something larger*, God's Spirit opens our mind to spiritual understanding that the *something larger* is God.

You reach a new level. But your needs are not complete yet. You need two other vital elements joined with God's Spirit.

God's Word and God's teachers

Christ came for several purposes. To teach God's Word and to prepare others, namely the Apostles and disciples, to go and teach the nations, to propagate evidence for God.

> **Romans 10:13-15**
>
> 13 For whosoever shall call upon the name of the Lord shall be saved.
>
> 14 How then shall they call on him in whom they have not believed? and how shall they believe in him of whom they have not heard? and how shall they hear without a preacher?
>
> 15 And how shall they preach, except they be sent? as it is written, How beautiful are the feet of them that preach the gospel of peace, and bring glad tidings of good things!

11. https://theexplanation.com/holy-spirit-of-god-interrelationship-humans/

Some preach verse 13 and stop there. *Just call on God and you're saved.* No, you must continue to the next verses. We need to *hear and believe in God.* For this, we *need a preacher, teacher.* Someone to explain the Word of God. I hope you realize you cannot imagine, think up or know God by yourself. The knowledge of God that builds belief, called faith, can only come from God's Word and a teacher versed in it. Here's a verse about faith and evidence for God, for things not seen, but understandable by those with the Spirit of God.

Hebrew 11:1

> Now faith is the substance of things hoped for, the *evidence* (G1650) of things not seen.

Look at the meaning of *evidence.* Strong's Concordance[12] helps us out.

G1650

> ἔλεγχος elegchos el'-eng-khos; From G1651; proof conviction:
>
> KJV - evidence reproof.

Interesting, Strong uses the word *proof.* Faith, belief, hope are the proof of God's future plan for humankind. Read the only other context where we find this Greek word.

2 Timothy 3:16

> All scripture is given by inspiration of God, and is profitable for doctrine, for *reproof* (G1650), for correction, for instruction in righteousness:

12. https://theexplanation.com/strongs-concordance-demon-or-angel-which-will-it-be/

All scripture, the Word of God, alone, tells us Who and What God is all about. There's no surmising, imagining, deciding, debating, brainstorming, conceptualizing, inner feeling about what God is. God's Word defines precisely all the parameters regarding God, His Mind, and Plan. You're on board with His Word, or you're not. There's no in-between.

Note in those two verses the meaning of spiritual evidence for God. It's the relationship between *evidence* and *reproof*. There's a two-sided approach.

- One hears the scriptures, the Word of God, the spiritual evidence for God and Who He is (Rom. 10:14).
- This hearing of the scripture influences the hearer. It impacts the mind and heart (2 Tim. 3:16).

The conviction operates a change, it reproves, it gives us doctrine, teaching, nurturing, reexamination, rectification of who we are as humans in relation to God our Creator. The hearer takes it to heart and follows with action. Our Godview is turned right side up[13], It's based on God's Word and the Holy Spirit revealing the deep things of God (1 Cor. 2:10, above). Here's the schema of spiritual evidence for God.

13. https://theexplanation.com/can-you-build-true-worldview-on-savvy-opinions-experience/

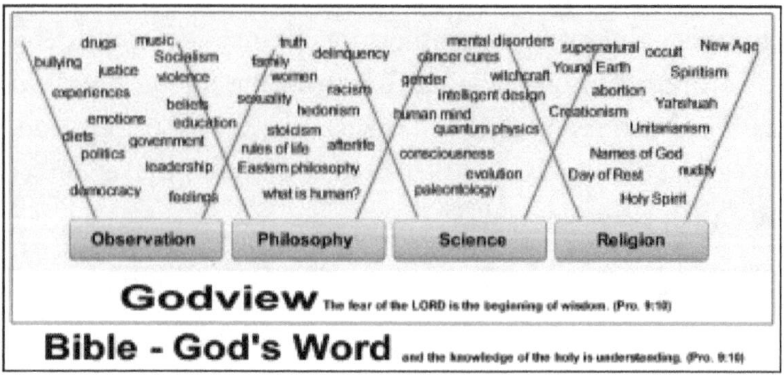

When God's Word filled me with evidence for God, I remember exchanging with my parents, especially my mother, who lived in Canada. I was excited. Unfortunately, my parents weren't. People talk about God, but when it comes to evidence for God, getting into God's Word, and listening to proper teaching, that's a different kettle of fish.

I lived in Belgium at the time and recall inviting an English religious friend over and going through some prophetical passages in Daniel 11. We agreed until we reached verse 32, which refers to the Coming of Christ. He refused allusions to the New Testament.

Because of my ignorance, I had never looked into the Bible, but because of my ancestry, I had a natural aversion to the New Testament. I remember the story of a little girl who was scolded for jumping on a bed with her arms held out. She looked like a cross, and that was bad. Silly, but those events leave an indelible mark on your mind. Negative attitude toward Christ.

Maybe because I had practically no religious background, I started my journey at 20 years old with a clean slate, so to speak, I had a lot less baggage of false teaching to shed. In fact, once I progressed in the Bible, I began to see the foundation and believe it makes sense.

I remember studying Isaiah 53 for the umpteenth time and finally being convicted; it predicted the First Coming of Christ.

Here are both the negative and positive results of our reaction to the spiritual evidence for God.

Luke 8:4-15

4 And when much people were gathered together, and were come to him out of every city, he spake by a parable:

5 A sower went out to sow his seed: and as he sowed, some fell by the way side; and it was trodden down, and the fowls of the air devoured it.

6 And some fell upon a rock; and as soon as it was sprung up, it withered away, because it lacked moisture.

7 And some fell among thorns; and the thorns sprang up with it, and choked it.

8 And other fell on good ground, and sprang up, and bare fruit an hundredfold. And when he had said these things, he cried, He that had ears to hear, let him hear.

9 And his disciples asked him, saying, What might this parable be?

10 And he said, to you it is given to know the mysteries of the kingdom of God: but to others in parables; that seeing they might not see, and hearing they might not understand.

11 Now the parable is this: The seed is the word of God.

> 12 Those by the way side are they that hear; then comes the devil, and takes away the word out of their hearts, lest they should believe and be saved.
>
> 13 They on the rock are they, which, when they hear, receive the word with joy; and these have no root, which for a while believe, and in time of temptation fall away.
>
> 14 And that which fell among thorns are they, which, when they have heard, go forth, and are choked with cares and riches and pleasures of this life, and bring no fruit to perfection.
>
> 15 But that on the good ground are they, which in an honest and good heart, having heard the word, keep it, and bring forth fruit with patience.

Note Christ's Words, *to you it is given to know the mysteries of the kingdom of God*. That is the spiritual evidence for God. It can only come from God's Word and its influence on our minds and actions. The devil hates the Words that enhance evidence for God; it pulls out all stops to sidetrack you. We must nurture this evidence for God to grow spiritually. Be focused, this isn't a one-time thing; it's a lifetime adventure. The benefits are a hundredfold, and that's an under-estimated manner of speaking.

The Explanation publishes this book to give you deeper insight into the evidence and mysteries of God's master plan for humankind in the 21st century and beyond. May it enhance your belief.

Let's start with God's definition of humanity. What is a human being? Who are you?

Consciousness, Human Nature, Mind. Definitions

What is humanity? Who are we? The definitions of human nature, consciousness, and mind. All clearly described.

We will define:

- Human nature
- Consciousness
- Mind

To show you how complex this issue is, here's the introduction to the *mind* entry in Wikipedia[1].

---

1. https://en.wikipedia.org/wiki/Mind

> One open question regarding the nature of the mind is the mind-body problem, which investigates the relation of the mind to the physical brain and nervous system. Older viewpoints included dualism and idealism, which considered the mind somehow non-physical. Modern views often center around physicalism and functionalism, which hold that the mind is roughly identical with the brain or reducible to physical phenomena such as neuronal activity, though dualism and idealism continue to have many supporters.
>
> Another question concerns which types of beings are capable of having minds. For example, whether mind is exclusive to humans, possessed also by some or all animals, by all living things, whether it is a strictly definable characteristic at all, or whether mind can also be a property of some types of human-made machines.

A lot of interrogations, particularly for such a fundamental subject. After all, *what is it to be human*? That question is basic and humankind, science, philosophy, and I'll add religion, can't furnish a clear, valid answer.

Let's do it.

Human Nature

Genesis 1 sounds like a good place to start. We're at the second part of Day six of Creation. On that day, God accomplished the initial part of His primary project. the Creation of man and woman. Four key verses reveal God's plan for Himself and humankind. Let's study.

Genesis 1:26-28, 31

> 26 And God said, Let us *make* (H6213) man in our image, after our likeness: and let them have dominion over the fish of the sea, and over the fowl of the air, and over the cattle, and over all the earth, and over every creeping thing that creeps on the earth.
>
> 27 So God *created* (H1254) man in his own image, in the image of God created he him; male and female created he them.
>
> 28 And God blessed them, and God said to them, Be fruitful, and multiply, and replenish the earth, and subdue it: and have dominion over the fish of the sea, and over the fowl of the air, and over every living thing that moves on the earth.
>
> 31 And God saw every thing that he had made, and, behold, it was very good. And the evening and the morning were the sixth day.

We're establishing a Godview; a worldview through the eyes of God. Theology[2] is what it's all about, what does God say, not human interpretations.

In one short verse 26, God gives His entire plan; make humans in His image and give them rulership over everything on Earth. The Biblical Hebrew meaning of *make* is below. Following the KJV are all the English translations of this word. In Strong's entry, H6213 is a very common word used abundantly in the Bible and modern Hebrew. Strong, author of Strong's Concordance, sums it up well, "to do or make, in the broadest sense and widest application."

---

2. https://theexplanation.com/deity-and-sound-reasoned-words-are-the-crux-of-theology/

The key is "God does, God makes," God performs all the meanings of this Hebrew word. God accomplishes, God advances, God appoints, God is apt, God becomes, God bears, God bestows, God brings forth, God bruises, God is busy, God has the charge of, God commits, God deals (with), decks, God displeases, God does, God (readies) dresses, God executes, God exercises, God fashions...

God accomplishes all these actions and tasks. God is not idle, He's occupied accomplishing His plan, second by second, hour by hour, day by day, week by week for all eternity. That is a human description of time. Obviously, God doesn't work under such constraints, you know what I mean.

> **H6213**
>
> עָשָׂה 'âsâh aw-saw'; a primitive root; to do or make, in the broadest sense and widest application:
>
> KJV - accomplish, advance, appoint, apt, be at, become, bear, bestow, bring forth, bruise, be busy, × certainly, have the charge of, commit, deal (with), deck, + displease, do, (ready) dress(-ed), (put in) execute(-ion), exercise, fashion, + feast, (fight-) ing man, +finish, fit, fly, follow, fulfill, furnish, gather, get, go about, govern, grant, great, + hinder, hold (a feast), × indeed, + be industrious, + journey, keep, labour, maintain, make, be meet, observe, be occupied, offer, + officer, pare, bring (come) to pass, perform, pracise, prepare, procure, provide, put, requite, × sacrifice, serve, set, shew, × sin, spend, × surely, take, × thoroughly, trim, × very, +vex, be (warr-) ior, work(-man), yield, use.

God executed His plan, "Make humans in His image and give them rulership over everything on Earth." In the next two verses 27-28, He created humans and gave them two commands; multiply and have dominion. *The Explanation* expresses these two orders as:

- **Relationships**. God married the couple, man and woman, and told them to have a family. That's socialization, the base of which is relationships between male and female, husband and wife, parents and children.
- **Rulership**. They are to manage or govern Earth and all its resources. In modern terms, we call this sustainable development[3]. Proper care, among others, in the areas of:
    a. Environment or ecology
    b. Economics
    c. Politics
    d. Culture

Here's the specific verb or action in Gen. 1:27, *create*, accomplished by God to start His plan.

H1254

בָּרָא bârâ' baw-raw'; A primitive root; (absolutely) to create; (qualified) to cut down (a wood), select, feed (as formative processes):

KJV - choose, create (creator), cut down, dispatch, do, make (fat).

Bara is familiar to you because it's the same word used in verse 1 to create the heavens and Earth[4].

The point is God has all the attributes of to *do*, to *make*, and to *create* in the broadest sense and largest application. And...

3. https://en.wikipedia.org/wiki/Sustainable_development

4. https://theexplanation.com/heaven-does-it-exist-yes-in-fact-there-are-three-heavens/

God created and made humans in His image, in His likeness.

This means humans have the same capacities as God but on a human scale. Please read that again. Yes, if humans have the image of God, which He says we do, then humans can do what God does! We are Godlike beings.

God makes, creates, and manages His Creation in the broadest sense and largest application. Meditate on the implication of these verses; we don't have the space to elaborate. It is grandiose. I'm going to sum it up with two words, *divine nature*. The essence of God, including the love and effort He puts into the *management*. I don't like that word, talking about God, maybe we could substitute other verbs; administer, oversee, guide... Throughout the Bible, Old and New Testaments, that's what God does. It's His *divine nature*. Actually, I borrowed those two words from Peter.

> **2 Peter 1:2-4**
>
> 2 Grace and peace be multiplied to you through the knowledge of God, and of Jesus our Lord,
>
> 3 According as his divine power has given to us all things that pertain to life and godliness, through the knowledge of him that has called us to glory and virtue:
>
> 4 Whereby are given to us exceeding great and precious promises: that by these you might be partakers of the *divine nature*, having escaped the corruption that is in the world through lust.

We can be partakers of God's *divine nature*. incredible goal! We'll be able to do, create, and manage like God! Hang on, wait a minute. Humans have the *image of God* now. Think about it, what do we accomplish? We *do*, *make*, *create* and *manage* in the largest sense of those terms. But we do it on a human level.

God has divine nature; we, in His image, have human nature. There's your first definition.

Let's add an important detail about Adam and Eve's human nature at their Creation on Day 6. "And God saw every thing that he had made, and, behold, it was very good." That means their human nature was very good. God creates perfectly.

> **Definition of Human Nature:** The ability of humankind to do, make, create and manage in two domains. **Relationships** (*multiply*, Gen. 1:28). We create couples, make marriages, make love, create and parent (manage) children. **Rulership** (*dominion* Gen. 1:28). We create and make myriad products and services and manage the environment, economy, government...

Consciousness

How, in reality, is this possible? To be like God, to have human nature like He has divine nature? This is not blasphemy, it is Bible theology, the plan of God for you and me. We're studying practical Bible wisdom. How can humans make, create, manage relationships and rulership?

Whereas Genesis 1 (through Gen. 2:3) focuses on God's overall plan, Genesis 2 gives us vital details regarding the *how* of the Creation. We're zeroing in on a verse regarding the Creation of the first human being. Here's the attribute God gives humanity to define the parameters, the attributes of human nature.

> **Gen. 2:7**

> And the LORD God formed man of the dust of the ground, and *breathed* into his nostrils the *breath* (H5397) of life; and man became a living soul.

The two words, *breathed* into his nostrils and *breath* of life, are different in Hebrew. I've expounded on this important distinction in this article[5]. God gave humanity, represented by the first human, *nishmat (H5397)* chayim, the *breath* of life.

First, who possesses this breath? This neshama? Only God and humanity. Read this article[6] explaining a context in Judges. God told the Israelites to annihilate everything with *neshama*. They wiped out all humanity but left the animals.

> Animals do not possess neshama; only humans do. Why? Because only humans are made in the image of God. Since God has neshama, humanity also possesses it.

What is neshama? Neshama is the unique ingredient setting humanity apart from animals. Neshama confers the image of God on humanity. It is God's imprint on humankind. Let me say *The Explanation* is exposing knowledge science, philosophy and religion have not understood and made known to humankind.

The Wikipedia article above makes it clear everyone is groping in darkness, and they have been ever since Descartes and others focused on this question[7]. Even Strong, in his definition below, is off-track. This should not be a surprise to you. But you must read the Biblical evidence in this article regarding God and humans alone possessing neshama[8].

---

5. https://theexplanation.com/god-breathed-nostrils-dust-man/

6. https://theexplanation.com/neshama-humankinds-relationship-god/

7. https://en.wikipedia.org/wiki/Consciousness

8. https://theexplanation.com/neshama-humankinds-relationship-god/

H5397

נְשָׁמָה n^{e}shâmâh nesh-aw-maw'; from H5395 (נָשַׁם); a puff, i.e. wind, angry or vital breath, divine inspiration, intellect. or (concretely) an animal:

KJV - blast, (that) breath(-eth), inspiration, soul, spirit.

God breathed into the first human something He possesses and animals do not possess. From Strong's entry above, I'd retain two words: *inspiration* and *intellect. The Explanation* adds another definition, *consciousness*. Yes, neshama defines consciousness in humanity.

How can we confirm this proposal? First, God's breathing in something invisible. It is not a part of the body, nor a part of the brain. You cannot see, touch, or measure this breath of life, the neshama. That is one reason consciousness is so elusive to science. They're trying to *locate* it in the brain and neurons. They won't find it, it's the breath-neshama of God.

It's the tool, I hate calling it that, conferring on humanity, the God-given image to multiply and dominate, have relations and rulership. Again, we do not have the space to elaborate. Neshama is all the qualities, the attributes, setting humanity light-years apart from animals, allowing them to relate to one another and govern Earth.

The Explanation wrote extensively about these spiritual, invisible qualities in *Audit of Humankind*[9]. a quick summary is;

- The singularities of humankind.
- How humanity functions.

---

9. *https://theexplanation.com/read-all-the-content-of-audit-of-humankind-online/*

- How humanity socializes.
- How humanity rules.
- How humanity reasons.

You and I and every human being ever to have walked Earth can only accomplish those five tasks because we have neshama, consciousness.

Here's the Wikipedia definition of consciousness[10], or rather an attempt at a definition. Humanity is lost in its quest for a definition of consciousness.

> Consciousness, at its simplest, is "sentience or awareness of internal or external existence." Despite millennia of analyses, definitions, explanations and debates by philosophers and scientists, consciousness remains puzzling and controversial, being "at once the most familiar and most mysterious aspect of our lives." Perhaps the only widely agreed notion about the topic is the intuition that it exists. Opinions differ about what exactly needs to be studied and explained as consciousness. Sometimes, it is synonymous with the mind, and at other times, an aspect of it.

After the messiness of science, philosophy, and religion, here's the clarity of the Bible:

> **Job 32:8**
>
> But there is a *spirit* (H7307 - ruach) in man: and the *inspiration* (H5397 - neshama) of the Almighty gives them understanding.

10. https://en.wikipedia.org/wiki/Consciousness

Definition of Consciousness: God's inspiration, the template of His image, a program[11] conferring on each human being the ability to possess human singularities and perform human accomplishments like functioning, socializing, ruling and reasoning.

Mind

The last of our three concepts, but not the least. You realize without knowledge and belief in the existence of a Supreme God, none of this wisdom would be available or understandable. Unfortunately, it shows how far humanity has yet to go to garner real understanding.

Let's recapitulate. Human nature is the image of God, or divine nature, on a human level. Consciousness is the program shaping all the elements (singularities, functions) of our human nature. Now we need the motor to run our consciousness, to activate all the parts so we can project our human nature.

The power humanity has to animate their human nature and consciousness is referred to in Job 32:8, above, alongside the neshama, *there is a spirit in man*. From a biblical perspective, this element is probably the best known. It is the *ruach*.

H7307

רוּחַ rûwach roo'-akh; from H7306 (רוּחַ); wind; by resemblance breath, i.e. a sensible (or even violent) exhalation; figuratively, life, anger, unsubstantiality; by extension, a region of the sky; by resemblance spirit, but only of a rational being (including its expression and functions):

11. https://theexplanation.com/human-software-god-breathed-neshama-adam/

KJV - air, anger, blast, breath, × cool, courage, mind, × quarter, ×side, spirit(-ual), tempest, × vain, (whirl-) wind(-y).

Ruach, also invisible, especially to science, is analogous to wind in all its strengths. From *breath* to *wind* to *blast* to *tempest* to *whirlwind.* The vicissitudes represent the ups-and-downs, extremes of movement, or swings of the mind. Below is a verse revealing two vital aspects of the mind.

1. It's where good and bad imagination and ideas, indeed all thinking, take place.
2. God knows what goes on in each person's mind! Mind-boggling, but God's Word reveals this power of God.

Ezekiel 11:5 (read verse 2 and the context)

And the Spirit of the LORD fell upon me, and said to me, Speak; Thus says the LORD; Thus have you said, O house of Israel: for I know the things that come into your *mind* (H7307), every one of them.

We cannot get into a deep study of mind here. You can read much more in *Origin of Humankind*[12]. I'd like to point out one key to studying *mind* in the Bible. Since it is a controversial and hard-to-understand subject, the translators and Strong mix up their terms. The Greek word *psuche* from which we get psychiatry[13] is often translated *soul* in the King James Bible. If you read *mind* instead, it makes more sense.

Allow me another analogy. If you have a metal and plastic computer equipped with Windows or iOS and a graphics program, nothing

12. *https://theexplanation.com/read-content-origin-humankind-online/*

13. https://en.wikipedia.org/wiki/Psychiatry#Etymology

works until you turn the electricity on. Similarly, if you have human nature and consciousness, nothing works until you turn mind on. Think about when you're asleep and not dreaming, your mind is turned off and there's no consciousness. The analogy breaks down because the *ruach* is still there, and plenty is going on, but it is in the sub-conscience. To be conscious, your mind must be on, functioning.

> **Definition of mind:** The ruach, the mind, animates the consciousness, the neshama. It's the mind power you use to animate your singular abilities to create experiences, emotions, character, personality, relationships, and rulership. All are recorded, like data, in your mind. Mind is the totality of every thought and action, the imprint of your being as an individual.

I always wondered why Genesis doesn't talk about *ruach* associated with the *mind* at Creation. Let me offer two, even three points.

1. When God created the first human, ruach was already present in the animals! Animals and humans have ruach[14] (Ecclesiastes 3:19), but animals are animated by instinct and humans by mind. Big difference. At birth baby animals, even blind and deaf rats, find their mother's teats. Not at all for human babies. Animal ruach confers only instinct. Human ruach activates consciousness with all its human traits. Read this article to learn the difference between animal and human ruach[15].
2. Since ruach was already present, neshama, consciousness, is solely mentioned in Gen. 2:7 because humans alone possess it, animals did not receive it and do not possess it.

---

14. https://theexplanation.com/gods-spirit-ruach-animates-living-beings/

15. https://theexplanation.com/gods-spirit-ruach-animates-living-beings/

3. Upon death, the ruach returns to God. Why? Because it is the imprint (as we saw in Ezek. 11:5) of a human being. If I may draw another analogy, the ruach, the mind, is the hard drive with all the memory, the data, of the person's entire life. Ecclesiastes 12:7, "Then shall the dust return to the earth as it was: and the *spirit* (H7307–the ruach, mind) shall return to God who gave it." Why does God keep each person's spirit?

Ezekiel 37:9-12

9 Then said he (the Lord) to me (Ezekiel), Prophesy to the *wind* (H7307), prophesy, son of man, and say to the *wind* (H7307), Thus says the Lord GOD; Come from the four *winds* (H7307), O *breath* (H7307 and mind), and *breathe* (H5301, the identical word in Gen. 2:7 God *breathed*... See Further Study below) on these slain, that they may live.

10 So I prophesied as he commanded me, and the *breath* (H7307 and mind) came into them, and they lived, and stood up upon their feet, an exceeding great army.

11 Then he said to me, Son of man, these bones are the whole house of Israel: behold, they say, Our bones are dried, and our hope is lost: we are cut off for our parts.

12 Therefore prophesy and say to them, Thus says the Lord GOD; Behold, O my people, I will open your graves, and cause you to come up out of your graves, and bring you into the land of Israel.

The Prophet Ezekiel describes a resurrection to physical life. The *ruach*, the *mind*, will be placed into each resurrected, healed body.

People will have their properly functioning minds (no more mental diseases or Alzheimer's) with the record of their past life. This is what they'll start working with at their resurrection with God's teachers in a Godly environment. This is another exciting story. The point here is, there's a reason humans have a mind-ruach, its purpose, and its future.

The Explanation expounds on Human nature, Consciousness, and Mind in two books. *Audit of Humankind*[16] explains the three concepts in a secular fashion. *Origin of Humankind*[17] deepens the subject using the Bible. This book not only explains *what* and *how* but also *why* there is animal nature, human nature, and divine nature. And the relationship among all three, and particularly the link between human and divine nature.

Further Study

Read Hebrews 2. It clearly delineates divine nature and human nature. Note the transformation of Christ's nature. As God, He possessed divine nature (by whom are all things, vs. 10) and took on Himself human nature (the seed of Abraham, vs. 16). Note in the same verse another nature, *angelic*. There's also *animal* nature, which you can study.

Hebrews 2:10, 16

> 10 For it became him (Christ), for whom are all things, and by whom are all things, in bringing many sons to glory, to make the captain of their salvation perfect through sufferings.

---

16. https://theexplanation.com/read-all-the-content-of-audit-of-humankind-online/

17. https://theexplanation.com/read-content-origin-humankind-online/

16 For verily he took not on him the nature of angels; but he took on him the seed of Abraham.

***

Ezekiel 37:9 ... Thus says the Lord GOD; Come from the four *winds* (H7307), O *breath* (H7307 and mind), and breathe (H5301, the identical word in Gen. 2:7 God breathed...) on these slain, that they may live.

In Genesis, for the first man, God breathed (H5301) the neshama (consciousness, the attributes of humans into him).

In Ezekiel, for all resurrected humans, God will have the winds (H7307 here, it is God's Holy Spirit) breath (H5301) the ruach (H7307) their minds back into each human being, the slain, now revived from the dead.

In Genesis, for the first human, at his Creation, the formed dust needed a *human template*, human attributes, the neshama, consciousness. At his Creation, there was nothing, no conscience, and no mind. God breathed the consciousness, the neshama, into him (think of artificial respiration, we blow in air to revive the person's consciousness), and gave him a mind, the ruach.

In Ezekiel at the resurrection, the raised humans will already have their neshama, because they are human. *Inserting* the ruach means giving them back *their minds, their character, their personality, memories, experiences, and talents.* The *ruach* activates their *neshama*-consciousness. This is their time for salvation, which they did not receive during their first lifetime. This is another future chapter in the story of humankind.

Our ancestors are neither lost nor in heaven. It's like a hard drive with the electricity turned off, the data is non-functional. They await the resurrection when, excuse the expression, they will be plugged in again. What a moment that will be. Everyone acquiring impeccable body and mind health (no physical or mental disorders) recognizing and hugging (no Covid!) one another. The work of conversion for these multitudes will begin.

Are you seeing evidence for Bible wisdom?

With short definitions of human nature, consciousness, and mind under our belts, it's time to let the Bible define what a *soul* is.

Nefesh Chaya, the Deep Meaning of Soul

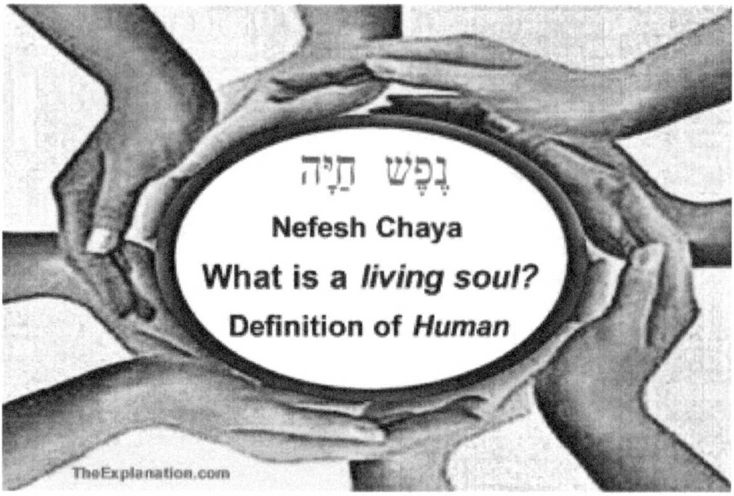

Nefesh Chaya. Here's the Godview and focused meaning of this Biblical Hebrew phrase. It's pivotal to Bible and Psychology comprehension.

In the last chapter, we studied *God breathed the breath of life* from Genesis 2:7. Now we reveal the meaning of the end of the verse; *man became a nefesh chaya*, translated *living soul* in the King James Bible. *Man* is a generic term referring to *humans*. This term occupies center stage in the entire Bible story. Why? Because both words are the story of humankind. Let me explain.

> NB If you want to know the definition of a human being, you need an open mind to read this chapter. Some scripture corroborated affirmations might shock you, but

> we must get this understanding of what a human is correct from the start. This knowledge is fundamental Bible wisdom.

In Genesis 1 the word *nefesh* (H5315) appears four times in verses 20, 21, 24, and 30 where it's translated *creature* and *life*. It refers to fish, beast, fowl, and everything that creeps on earth. In other words, *nefesh* refers to every single living creature God created before the first human.

Likewise, Genesis 1 uses the word chai, chaya (H2416) eight times in verses 20, 21, 24, 25, 28, and 30. It also refers to every living thing created by God before the first human.

Please verify this at UnlockBibleMeaning.com[1], where you'll find an Interlinear Bible with Strong's Concordance numbers. See it with your own eyes, don't take my word for it. It is so important I've also included an image of both the Interlinear and KJV translations. Here's the point. Both these words, nefesh chaya, are present. They are used together as *nefesh chaya* in Gen. 1:30, translated in the Interlinear, "in which *life is living*." (reading Hebrew right to left). Whereas in the KJV, the translators omitted a word with "wherein *is life*."

1. https://unlockbiblemeaning.com

Ge 1:30 **Interlinear Bible**

H8064	H5775	H3605	H776	H2416	H3605
haš·šā·ma·yim	'ō·wp̄	ū·lə·ḵāl-	hā·'ā·reṣ	ḥay·yaṯ	ū·lə·ḵāl-
הַשָּׁמַיִם	עוֹף	וּלְכָל־	הָאָרֶץ	חַיַּת	וּלְכָל־
of the air	bird	and to every	of the earth	beast	and to every

H5315		H834	H776	H5921	H7430	H3605
ne·p̄eš	bōw	'ă·šer-	hā·'ā·reṣ,	'al-	rō·w·mêś	ū·lə·ḵōl
נֶפֶשׁ	בּוֹ	אֲשֶׁר־	הָאָרֶץ	עַל־	רוֹמֵשׂ	וּלְכֹל
life	in	which	the earth	on	that creeps	and to everything

H402	H6212	H3418	H3605	H853	H2416
lə·'āḵ·lāh	'ê·śeḇ	ye·req	kāl-	'eṯ-	ḥay·yāh,
לְאָכְלָה	עֵשֶׂב	יֶרֶק	כָּל־	אֶת־	חַיָּה
for food	plant	[I have given] green	every thing	-	is living

H3651	H1961
kên.	way·hî-
כֵן׃	וַיְהִי־
so	and it was

King James Version Bible + Strong's numbers

30 And to every beast H2416 of the earth, H776 and to every fowl H5775 of the air, H8064 and to every thing that creepeth H7430 upon the earth, H776 wherein there is life H5315 * H2416, I have given every green H3418 herb H6212 for meat: H402 and it was so.

Please grasp the vital difference between the Hebrew and KJV translations. The Hebrew says in every beast there is a *living life*. The KJV says in every beast is *life*. The Hebrew implies there is life happening inside the living beast. What is that life animating the animal kingdom?

The Bible says it is the *ruach*. This life-giving breath and spirit confer on beasts, fish, fowl, and crawlers, their instinct and special traits for sleeping, hunting, eating, and reproducing. The specific survival qualities each species demonstrates since its Creation.

God's ruach (careful, this has a small *r*, not the capital *R* associated with the Holy Spirit) animates every single living animal.

Ecclesiastes 3:19-21

> 19 For that which befalls the sons of men befalls beasts; even one thing befalls them: as the one dies, so dies the other; yea, they have all one *breath* (H7307 - ruach); so that a man has no preeminence above a beast: for all is vanity. (Sam: when it comes to *breathing*, humans and animals are identical)
>
> 20 All go to one place; all are of the dust, and all turn to dust again. (Sam: God created animals and humans from the earth, dust, and that's where their bodies return)
>
> 21 Who knows the *spirit* (H7307 - ruach) of man that goes upward, and the *spirit* (H7307 - ruach) of the beast that goes downward to the earth? (Sam: in addition to *breathe*, ruach means *spirit*. Here there's an enormous difference between animals whose spirit follows the body. But the spirit of humans returns to God who gave it. Read Eccl. 12:7)

The proper Interlinear translation of Genesis 1:30 tells us there is an essence, something living within a live, breathing animal. This essence is the *ruach*. This is an inaccuracy of science, it doesn't believe there's a non-material essence. From this point on, there's irreconcilable understanding.

But that's not the only comprehension problem. The *ruach*, the essence animating animals, emanates from God, that's clear, but more precisely from God's Ruach, the Holy Spirit. The point the Bible makes, here and elsewhere, is the Holy Spirit is an Essence, the Essence of God. Why can *The Explanation* affirm this? Because of Genesis 1:2, "The Spirit of God[2] moved over the waters." The

2. https://theexplanation.com/spirit-of-god-moved-face-waters-meaning/

presentation and movement of the Spirit in this context reveals it is the Essence belonging to and used by God to make the Creation. Please read the article at this link for all the details[3].

This is the first inaccuracy of traditional Christian religion; it doesn't believe the Holy Spirit is an essence. From this point on, there's irreconcilable understanding.

I forewarned you about needing an open mind. *Mind* and *soul* are among the biggest enigmas of science and religion. There's no consensus between the two domains or within each as to the understanding of these two fundamental aspects of what a human is. We're turning to Bible wisdom for clarification.

Humans and Nefesh Chaya

Until the Creation of humans, on Day 6 of Creation, it's been about animals multiplying and eating. In one word, animals survive as *nefesh chaya*, the identical phrase we see in Gen. 2:7. From this point forward, it's about humans and how they thrive. Let's analyze Genesis 2:7.

> **Genesis 2:7**
>
> And the LORD God formed *man* (adam) of the dust of the ground, and breathed into his nostrils the breath of life; and man became a *living* (chaya) *soul* (nefesh).

Genesis 2:7 and nefesh chaya are the beginning, the moment of Creation of the first human. By the way, in Biblical Hebrew, it uses the term adam, but NOT in the sense of either a name or a gender[4]. We know, of course, the first human created was male, but here in

3. https://theexplanation.com/spirit-of-god-moved-face-waters-meaning/

4. https://theexplanation.com/human-beings-god-created-them-equal-but-different/

2:7 it is a generic term referring to *human*, including male and female (Gen. 1:27), but excluding animals. This is vital comprehension for understanding *nefesh chaya* in Gen. 2:7. It is not the same *nefesh chaya* as in Gen. 1:30.

How can *The Explanation* affirm this?

There are at least a couple of reasons:

1. Because Gen. 2:7 says God *formed* humans[5]. There is no such reference to the animals.
2. God breathed the *neshama chayim* (*nishmat chayim* in Hebrew) into the human's nostrils. There's no such reference to animals. Gen. 2:7 is the very first mention of neshama.

The *nefesh chaya* in Gen. 2:7 for humans includes three elements.

1. The body is made from *dust.*
2. The *ruach* is a similar essence, but different in nature to animals. Confirmed in Ecclesiastes, as we saw above, and we'll see below.
3. The *neshama chayim*. Which no other physical living being than humans possess.

The *nefesh chaya* in Genesis 1:30, referring to animals, ONLY includes the ruach, there's no neshama. This puts humans in a category of their own. The human species, the human race. In Biblical terms, following on from the vocabulary used in Genesis 1, *after their kind*[6], we can say, "And God made humans from the dust after their kind."

---

5. https://theexplanation.com/god-created-man-bible-god-formed-man/

6. https://theexplanation.com/were-humans-created-or-did-humans-originate-creation-day-6/

> And the human kind is heavily related to God because only God and humans possess neshama! That's the meaning of "God created humans in His Image after His Likeness."

Genesis 2:7 tells us there is a material body + the immaterial ruach + the immaterial neshama. ALL three together make up the *nefesh chaya*. The KJV translators used one word *soul*. And science and religion have been at loggerheads with each other and each is lacking in comprehension about this primary subject.

The entire Bible is the story of humankind, of billions of *nefesh chaya*. And neither science nor religion understand what a *human being* is. Wow. How can they get the story right if they don't know what or whom they are referring to?

Human Nature

We now know what human and nefesh chaya in Gen. 2:7 mean. And we know there are three elements. Let's move on to a more comprehensive understanding of *human nature*. It has two parts, *human* and *nature*. We'll examine the immaterial aspects of these elements, you can't touch or measure them. In the preceding chapter we saw in scholarly circles there's no [7]consensus about what this is. The Bible reveals two non-physical essences compose a human, a nefesh chaya. Let's see how *human nature* corresponds to the *neshama ruach* combination.

Neshama = Human

What does it mean to be human? The million-dollar question. Let the Bible do the talking. Immediately following Gen. 2:7, the Creation of the first human, God interacts with him. An exchange

7. https://theexplanation.com/humanity-definition-human-nature-consciousness/

did not take place with any of God's other Creations. This interaction reveals what the *neshama* and *ruach* accomplish together. This is *human,* nefesh chaya. This is what humans alone can accomplish with the neshama.

- Manage the Garden God planted. *Dress it and keep it.* In Biblical Hebrew, this phrase means worship and serve[8]; the implication is worship and serve God.
- The human can choose between two Trees and a lot more to choose their food.
- Humans can name animals and many other items, including their babies.
- The male could reason there was no mate for him among the animals.
- The male saw and reasoned the female resembled himself. He said, "she's bone of my bone."
- The male understood he'd leave the home of his parents and set up a new home in the institution of marriage, which forms a new family. As a couple, they would multiply their children.
- They would have dominion over the Earth, including the animals.

That's the meaning of human. That's what the human *nefesh chaya* can undertake! Only possession of the neshama makes all the above possible. An animal nefesh chaya without the neshama, only possessing ruach, cannot do any of the above.

Without neshama, you're just an animal... No matter how much you may bodily resemble (like prehistoric beings) a human being. It's not the body and brain that make a human. The immaterial essences, the ruach, and in particular the neshama produce a human.

---

8. https://theexplanation.com/dress-keep-garden-of-eden-man-destined-to-be-a-gardener/

This is the *human* in *human nature*. In this context, let's discuss two other hard-to-define descriptions referring to humans; consciousness and cognition.

Consciousness and Cognition

The first human had consciousness and cognition. He was aware of himself, had knowledge, and could reason. These attributes are apparent in his singular statement, "she is bone of my bones, flesh of my flesh." Adam recognized what he was, what she was, and reasoned about their similarity. All because God equipped him with neshama.

The Explanation elaborates on the neshama aspect of nefesh chaya by laying out the singularities of humankind. The human singularities[9] allow each of us to *master space-time*, be *creative* by using our *imagination*. Once we've imagined our project, we need the *education* and right *choices* oriented towards the accomplishment of our project. We then make *progress* towards that goal meeting the arising *challenges* along the way; this alone leads to a sense of success and fulfillment. Only humans can follow such a trajectory because of the neshama.

This is not intended to be an exhaustive list; there are other singularities, all of which are immaterial. You cannot locate them in the brain. Yes, they all affect the brain, but they do not originate there. Read the relationship between consciousness (non-material) and the brain[10] (material neurons, synapses, etc.).

The neshama defines *human*. It is what differentiates us from animals. Every single human being who has ever lived or is living is animated by the neshama. Humans are one race with a multitude of cultures and languages. But we all have the same needs, desires, and

9. https://theexplanation.com/rule-life-responsibly-the-key-human-singularity/

10. https://theexplanation.com/human-brain-role-consciousness-mind/

aspirations. Neshama is the *human* in the *human nature* each person possesses.

Ruach - Nature

In *human nature, ruach* is the *nature* part. Here's the definition of *nature* from the article human nature in Wikipedia[11].

> Human nature is a concept that denotes the fundamental dispositions and characteristics—including ways of thinking, feeling, and acting—that humans are said to have naturally. The term is often used to denote the essence of humankind, or what it 'means' to be human. This usage has proven to be controversial in that there is dispute as to whether or not such an essence actually exists.

Wikipedia included the controversial, for science, *human essence* aspect as well. I'd draw your attention to the *thinking, feeling, acting*, the *doing* part of this definition. A verse in Job shows we have an active, *doing* spirit. The second context in Ezekiel reveals how God adds to and later replaces the human spirit with His Spirit.

> **Job 32:18** For I (Elihu, friend of Job) am full of matter, the *spirit* (H7307) within me constrains me.

> **Ezekiel 36:26** A new heart also will I give you, and a new *spirit* (H7307) will I put within you: and I will take away the stony heart out of your flesh, and I will give you an heart of flesh.

11. https://en.wikipedia.org/wiki/Human_nature

> 27 And I will put my *spirit* (H7307) within you, and cause you to walk in my statutes, and ye shall keep my judgments, and do them.

The *neshama* gives rise to the characteristics describing what human is. Whereas the *ruach* is what humans do, their action in the form of thinking, feeling, and acting. Elihu's ruach, his spirit, was pushing him to get involved in the conversation, which he did decisively.

In Ezekiel, God adds His Holy Spirit. It also causes and helps the receiver take positive action regarding God's way of life. Whether it's the human or God's *s/Spirit* (r/Ruach), it involves action.

Note verse 26, there's mention of a stony heart replaced by a fleshly heart. We have to be careful because there are poetic images here. Just as we'd say, *he was petrified with fright*. He wasn't turned to stone any more than a heart can be real stone. There is imagery and use of vocabulary not always easy to define.

Sometimes the KJV uses the following translations interchangeably: *soul, mind, heart, understanding, wisdom, spirit*. Remember, *soul* covers all three aspects of *human*. And two of them, neshama and ruach, are non-material, spiritual, both functioning together as a tandem. These elements are all present, but sometimes it is hard to separate and identify each, particularly given the interchangeable translations. My intention in this chapter is not to define or untangle definitively every minute aspect of what a human is or does.

> **Job 32:8** But there is a *spirit* (H7307 - ruach) in man: and the *inspiration* (H5397 - neshama) of the Almighty gives them understanding.

There is the tandem of immaterial essences animating each human being. The neshama is analogous with an imprint of God's qualities on a human scale that He infuses into every human being. Coupled with it is the ruach, the action each person takes by capturing information, thoughts, feelings and transforming them into activity. *The Explanation* summarizes this human action in four parts. Here's a link to the index of *Audit of Humankind*[12] where you'll find these sections of the book.

1. How humans function.
2. How humans socialize.
3. How humans rule.
4. How humans reason.

Elaborating neshama and ruach helps you see the basics Genesis lays out at the very Creation of humans. This is evidence of Bible wisdom.

Mind and Conscience

Conscience is an element associated with humans and their minds. It is the ability to exercise a moral sense of right and wrong, humans evaluate situations and subsequent emotions. Please refer to *How humans function* in *Audit of Humankind* to see the relationship between behavior, rules, and self-reproach. The Bible associates mind and conscience with the ruach, the spirit in humans.

> **Genesis 26:35** Which were a grief of *mind* (H7307 - ruach) to Isaac and to Rebekah.
>
> **Genesis 41:88** And it came to pass in the morning that his *spirit* (H7307) was troubled; and he sent and called for all the magicians of, and all the wise men thereof: and Pharaoh told them his dream; but there was none that could interpret them to Pharaoh.

12. https://theexplanation.com/read-content-origin-humankind-online/

In the New Testament, there are many references to the mind and conscience. Behavioral and spiritual conversion takes place at the mind-conscience level. The Apostle Paul is well aware of this and is a primary source of information and inspiration by his personal example.

> **Romans 8:6-7** Read the whole context
>
> 6 For to be carnally minded is death; but to be spiritually minded is life and peace.
>
> 7 Because the carnal mind is enmity against God: for it is not subject to the law of God, neither indeed can be.
>
> **Rom 7:22-23** The war in Paul's conscience
>
> 22 For I delight in the law of God after the inward man:
>
> 23 But I see another law in my members, warring against the law of my mind, and bringing me into captivity to the law of sin which is in my members.

Like Paul, the repentant Christian has embarked on their second life, their spiritual journey. They see the war of lawlessness in their body and God's law in their mind. Their conscience is active, like Paul told Timothy, they are fighting the good fight.

> **I Timothy 6:10-14**
>
> 10 For the love of money is the root of all evil: which while some coveted after, they have erred from the faith, and pierced themselves through with many sorrows.

11 But you, O man of God, flee these things; and follow after righteousness, godliness, faith, love, patience, meekness.

12 Fight the good fight of faith, lay hold on eternal life, whereunto you are also called, and have professed a good profession before many witnesses.

13 I give you charge in the sight of God, who quickens all things, and before Christ Jesus, who before Pontius Pilate witnessed a good confession;

14 That you keep this commandment without spot, unrebukeable, until the appearing of our Lord Jesus Christ:

God's Plan in Gen. 2:7 through nishmat chayIM and nefesh chayA

Above, I mentioned how Gen. 2:7 incorporates the entire plan of God. Here's how. It is the usage of the Hebrew word *chai, life*. Nishmat chayim (the breath of live*s*) is plural, whereas nefesh chaya (living soul) is singular. Here's why.

Nishmat chay*im* (breath or inspiration of live*s*) is plural. Important because it's life + life = 2 lives. This relates to the Tree of Lives, yes it's not the Tree of Life but the Tree of Lives, plural. When you eat from the Tree of Lives, it's life + life = 2 lives. To understand, you need to know what the first life and the second life are. How many know? The plural lives of the inspiration of God give you access to the plural lives of the Tree. Hold this thought.

Nefesh chay*a*. The word chaya and chayim are identical except nefesh chaya is singular. Only one nefesh. Why? To make a long story short. Because when God breathed the nishmat chayim into the human nostrils, the Biblical Hebrew *breathe* means both give and take life. With His breath[13] (please read that article), God can resuscitate or blow you away. The neshama gives you access to two lives, but the nefesh only has one life. If humans don't receive access to the second life, God will blow them away.

The Tree of Lives symbolizes the two lives, a physical and a spiritual life. The spiritual life starts with repentance and baptism, leading to eternal life. The Tree of the Knowledge of good and evil leading to death symbolizes one life. Only physical life for the single nefesh chaya, the person who chooses not to repent. They refuse the fulness of the neshama chayim, the second spiritual life.

Here's Bible corroboration, the conclusion of the story of humankind. The just who go on to eternal life (chayIM), while the unjust lose their life (chayA) (read Revelation 21). The righteous receive the neshama chayim, God's essence of lives forever. The unrighteous receive only the nefesh chaya, one worldly life. They forfeit eternal life.

Rev. 22:11-15

> 11 He that is unjust, let him be unjust still: and he which is filthy, let him be filthy still: and he that is righteous, let him be righteous still: and he that is holy, let him be holy still.
>
> 12 And, behold, I come quickly; and my reward is with me, to give every man according as his work shall be.

13. https://theexplanation.com/god-breathed-nostrils-dust-man/

> 14 Blessed are they that do his commandments, that they may have right to the tree of life, and may enter in through the gates into the city. (physical + spiritual life = chayIM)
>
> 15 For without are dogs, and sorcerers, and whoremongers, and murderers, and idolaters, and whosoever loves and makes a lie. (only physical life = chayA)

The Bible story is about humankind. Nothing more, nothing less. Christ is the focal point. Why? Because He's devoted to human beings and their salvation. That's the relationship between God and humans. God is focusing this part of His plan on the salvation of humankind. The conclusion of Rev. 22, the entire Bible story, is God saves humans. The nishmat chayim God breathed into the first human nostrils is now a massive multitude who have fulfilled the nishmat chayim. Their physical life and their spiritual life have led to God's goal, eternal life.

Further Study

The verses below are directly related to Genesis 2:7. What God did at the Creation of the first human, and what God has in mind and inspired Moses to write as scripture, already included the sure accomplishment of Christ's First and Second Comings. It was already known there would be a resurrection, a new, second spiritual life leading to eternal life. It was known Christ will *make alive* the dead.

Paul emphasizes this point over and over in 1 Corinthians 15. This *make alive* to eternal life is why we have the Tree of Live*s* and nishmat chay*im* (plural), the essence of *lives*. Carrying the neshama means we carry the essence of a second spiritual life leading to eternal life. The nefesh chaya including neshama animates every human, conferring on each one the potential to be quickened, made alive with eternal life. It is the sign of being human.

> **1 Corinthians 15:45** (Study the whole context to see its relation to Gen. 2:7)
>
> 45 And so it is written, The first man Adam was made a living soul; the last Adam was made a quickening spirit.
>
> 21 For since by man came death, by man came also the resurrection of the dead.
>
> 22 For as in Adam all die, even so in Christ shall all be made alive.

We saw Paul's combat, "But I see another law in my members, warring against the law of my mind, and bringing me into captivity to the law of sin which is in my members." (Rom. 7:23). He knew about the downward pull of the Tree of Knowledge leading to death and the upward pull of the Tree leading from physical life to spiritual and eternal life. How many do today? The next chapter gives this internal battle of the mind a name and reveals its gangrene effect on individuals and society. Here's one reason humankind suffers. Bible wisdom tells us how we can lessen its grip and become a twice-living soul.

Hardness of heart. How to deal with it

Hardness of heart in modern English has the meaning, obstinacy. It is the key reason for the Agony of Humankind and human misunderstanding of practical Godly wisdom.

Here's a question about *hardness of heart.* If God is God, Power of Powers, Miracle of Miracles, why doesn't He intervene now and manifest His Magnificence this instant? Humans have been around for thousands of years and gone through hell frequently. Why doesn't the Power of Powers just come and take care of it... collectively or individually?

So far, we see Godview, based on God's Word, is the foundation of solid Bible wisdom. We are wiser about what a human is, with the neshama, consciousness with its singular human characteristics, and physical life as a nefesh chaya, a living soul. Now we need to investigate a defining trait of humankind. This unique temperament is a prerequisite for understanding how God works with human beings. Particularly why God appears to be so cruel in the Old Testament. Grasping this one attribute unlocks much Bible wisdom.

Dictionaries define *hardness of heart* as obstinacy, refusing to change your course of action or opinions. A synonym is *stubbornness*. We all possess it to one degree or another depending on the subject, often influenced by education or an unfortunate experience. Even when others encourage us or try persuasion, hardness of heart prevents budging from one's position.

What is Hardness of Heart?

Let the Bible do the talking. We understand hardness of heart is a word picture, a manner of speaking. It's the objective referring to the subjective. The physical pointing to the non-physical. Even today, we employ another term, stiff-necked. Physically, when someone takes an adamant position in a discussion, veins pop out of their neck, it seemingly becomes unmovable, stiff.

> **Psalms 78:8** And might not be as their fathers, a **stubborn** and rebellious generation; a generation that set not their heart aright, and **whose spirit** was not stedfast with God.

> **Daniel 5:18** O you king, the most high God gave Nebuchadnezzar your father a kingdom, and majesty, and lory, and honour:

> 19 And for the majesty that he gave him, all people, nations, and languages, trembled and feared before him: whom he would he slew; and whom he would he kept

alive; and whom he would he set up; and whom he would he put down.

20 But when his heart was lifted, and his **mind hardened in pride**, he was deposed from his kingly throne, and they took his glory from him:

2 Chronicles 36:13 And he also rebelled against king Nebuchadnezzar, who had made him swear by God: but he stiffened his neck, and **hardened his heart from turning to the LORD** God of Israel.

Nehemiah 9:16 But they and our fathers **dealt proudly, and hardened their necks**, and hearkened not to your commandments,

Rom. 2:5 But after **your hardness and impenitent heart** treasure up to yourself wrath against the day of wrath and revelation of the righteous judgment of God;

Mark 6:52 For they **considered not the miracle of the loaves**: for their heart was hardened.

Mark 8:17 And when Jesus knew it, he said to them, Why reason you, because you have no bread? **perceive you not** yet, **neither understand**? have you your heart yet hardened?

Mark 16:14 Afterward he appeared to the eleven as they sat at meat, and upbraided them with their **unbelief and hardness of heart**, because they believed not them which had seen him after he was risen.

Whether it's the Old or New Testaments, it's the same notion. There are two points to retain.

1. The mind. The seat of hardness is not the physical heart. That is just a picture of the central physical life-giving organ of the body directing us to the central spiritual life-giving element, the human mind[1]. *The Explanation* continues to write reams on this matter[2] because we cannot overemphasize the sheer importance of the mind[3]. Our ideas, imagination, reasoning, moods, attitudes stem from the mind. Block the mind, and the individual is out of circulation. As goes the mind, so goes the person. Possessing a stable mind is the key for each human being[4].
2. Notice the adjectives used to describe this state of hardness of mind: impenitent, considered not, perceive not, neither understand, unbelief.

The Merriam-Webster dictionary provides these synonyms for obstinacy, which is hardness of heart. Using worldly terms, we'd say their states of mind are psychological factors. They are negative spiritual characteristics of human beings: adamant, bullheaded, dogged, hard, hardened, hardheaded, hard-nosed, headstrong, immovable, implacable, inconvincible, inflexible, intransigent, mulish, obdurate, opinionated, ossified, pat, pertinacious, perverse, pigheaded, self-opinionated, self-willed, stiff-necked, stubborn, unbending, uncompromising, unrelenting, unyielding, willful (or wilful).

Stubbornness and obstinacy

1. https://theexplanation.com/nature-of-humans-consciousness-mind-reveal-adroit-humans/
2. https://theexplanation.com/?s=mind
3. https://theexplanation.com/mind-control-the-serpents-number-one-goal/
4. https://theexplanation.com/understanding-the-human-mind-key-to-gods-plan/

Stubbornness or hardness of heart must be understood correctly to grasp God's actions, both in the Old and New Testaments. Hardness of heart is NOT a onetime disobedience, or even a ten-time demeanor. In fact, it has nothing to do with the number of crimes or depth of depravity or immorality. How can I say this? Read the parable of the prodigal son in Luke 15, "he wasted his substance with riotous living." The riotous living covers every crime you can imagine and probably many you can't imagine.

All of God's servants have committed crimes, some terrible ones, like Paul, who killed who knows how many men and women (Acts 22:1-5). Or King David, likewise with Uriah (2 Sam. 11), even after he was in the good graces of God. We are not talking about temper tantrums, or disobedient criminals.

We are talking about an ongoing frame of mind, an attitude rigidly set in stone. The following two passages need to be understood in these terms. The prodigal son had a *change* of heart. That means he did *not* possess hardness of heart. While he was deep into riotous living, yes, it appeared that way, agreed, but he came to his senses. The key to this story and all stories is coming to one's senses, no matter what the crime. But there is a point of no return, and that's hardness of heart, the crux of these two examples.

> **Deuteronomy 21:18, 20**
>
> 18 If a man have a stubborn and rebellious son, which will not obey the voice of his father, or the voice of his mother, and that, when they have chastened him, will not hearken to them:
>
> 20 And they shall say to the elders of his city, This our son is stubborn and rebellious, he will not obey our voice; he is a glutton, and a drunkard.

Judges 2:19

> And it came to pass, when the judge was dead, that they returned, and corrupted themselves more than their fathers, in following other gods to serve them, and to bow down to them; they ceased not from their own doings, nor from their stubborn way.

These examples of hardness of heart have to do with disobedience, a way of life, disobeying laws, doing what's wrong. There is another hardness of heart characterizing people's minds, even good people who are leading decent lives and obeying the laws of the land. Good people also have hardness of heart.

Hardness of Heart = Blindness of those who refuse God

From the start, Adam and Eve hid themselves among the trees. They didn't want God in their lives. This is the underlying cause for the 6000 years of human history. Christ summed it up by quoting Isaiah in John 12:40, "He has blinded their eyes, and hardened their heart; that they should not see with their eyes, nor understand with their heart, and be converted, and I should heal them."

That sounds harsh. Yes, God blinded and still blinds people so they will not be converted. Why? Because God allows humankind to exercise its free will to the nth degree to prove to itself just how hard-headed humanity is. From the start, God told humankind to remember Him[5]. But that was and is not the case. This attitude is still rampant today, "And all the people shall know, even Ephraim and the inhabitant of Samaria, that say in the pride and stoutness of heart, The bricks are fallen down, but we will build with hewn stones: the sycomores are cut down, but we will change them into cedars" (Isa. 9:9-10).

5. https://theexplanation.com/creation-week-reveals-gods-plan-remember-it/

That is what Science, leaders, philosophy, and religion are trying to do today with more or less success. We see the problems in the world, health, war, conflict, etc., and instead of looking for God's solutions, we say we'll find a better way, the way of hewn stones and cedars. God is letting humans exhaust all potential solutions.

Practical Bible wisdom on how to handle hardness of heart

The first thing to realize is God is responsible for the hardness of heart, the blinding of their minds. We have difficulty with that, thinking God is good, He wouldn't voluntarily stop people from being converted. Yes, He would, yes He does.

Romans 1:28

> And even as they did not like to retain God in their knowledge, God gave them over to a reprobate mind, to do those things which are not convenient;

From Adam and Eve onward, Earth's population does not retain God in their knowledge, they do not have Godview but rather personalview. From the time of Noah's flood, and even before, God knew even warnings and punishment would not keep people God-centered. He's turned the reins over to humankind to write their own story and learn the lesson the hard way.

Genesis 9:5-6

> 5 And surely your blood of your lives will I require; at the hand of every beast will I require it, and at the hand of man; at the hand of every man's brother will I require the life of man.

> 6 Whoso sheds man's blood, by man shall his blood be shed: for in the image of God made he man.

> **Luke 8:10**

> And he (Christ) said, to you it is given to know the mysteries of the kingdom of God: but to others in parables; that seeing they might not see, and hearing they might not understand.

God is letting Science, leaders, philosophy, and religion have their *day* to channel *all* their human mind power + human imagination + free will to find solutions for living in peace and prosperity! He is patiently letting them do their thing. Humankind has to write the *full* book of their experience, finish the experiment *before* God can step in! Even then, some will oppose Him.

The first way to handle hardness of heart; understand God causes it. Second, be patient and let it be. Before getting into an argument, think about the consequences. It might seem like the right thing to say, but do you really think it will solve the problem in the long run? We can talk about God, but it is not our role to go on a crusade to push, convince, and insist about God. Think before you speak or act.

> **Proverbs 15:11** A soft answer turns away wrath: but grievous words stir up anger.

A third way, and a suitable compromise to help the hard-hearted, is asking pertinent questions to make people think. It's up to the person. This is not always possible. I know I'm guilty of pushing people too far with strong words, and I have to be careful. Sometimes I even wonder whether I'm too strong in articles and books. However, here, people choose to read them or not.

The solution to hardness of heart must come from the person

You can't convince someone against their will. They alone can initiate their own change.

> **Lamentations 3:39-41**
>
> 39 Wherefore does a living man complain, a man for the punishment of his sins?
>
> 40 Let us search and try our ways, and turn again to the LORD.
>
> 41 Let us lift up our heart with our hands to God in the heavens.

A fourth way to help is to put stubborn people in another environment.

1. God allows a situation to disintegrate... deteriorate. You can do a study, both in Old and New Testament times. There are many examples (the up and downs[6] of the nation of Israel and individuals like Jonah and Job). In 1 Cor. 5:5 this principle is clear, "To deliver such an one to Satan for the destruction of the flesh, that the spirit may be saved in the day of the Lord Jesus."
2. We do this on a human level for rehabilitation of hard-to-handle kids. or wayward boys[7] (and girls, for that matter).

By putting a person through the paces, it makes them think and allows the individual to make a comparison. Which do I really want?

---

6. https://theexplanation.com/ups-and-downs-order-confusion-order-bible-cycle/

7. https://gallery.records.nsw.gov.au/index.php/galleries/50-years-at-state-records-nsw/4-02/

Hardship can bring a person to their senses, as the example of Job shows us.

> God challenges Job about Leviathan, an animal much more powerful than him. Job woke up...
>
> **Job 43:1-6**
>
> 1 Then Job answered the LORD, and said,
>
> 3 Who is he that hides counsel without knowledge? therefore have I uttered that I understood not; things too wonderful for me, which I knew not.
>
> 5 I have heard of you by the hearing of the ear: but now mine eye sees you.
>
> 6 Wherefore I abhor myself, and repent in dust and ashes.

Christ also used other methods despite their hardness of heart

Christ has a mission, which we do not have. Therefore, we need to be careful. He took action despite their hardness of heart. He needed to show them unequivocally who He is, and He did so through the miracles He performed. In the second example below, in John 6, Christ tested His disciples to see who would stay with him. He forcefully said something difficult to test and see their attachment to Him, and especially to the Word.

> **Mark 3:5**
>
> And when he had looked round about on them with anger, being grieved for the hardness of their hearts, he

said to the man, Stretch forth your hand. And he stretched it out: and his hand was restored whole as the other.

John 6:53-62

53 Then Jesus said to them, Verily, verily, I say to you, Except you eat the flesh of the Son of man, and drink his blood, you have no life in you.

54 Whoso eats my flesh, and drinks my blood, has eternal life; and I will raise him up at the last day.

55 For my flesh is meat indeed, and my blood is drink indeed.

59 These things said he in the synagogue, as he taught in Capernaum.

60 Many therefore of his disciples, when they had heard this, said, **This is an hard saying**; who can hear it?

61 When Jesus knew in himself that his disciples murmured at it, he said to them, Does this offend you?

62 What and if you shall see the Son of man ascend up where he was before?

Because of the *hard saying*, many could not bear it. The stamina of their hearts could only bear so much, after which it got harder and harder until finally, no more of the Words of Christ would enter.

God's laws in function of hardness of heart

We now come to the reason I broached this subject. Over the next chapters, I will cover a few subjects, including slavery, parenting, corporal punishment, and the treatment of women in the Old Testament. These are hard subjects of division and miscomprehension. It is impossible to grasp God's view (Godview) without understanding the depth of the concept *hardness of heart*.

> Here's a hard saying to show you how far it goes: *All* laws, bar two, in the Old and New Testament were and are written because of hardness of heart.

Those two exceptions are to love God and love your neighbor. Understand, *if* we fully applied those two Laws, we would *not* need any other law. All the law hangs on the two Great Laws. Overall law in the Old Testament is *do NOT* because of hardness of heart. In the New Testament, it's the opposite, *do*, love God and neighbor, because of the openness of the converted heart.

Christ answered a question about divorce, "Why did Moses then command to give a writing of divorcement, and to put her away? He said to them, Moses because of the hardness of your hearts suffered you to put away your wives: but from the beginning it was not so" (Mat. 19:7-8).

If they'd have asked him about the laws regarding slavery, parenting, corporal punishment, and the treatment of women, Christ would've given exactly the same answer, *because of the hardness of your hearts, but from the beginning it was not so*. Please grasp this point. This is the answer to all the queries regarding all the laws. Why?

"Because from the beginning it was not so." What was "in the beginning?" Love God and love your neighbor. Two simple laws encompassing *all* the law. Of course, *simple* is a manner of speaking.

At Mount Sinai, God officializes the Ten Commandments to the nation of Israel *and* all peoples who accompanied them on departure from Egypt. This latter observation means the law is for *all* people.

Referring to that law, "Jesus answered and said to them (the Pharisees), For the hardness of your heart he wrote you this precept" Mark 10:55. God gave them rules for ethical behavior[8]. Those rules, or *laws*, were in function of their hardness of heart. Slavery, parenting, corporal punishment, and the treatment of women, as mentioned, and as practices according to God's rules, were necessary to maintain law and order of hard-hearted citizens and a world of hard-hearted people.

That might be hard to accept, I hope not. The key to peace and prosperity for Old Testament Israel and all of humanity is to follow God's way of life. They were characterized, and the world today is bitten by hardness of heart toward God, their Creator. The law is the best way to maintain order in the face of stubbornness.

The antidote to hardness of heart is...

God pleaded with Israel and His people everywhere to rid themselves of hardness of heart. To open up their minds to His ways of peace and prosperity. This is so, both in the Old and New Testaments.

> **Psalms 95:8** Harden not your heart, as in the provocation, and as in the day of temptation in the wilderness:
>
> **Hebrews 3:8, 15**

---

8. https://theexplanation.com/ethical-behavior-break-the-rules-heres-the-outcome/

> Harden not your hearts, as in the provocation, in the day of temptation in the wilderness:
>
> While it is said, To day if you will hear his voice, harden not your hearts, as in the provocation.

Christ upbraided the disciples for not seeing what should've been evident. "For they considered not the miracle of the loaves: for their heart was hardened." They had seen Christ feed about 5000 people with 12 baskets of leftovers (Mark 6). This miracle should've been enough to convince them Christ could walk on water. But no, they didn't put two-and-two together. The solution is right there before their and our eyes, but we don't want to see it.

God has always made available evidence for Bible wisdom. Because of obstinacy, people reject such testimony. They display hardness of heart and rebuff what God lays out in His Word.

Repentance

The opposite, hence the antidote to hardness of heart, is repentance, an open heart desiring to hear and follow God's way. This is just as true in the Old as in the New Testament. But the rules and stakes are different for a carnal and a spiritual mind. In the Old, for the carnal mind, you can do a study on the word *hearken*. Go to UnlockBibleMeaning.com and search for it, switch to Strong's, and check H8085. It means *listen, perceive, obey*. Moses' last exhortation revolves around this word as he focuses the nation's attention on God's way of life and the consequences of following or not His injunctions.

> **Deuteronomy 30:10-18**

> 10 If you shall **hearken** to the voice of the LORD your God, to keep his commandments and his statutes which are written in this book of the law, and if you turn to the LORD your God with all your heart, and with all your soul.
>
> 11 For this commandment which I command you this day, it is not hidden from you, neither is it far off.
>
> 14 But the word is very near to you, in your mouth, and in your heart, that you may do it.
>
> 15 See, I have set before you this day life and good, and death and evil; (remind you of the two Trees in the Garden of Eden?)
>
> 16 In that I command you this day to love the LORD you God, to walk in his ways, and to keep his commandments and his statutes and his judgments, that you may live and multiply: and the LORD your God shall bless you in the land whither you go to possess it.
>
> 17 But if your heart turn away, so that you will not hear, but shall be drawn away, and worship other gods, and serve them;
>
> 18 I denounce to you this day, that you shall surely perish, and that you shall not prolong your days upon the land, whither you pass over Jordan to go to possess it.

Individually and collectively, God always leaves us with the choice of a hard or an open heart. Make the right decision. God is forever ready to overlook the period of hardness of heart when there is a change of heart and mind.

Acts 17:30 And the times of this ignorance God winked at; but now commands all men every where to repent:

Acts 3:19 Repent you therefore, and be converted, that your sins may be blotted out, when the times of refreshing shall come from the presence of the Lord;

Conversion, changing from hardness of heart to repentance, is part of the covenant with God. On repentance, we show God we want His way of life. In the future, God will put His full law, the two laws, in our hearts forever. Hardness of heart will be a thing of the past. For now, the evidence of Bible wisdom is there, but few heed it as the next chapter reveals. How many remember the Sabbath?

Sabbath Day. God Rested & We Rest. That's it?

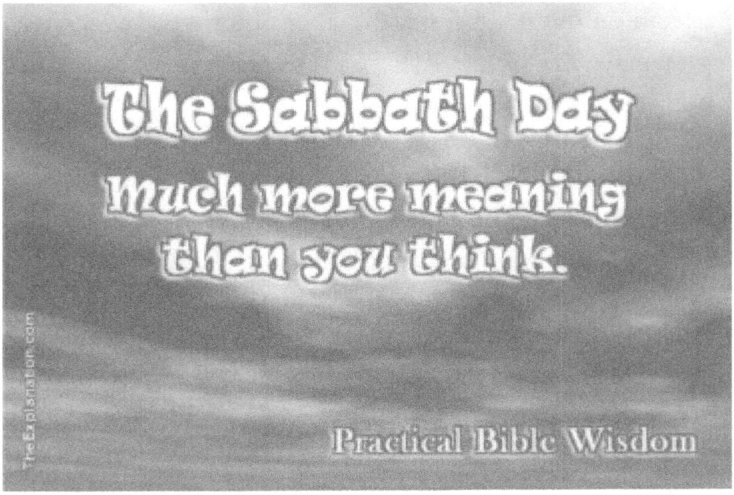

Of the Ten Commandments, which is the longest? The strangest? The least understood? The only one modified in Deuteronomy? The Sabbath day.

What is the meaning of the Sabbath day? Why is it so controversial? Practical Bible wisdom asserts God set aside a day for a good reason. Here's the purpose of the Sabbath day.

In Chapter 1.1, we addressed evidence for God and I said *The Explanation* will give you some deep insight into the mysteries (Luke 8:10) of His Master plan for humankind to further enhance evidence for God. The Sabbath day is one of those mysteries the Lord of the Sabbath (Mark 2:27), Jesus Christ, explained, as recorded in all four Gospels.

God inaugurated The Sabbath day, the seventh day of the week, at Creation.

Genesis 2:2-3

> 2 And on the seventh day God *ended* his work which he had made; and he *rested* (H7673) on the seventh day from all his work which he had made.
>
> 3 And God blessed the seventh day, and sanctified it: because that in it he had *rested* (H7673) from all his work which God created and *made* (to make H6213).
>
> 4 These are the generations of the heavens and of the earth when they were created, in the day that the LORD God made the earth and the heavens,

For a detailed explanation of these verses, read this article[1]. Use the Bible tools at UnlockBibleMeaning.com[2] to verify the Biblical Hebrew meaning of *Sabbath*. This is an important context for several reasons I will summarize here, read this article for a detailed explanation[3]. God ceased the physical Creation and on the Sabbath, the seventh day (not the sixth or the first). On the Sabbath, He worked with His special Creation, humans to make (H6213) them[4], to teach them how to lead their lives.

The KJV translation is hard to grasp, "he had rested from all his work which God created and made." Here's a more comprehensible translation, as the two articles explain, "he rested WITH[5] all his

1. https://theexplanation.com/god-to-do-with-his-work-to-make-them-on-7th-day-to-take-care-his-creation/
2. https://unlockbiblemeaning.com
3. https://theexplanation.com/god-made-something-on-the-climactic-7th-day-of-creation/
4. https://theexplanation.com/god-made-something-on-the-climactic-7th-day-of-creation/

work (the humans) which God created TO MAKE[6]." Whereas ALL the rest of the Creation was finished, humankind was physically finished but NOT spiritually. The meaning of the word Sabbath reveals what the Sabbath day is for, what God did on that day with Adam and Eve.

I need you to note Genesis 2:4 is the first time in the Bible the term *Lord God* (Yahveh Elohim) is used. This refers to the entire seven-day Creation week, but specifically the Lord's relation to the seventh day and what He did with the humans on that original Sabbath day.

> **H7673**
>
> שָׁבַת shâbath shaw-bath'; a primitive root; to repose, i.e. desist from exertion; used in many implied relations (causative, figurative or specific):
>
> KJV - (cause to, let, make to) cease, celebrate, cause (make) to fail, keep (sabbath), suffer to be lacking, leave, put away (down), (make to) rest, rid, still, take away.

Most people associate one word with the Sabbath day, *rest*, which is the translation in Gen. 2:3. But elsewhere *shabbat* (שָׁבַת, H7673) translates many other ways. Space lacks for in-depth development of this subject. For now, retain the second meaning of Sabbath day, *cease*. It is a day of ceasing from regular weekday activities. This aspect is well-known but both *ceasing* and *resting* have deeper meaning, as we'll see in just a moment.

---

5. https://theexplanation.com/god-to-do-with-his-work-to-make-them-on-7th-day-to-take-care-his-creation/

6. https://theexplanation.com/god-made-something-on-the-climactic-7th-day-of-creation/

There's an important *third* event mostly overlooked, God did on the Sabbath day. We must consider it for a more complete understanding of the wisdom of the Sabbath. Here it is.

Exodus 31:16-17

16 Wherefore the children of Israel shall keep the sabbath, to observe the sabbath throughout their generations, for a perpetual covenant.

17 It is a sign between me and the children of Israel for ever: for in six days the LORD made heaven and earth, and on the seventh day he *rested* (H7673), and was *refreshed* (H5314).

The Sabbath day is a day of rest. Some people think this means doing nothing. On the contrary, it is a day of directed activity with a specific goal, to *refresh* individuals and the community. We use the term refreshments when we take a break from any activity, it generally refers to a drink or snack to renew our physical strength. In the context of God and the fourth Commandment, it refers to *refreshing* our spiritual strength.

H5314

נָפַשׁ knavish naw-fash'; a primitive root; to breathe; passively, to be breathed upon, i.e. (figuratively) refreshed (as if by a current of air):

KJV - (be) refresh selves (-ed).

H5315

> נֶפֶשׁ nephesh neh'-fesh; from H5314 (נָפַשׁ) properly, a breathing creature, i.e. animal of (abstractly) vitality; used very widely in a literal, accommodated or figurative sense (bodily or mental):
>
> KJV - any, appetite, beast, body, breath, creature, × dead(-ly), desire, × (dis-) contented, × fish, ghost, + greedy, he, heart(-y), (hath, × jeopardy of) life ([idiom] in jeopardy), lust, man, me, mind, mortally, one, own, person, pleasure, (her-, him-, my-, thy-) self, them (your) -selves, + slay, soul, + tablet, they, thing, ([idiom] she) will, × would have it.

On the Sabbath day, God *rested* and was *refreshed*. When you read the Hebrew for *refreshed* (H5315) you might've been struck by this word because you've heard it before. Indeed, it's the recognized word *nefesh* for *soul* in Gen. 2:7 "And he (the first man) became a living *soul*." We discussed it a couple of chapters ago. It comes from H5314, *refresh*, as from a current of cool air after you've exerted an effort. Exactly what you've done over the six day work week. You need a day of ceasing from physical activity to focus on spiritual rejuvenation.

Cease, refresh, rest

The Sabbath day, by God's actions, projects three primary themes: *ceasing*, *refreshing*, *resting*. To say the Sabbath day is a day of *rest* is correct. But it also means we miss two-thirds of the meaning. The Sabbath day includes *ceasing* and *refreshing*.

Here's how this applies to the original Sabbath when the Lord God was with the first two humans in the Garden of Eden viewing the two Trees.

1. **Cease**: The Lord God told the humans to always *cease* from

eating from the Tree of the knowledge of good and evil or they would *decease*. They would die. It is vital to understand the meaning of *sabbath* includes this concept. For confirmation, look at (and study them) the fuller significance of *shabbat* (H7673): *cause (make) to fall, leave, put away (down), (make to) rest, rid, still, take away*. That means if you don't cease eating the forbidden fruit of the Tree, you will die.

2. **Refresh**: The Lord God told them to eat of the Tree of Life. This represents the spiritual path of growth humans were created to follow. It is the reason God created perfect physical beings *to make* (H6213) them spiritually. The Lord God established the Sabbath day for human spiritual activity. It's the day for spiritual creation, learning to cease from the Tree of Death and eat of the Tree of Life.
3. **Rest**: This is the peace that comes from the Lord God. Christ said in John 14:27, "Peace. I leave with you, my peace I give to you: not as the world gives, give I to you. Let not your heart be troubled, neither let it be afraid." The world's way (of the forbidden Tree) leads to death. God's way (the Tree of Life) leads to real rest, ultimately Eternal Life. Sabbath, H7673, also means *celebrate*. Yes, the Sabbath is a day of celebration.

The Sabbath day was inaugurated at Creation by the Lord God for humans. The Sabbath day was later codified as the fourth of the Ten Commandments. Are these commandments only for the Israelites or for all peoples everywhere? Again, a controversial subject where much could be said. Let's slash through the Gordian knot and go to the crux of the matter.

First, it was given at Creation to the representatives of all humankind. Second, Christ said, "On these two commandments hang all the law and the prophets" (Matthew 22:40). Those two commandments are for all humanity. They are the spiritual application of everything stated by all the prophets, of which Moses was one.

The Sabbath is for all humankind. It is in the fourth position of the list of ten because it joins the first three commandments specifically referring to God to the last six commandments specifically referring to humankind, all nations. It is the link command. Interestingly, it is the only command having two versions. The first edition is in Exodus.

Exodus 20:10-11

10 But the seventh day is the sabbath of the LORD your God: in it you shall not do any work, you, nor your son, nor your daughter, your manservant, nor your maidservant, nor your cattle, nor your stranger that is within your gates:

11 For **in six days the LORD made heaven and earth, the sea, and all that in them is**, and rested the seventh day: wherefore the LORD blessed the sabbath day, and hallowed it.

The second edition is in the last book of Moses.

Deuteronomy 5:13-15

13 Six days you shall labour, and do all your work:

14 But the seventh day is the sabbath of the LORD your God: in it you shall not do any work, you, nor your son, nor your daughter, nor your manservant, nor your

> maidservant, nor your ox, nor your ass, nor any of your cattle, nor your stranger that is within your gates; that your manservant and your maidservant may rest as well as you.
>
> 15 And remember that you were a servant in the land of Egypt, and that **the LORD your God brought you out thence** through a mighty hand and by a stretched out arm: therefore the LORD your God commanded you to keep the sabbath day.

This is the only modified commandment because God associates the Sabbath day with creation and progressing from slavery to freedom. Briefly, here's the point.

1. God created humans and continued to make them spiritually by giving them instruction (physical and spiritual *creation* Ex. 20).
2. They disobeyed and went into slavery to their own ways and literally in Egypt.
3. God brings them out of slavery in Egypt and sends His Son, Jesus, to release us from the slavery of this world (Deut. 5, *cease* slavery and own ways, *refresh* in God's way). God gave the Israelites freedom from physical slavery and to us freedom from sin (*rest*).

> The Sabbath day is an amazing summary of the entirety of God's plan; *creation*, *refreshing* from sin, and the ultimate *rest* for humankind.

Remember ceasing, refreshing, resting.

1. **Ceasing.** The Sabbath day represents humans ceasing from

their regular daily activities. Spiritually this means ceasing from anything opposed to God's ways, ceasing from sin.

2. **Refreshing.** The current of cool air, the breathing of the Holy Spirit on a human being, is the only way humans can become *a new man* in Christ. They can refresh "For they have re*freshed* (G373) my spirit and yours therefore acknowledge you them that are such" (1 Corinthians 1:18).
3. **Resting.** "There remains therefore a *rest* to the people of God. For he that is entered into his *rest*, he also has *ceased* from his own works, as God did from his. Let us labour (*refresh ourselves*) therefore to enter into that *rest*, lest any man fall (*decease*) after the same example of unbelief" (Hebrews 4:9-11).

All the spiritual elements of the profound meaning of the Sabbath are present in the passage in Hebrews; *ceasing* from the works of the Tree of the Knowledge of Good and Evil. *Refreshing* by partaking of the Tree of Life. Leading to full *rest* in eternal life or, if one refuses God's ways, *deceasing* as per the Tree leading to death.

Lord of the Sabbath & Sabbath made for man

Now we can understand two related statements, both by Christ, recorded side-by-side in the book of Mark.

Mark 2:23-3:5

23 And it came to pass, that he went through the corn fields on the sabbath day; and his disciples began, as they went, to pluck the ears of corn.

24 And the Pharisees said to him (Christ), Behold, why do they on the sabbath day that which is not lawful

25 And he said to them, Have you never read what David did, when he had need, and was an hungred, he, and they that were with him?

26 How he went into the house of God in the days of Abiathar the high priest, and did eat the shewbread, which is not lawful to eat but for the priests, and gave also to them which were with him?

27 And he said to them, **The sabbath was made for man**, and not man for the sabbath:

28 Therefore the Son of man is **Lord also of the sabbath**.

3:1 And he entered again into the synagogue; and there was a man there which had a withered hand.

2 And they watched him, whether he would heal him on the sabbath day; that they might accuse him.

3 And he said to the man which had the withered hand, Stand forth.

4 And he said to them, Is it lawful to do good on the sabbath days, or to do evil? to save life, or to kill? But they held their peace.

5 And when he had looked round about on them with anger, being grieved for the hardness of their hearts, he said to the man, Stretch forth your hand. And he stretched it out: and his hand was restored whole as the other.

These two examples illustrate how the Sabbath serves the welfare of all humans (the sabbath was made for *man*). How Christ, our Lord, decides what the use of the Sabbath is for (the Son of man is Lord of the Sabbath).

1. **Cease.** David ceased from war, Christ and His disciples ceased from their intensive work, but continued to preach and teach. The withered hand ceased.
2. **Refresh.** David and the disciples were refreshed physically. Spiritual teaching on the Sabbath refreshes spiritually. The man's hand was refreshed.
3. **Rest.** The result of ceasing and refreshing leads to resting for David, Christ, the disciples, and the healed man.

The entire process of ceasing, refreshing, resting is the pathway for coming out of slavery to sin (Deut. 5) and becoming a new spiritual creation (Ex. 20). This next passage can be a little enigmatic, but with the principles developed in this chapter, you should understand the meaning.

Matthew 12:5-8

5 Or have you not read in the law, how that on the sabbath days the priests in the temple profane the sabbath, and are blameless?

6 But I say to you, That in this place is one greater than the temple.

7 But if you had known what this means, I will have mercy, and not sacrifice, you would not have condemned the guiltless.

8 For the Son of man is Lord even of the sabbath day.

Priests and present-day pastors in God's Church *work* on the Sabbath. They work *to make* the people of God as the Lord God did in Genesis 2:3 with the first humans. They do not profane the Sabbath in God's Church, the spiritual Temple, the Church of which the Lord Jesus Christ is the Foundation, Cornerstone, and Builder. He's greater than the Church, as He is to the temple, and His desire is for us to cease and refresh ourselves in God's mercy to be at rest with ourselves and with Him.

All the Gospels refer to Christ's activity on the Sabbath, Luke 6:2-10, John 7:19-23, etc. and whether it's His instruction or actions, they always include the principles of ceasing, refreshing, and resting. When we understand the deep meaning of the Sabbath day, encompassed by these three principles, then we will see the significance of the Sabbath day in many other verses. For instance.

Romans 12:2

> And be not conformed to this world: but be you transformed by the renewing of your mind, that you may prove what is that good, and acceptable, and perfect, will of God.

Non-conformation to the world is synonymous with *ceasing*. Transforming and renewing are synonymous with *refreshing*, while the perfect will of God is synonymous with *resting*. That's the mystery of the Sabbath day for humankind, the Lord God of the Sabbath's plan for the salvation of humanity.

The next chapter goes further in-depth by expounding on God's story for humanity with practical Bible wisdom about another mystery of God, His festivals.

Biblical Feast Days. Meaning for You

Feast days in the Bible are an enigma. Are they Jewish? Should Christians observe them? Are they rituals or do they have meaning?

God's feast days are one of the biggest puzzles of religion and Bible theology. Books like Exodus and Leviticus record them, and many consider them therefore as festivals for the Israelites. In the New Testament, Christ seems to have observed some of them. But He's Jewish, so it's normal. When you get into the post-Jesus Christian era, there are vague allusions to Passover, Unleavened Bread, a fast alluded to in Acts 27:9, but no clear injunctions for their observance.

Do we? Don't we? Are they necessary under the new dispensation? Which Feasts? And the questions go on and on. As with a lot of Bible commentaries showing Old Testament principles are no longer binding, they emphasize the triviality of events, often quoting Bible experts to back up their suppositions.

You can look at all the arguments against Feast-keeping by searching in Google, "why old testament feast days are no longer valid." Supposedly, verse after verse proves the abolition of the Feast days. Paradoxically, one Church that observes these days proposes their primary reason, "Christ did, so we do too." Should that be the primary reason? It certainly is a good one, but is it the essential purpose?

What is the underlying aim of the Feast Days? They are vital lessons God teaches humankind. Yes, not just Israelites, or Old Testament Israel, or a few Christian observers of these days. The Feasts teach incredible lessons about God, His plan, and humankind's relation to their Creator.

Consider this chapter as an introduction to the subject. It will give you Bible reasons to motivate your closer study of this exciting subject. We want a Godview[1], what God has in mind. Why God instituted the Feast days. Is there something He wants us to learn beyond simple observance because the Old Testament Israelites kept them with sacrifices and Christ observed them because He was Jewish?

The Explanation always starts at the beginning, in Genesis. The first five minutes of the movie establish the characters and plot. Let's start with a regular remark from detractors. Light on Day 1, when the Sun only appears on Day 4 of Creation. May I point out, whoever wrote Genesis would've been aware of such a blatant discrepancy and made amends, were it a mistake, but it isn't.

---

1. https://theexplanation.com/evidence-for-god-can-you-prove-god-exists/

Please read this article for a detailed explanation[2]. The brief answer is the sun was already there on Day 1, having been set in place billions of years previously[3]. Day 4 says, "God *made* two great lights..." The *made* does not imply creation but adjustment of the sun and moon to govern the calendar[4].

In our 21st century Western society, we tend to forget the importance of seasons. Yes, we know it's too hot in summer and too cold in winter because of the upset climate. But what I mean is we don't see the relation between seasons and harvests. Our food comes from a supermarket and with globalization, we purchase all products year-round. We don't know what *fruit or vegetables in season* means. In a geographical location, it doesn't work that way. There are seasons; spring, summer, fall, and winter. And there are crops grown and harvested only at precise times in the year.

Genesis 1:14 says, "let there be lights in the firmament of the heaven to divide the day from the night; and let them be for signs, and for *seasons* (H4150), and for days, and years." That is the key to Day 4. Do a study of Christ's parables and see how many of them refer to seed, crops, and harvesting. Christ gave the parables to teach us lessons of life, particularly Christian life. Could it be these lessons from agriculture are keys to understanding times, seasons, and Feast Days? Yes, as we shall see.

Sabbath and Feast Days

Let's grasp the relationship between the first and last days of Creation week[5]. *The Explanation* elaborated on this subject in *Origin*

---

2. https://theexplanation.com/day-4-of-creation-sun-and-moon-establish-calendar/

3. https://theexplanation.com/timeline-history-universe-earth-humans/

4. https://theexplanation.com/day-4-of-creation-sun-and-moon-establish-calendar/

5. https://theexplanation.com/creation-day-5-and-6-god-created-fish-fowl-and-fauna/

of the Universe. Please read the background[6]. On the first days comes the framework; light-dark, water-sky, and land, then the details; sun-moon, fish-fowl, and fauna. I wrote,

- **Days 1** / **4**: Light-Dark / Sun-Moon.
- **Days 2** / **5**: Water-Sky / Fish-Fowl (Genesis 1:20-23).
- **Days 3** / **6**: Land / Fauna (Genesis 1:24-25).

There are rhyme and reason for this creation parallelism which continues to Days 4 /7: Sun, moon / The Sabbath teaching of creation, refreshing, and resting[7].

- **Days 4** / 7: Annual Sabbaths / Weekly Sabbath.

Day 4 instructs us in the same lessons of creation, refreshing, and resting on a monthly and yearly basis, according to God's established calendar, as the weekly Sabbath. That's why I explained the meaning of the Sabbath day[8] and Christ's words, "the Sabbath was made for man." Similarly, the calendar, seasons, and the Feasts were made for man.

The link between the *Sabbath* (established Day 7 of Creation week), the *Feasts, seasons*, and *calendar* (Day 4) is in Leviticus 23:1-4.

Leviticus 23:1-5

1 And the LORD spake to Moses, saying,

2 Speak to the children of Israel, and say to them, Concerning the *feasts* (H4150) of the LORD, which you

6. https://theexplanation.com/creation-day-5-and-6-god-created-fish-fowl-and-fauna/

7. https://theexplanation.com/meaning-of-the-sabbath-day-god-rested-we-rest/

8. https://theexplanation.com/meaning-of-the-sabbath-day-god-rested-we-rest/

shall proclaim to be holy convocations, even these are my *feasts* (H4150).

3 Six days shall work be done: but the seventh day is the *sabbath* (H7676) of *rest* (H7676), an holy convocation; you shall do no work therein: it is the *sabbath* (H7676) of the LORD in all your dwellings.

4 These are the *feasts* (H4150) of the LORD, even holy convocations, which you shall proclaim in their *seasons* (H4150).

5 In the fourteenth day of the first month at even is the LORD's passover.

- The Sabbath is the first of the Feast Days (Lev. 23:1).
- The *Feasts* (verse 2) and the *seasons* (verse 4) are the identical Hebrew word, *moadim* - H4150. Verify this in Strong's Concordance with the Bible tools at UnlockBibleMeaning.com[9]. God established the seasons (moadim) so we can know when the Feasts (moadim) occur on the calendar. Without the movement of the sun and moon, no calendar, no seasons, no knowing when these Feasts occur.

The fourth day of Creation establishes the movement of our key calendar pointers, the sun and moon. They are not to be worshipped, but to designate, for humankind, the Feasts during which we worship God. These same Feasts, through the seasons and harvests, also reflect the plan of God for the individual and collective salvation of all humankind, as we shall see.

9. https://unlockbiblemeaning.com

> These Feasts are the *Feasts of the Lord* (Lev. 23:4), just as the seventh-day *Sabbath is of the Lord* (Lev. 23:3). As Christ is the *Lord of the Sabbath*, He's also *Lord of the Moadim*, the Feasts.

In this respect, Creation week is a literal period of seven 24-hour days. Why? Whereas the movements of the sun and moon in relation to Earth establish the length of a day, month, seasons, and year, no celestial movements establish the period of a week! Only the seven 24-hour days of Creation establish the duration of a calendar week.

Worldwide, we observe the 7-day week without realizing its origin at the Creation. Christ, as Lord of the Sabbath, rested on the original Sabbath to refresh, so to speak, the first two humans[10]. That 24-hour period followed the previous six 24-hour days, inaugurating the cycle of a week.

The length of a week is not a mystery, and neither is the seventh day, it's Saturday. It is the Day of the Lord, the Sabbath, with its name revealing the plan of God[11]. It is the only day with a name and names, in Hebrew, are vital for teaching meaning[12]. An ordinal number (first, second, third...) designates all the other days; they are regular working days "Six days shall you labour, and do all your work. (Exodus 20:9)."

Moad

The link between Leviticus 23 and Genesis 1 clearly reveals what God did on the fourth day of Creation.

---

10. https://theexplanation.com/god-pursued-his-work-resting-with-adam-and-eve-whom-he-created-to-make/

11. https://theexplanation.com/meaning-of-the-sabbath-day-god-rested-we-rest/

12. https://theexplanation.com/bible-names-have-descriptive-personal-meaning/

Genesis 1:14-15

14 And God said, Let there be lights in the firmament of the heaven to divide the day from the night; and let them be for signs, and for *seasons* (H4150 - moadim), and for days, and years:

15 And let them be for lights in the firmament of the heaven to give light upon the earth: and it was so.

This is where you have to be very careful studying translations[13]. In verse 14, these are not the *seasons* of spring, summer, fall, and winter. The Biblical Hebrew name *moadim* tells us what they are.

H4150

מוֹעֵד môw'êd mo-ade'; or מֹעֵד; or (feminine) 2) ;מוֹעָדָה Chronicles 8:13), from H3259 (יָעַד); properly, an appointment, i.e. a fixed time or season; specifically, a festival; conventionally a year; by implication, an assembly (as convened for a definite purpose); technically the congregation; by extension, the place of meeting; also a signal (as appointed beforehand):

KJV - appointed (sign, time), (place of, solemn) assembly, congregation, (set, solemn) feast, (appointed, due) season, solemn(-pity), synogogue, (set) time (appointed).

Moadim are *times appointed* by God, on Day 4 of Creation. They designate *congregation* at *set times* in places for a *solemn assembly*. God established these appointed times before He created humankind. He is Lord of the Moadim and He made the Feasts for man.

13. https://theexplanation.com/bible-translations-are-the-basis-of-your-beliefs/

The Moadim, the Feast Days, intricately weave into the planting of seed, the harvesting, and the offerings and blessings of the resultant crops. The entire story of humankind from a Godview revolves around a *land of milk and honey* (a description of the Holy Land, but also the Garden of Eden), and bread and wine, from Melchizedek to Christ. The flora (flowers > bees > honey), fauna (cows > milk), crops (grains > bread, grapes > wine) are all a result of establishing the calendar on Day 4 of Creation.

Milk and honey, bread and wine are vital for our physical sustenance. I don't need to go into details here for you to know the relevance of the *bread* and *wine*, the *body* and *blood* of Jesus Christ, for our spiritual sustenance. Without them we are spiritually dead, with them we come alive and can access eternal life. The physical food and crops prefigure the spiritual food and crops.

Passover

The first of the Feast Days is Passover, (Lev. 23:5) the Feast of the *blood of an unblemished lamb* smeared on the doorposts to identify the occupants to be saved. The very symbolism of the *blood of Christ* so we do not die of our sins. *Unleavened bread*, because the Israelites left in haste (Exodus 12:8, 39), represents His body so we can be healed from our past life. On the 14th day of the month, why? Because that day is a full moon[14] when the light of Christ shines fully on Christ's brothers and sisters. The wine and bread of Passover symbolize this transitional moment in a Christian's life.

I could go on and explain the meaning of each of the seven Feast Days evoked in Leviticus 23. In fact, you can write a book about them as they relate to Christ's parables and reveal God's plan of salvation for all of humankind.

---

14. https://theexplanation.com/day-4-of-creation-sun-and-moon-establish-calendar

Let's take another approach because of what a human being is. Unfortunately, today, humans do not know who they are. Science is continually telling us we are the continuum of the animal kingdom. It keeps highlighting animal intelligence and the mere 5% difference in the genome of apes compared to humans. In other words, we're pretty closely related.

No, there isn't any such relationship between humankind and apes or any animal. There is an impassable chasm dividing us, too deep, too wide to be crossed. The Moadim, the Feasts, demonstrate this night and day reality.

The first injunction Peter gave people to become Christian was "repent and be baptized" (Acts 2:38). What is the meaning of repent? Repent from what? How? *The Explanation* expounded on *How Humans Function* in Section 2 of the book *Audit of Humankind*[15].

There are seven steps relevant to human functioning. We must understand each in its role regarding repentance:

1. Dual human nature[16].
2. Free will[17].
3. Human Behavior[18].
4. Ethics[19].

---

15. https://theexplanation.com/read-all-the-content-of-audit-of-humankind-online/

16. http://theexplanation.com/20_mans-singularity-dual-nature

17. http://theexplanation.com/free-will-we-all-possess-it-but-we-cant-always-utilize-it/?swcfpc=1

18. http://theexplanation.com/human-behavior-is-the-expression-of-human-nature-and-free-will/?swcfpc=1

19. http://theexplanation.com/ethics-are-the-blueprint-for-behavior-how-humanity-should-function/?swcfpc=1

5. Justice[20].
6. Self-Reproach[21] - Repentance comes before forgiveness, therefore preceding baptism, as Peter said.
7. Forgiveness[22] - Passover, corresponding to baptism by immersion for the burial of our sins. Followed by a resurrection from the watery grave as a new, clean, spiritual creation, the new hu(man) (Ephesians 4:24, Colossians 3:10).

The first Feast is Passover, corresponding to the seventh step of how humans function. Note that repentance, or self-reproach, as I called it, is the sixth step, just before forgiveness. Here's the key. A being can *not* repent without understanding and accepting the first five steps of how humans function, in particular, themselves. Every human must recognize their dual nature, their free will, their behavior, where they have fallen short of God's ethics and His justice. When they do, they're repentant and ready for baptism and forgiveness. I hope you realize there's a lot of baptizing going on withOUT this perception, withOUT repentance.

I hear some saying, "not so. All you have to do is give your heart to the Lord," and He will save you. Practical Bible wisdom dismisses such affirmations. Bible evidence is in the Old and New Testaments. I will limit this chapter to the Old because most people think the ten plagues of Egypt leading to the Passover are a myth, or a nice plot for a Charlton Heston, Yul Brynner movie.

---

20. http://theexplanation.com/justice-goes-hand-in-hand-with-ethics-to-obtain-peace/?swcfpc=1
21. http://theexplanation.com/self-reproach-the-essential-beginning-step-toward-real-peace/?swcfpc=1
22. https://theexplanation.com/forgiveness-the-healing-bond-for-humans-to-function-peacefully/?swcfpc=1

The ten plagues reveal the first five points of how humans function. Each plague showed the dual nature (1) of the Egyptians and their Pharaoh. The free choice (2) of being in favor or against the Word of God in the mouth of Moses to let His people go. By the seventh plague, even some Egyptians changed their minds, exercising their free will (2) to oppose Pharoah (Exodus 9:20). But Pharoah's ten choices against God's will revealed his behavior (3). He disobeyed the orders, the ethics (4), God set for him and his people. The ensuing plagues were God's justice (5) for his free will decisions and behavior.

There are no less than ten examples to drive the necessity of proper human behavior home. The Egyptians didn't learn and frankly, as the story develops, neither did the Israelites. Their disobedience (3) to God's ethics, His commandments (4), is the reason they spent 40 years, God's justice (5), in the desert. It's the reason Joshua and Caleb went into the Promised Land (Numbers 14:24), their dual nature (1) exercised the proper free choice decision (2) to believe God's ethical guidelines (4), and they were blessed (the upside of God's justice) by crossing the Jordan River.

No animal can follow any of these steps of how humans function, that's the impassable chasm. The genome does not make us human. Even if apes had 100% correspondence, they would not be human. Why? We saw it in Chapter 3, the neshama. It is this unseen but central God-given element that confers consciousness on humans, allowing us to exercise self-reproach and forgiveness of ourselves and others. No animal possesses neshama, humans are on a spiritual plane, animals are not.

Every human being who has lived on Earth, regardless of gender, race, or creed, will have the opportunity for repentance and baptism, in God's timeframe. I realize there are mental and other reasons this is not possible now and will return to this point. But recognize that in Christ's day, since then, and even today very few people are aware of how humans function naturally and spiritually with godly sorrow, repentance, and His forgiveness (Matthew 22:14, 2 Corinthians 7:10).

If the seven steps of how humans function culminate in forgiveness, corresponding to the first Feast, Passover, what do the other six Feasts represent?

Individual Salvation

Feast 2 - Following the forgiveness of Passover, **Unleavened Bread** (15th day of 1st month) is the correct application of the first five steps of how a human functions. Unleavened signifies we're taking the self, our vanity, our sin, out of our behavior (1 Corinthians 5:6-8). Our nature (1) opts to choose (2) and behave (3) in accordance with God's way (4). We learn the Biblical ethics and apply them.

Feast 3 - **Pentecost**. Reception of the Holy Spirit, becoming part of God's community, the Church of which He is the Cornerstone (Isaiah 28:16). Biblically, this is the Spring, early harvest, the firstfruits of the harvest, in the form of two loaves offered to God on the Day of Pentecost (Lev. 23:16-22). Humans cannot function in a Godly manner only with the human mind. We need God's mind, which He gave on Pentecost through the power of the Holy Spirit. This makes us a new (hu)man, a new spiritual creation (Ephesians 4:24). This is the whole meaning of God making (hu)man(s) on the Sabbath day[23].

Collective Salvation for Everyone

23. https://theexplanation.com/god-to-do-with-his-work-to-make-them-on-7th-day-to-take-care-his-creation/

Feast 4 - The **Feast of Trumpets** (1st day of the 7th month. Completion of spiritual creation). A new moon, in other words, a dark time for the world. But a bright time for God's chosen because it inaugurates the salvation of all of humankind. No details here because of space. The key is, it corresponds to justice (5).

1. Justice for God's saints, those who have God's nature (1), made right choices (2) with proper behavior (3) following God's ethics (4). They will be resurrected or transformed into Spirit beings and rule on Earth with Christ. This group is all of God's people from the Creation to the Second Coming of Christ, the early harvest.
2. Justice for the world, which has wrongly applied the 4 points of how humans should function, a time of trouble culminating in Armageddon and the putting away of rebellion to God's ways.

Feast 5 - **Atonement** (10th day of 7th month), The remaining world population begins a period of re-learning, self-reproach (6). The spirit beings, the saints, the Apostles, the early harvest, led by Christ, are the teachers of the world population, who will begin to see the spiritual light, how they should function God's way.

Feast 6. - of **Tabernacles** (7 days from the 15th of the 7th month). The Fall great harvest begins. This is 1000 years of peace and prosperity on Earth. The goal will show humankind living by God's ethics with His government, developing God's nature (1), making right choices (2), proper behavior (3) according to His ethics (4) will lead to repentance (6) and forgiveness (7) of the population, resulting in their transformation into spirit beings. This transformation of multitudes of people who live their family lives giving birth to children during the Millenium is the beginning of the Fall harvest.

Feast 7 - The **Last Great Day**. The day immediately following the Feast of Tabernacles. Possibly the least understood of the Feast Days. This is when ALL the dead will rise. ALL the dead from and including Adam and Eve to Christ's Second Coming. A timeframe of about 6000 years corresponding to the period when God gave domination, the rule of Earth, over to humankind.

These multiple billions will be resurrected (Ezekiel 37, Revelation 20:5). They will have healthy flesh on healthy bones with healthy minds. They will receive their own spirit, the one that returned to God at their death with the record of their life on Earth. During the Last Great Day, they will be in the Millennial world of God's way with God's teachers, all the saints from the Spring and Fall harvests. This is when all families and loved ones will be reunited. An incredible gathering.

It will be their time to learn and apply how God wants humans to function. They will compare their former world and ways of war, famine, sorrow, sickness... to God's society and ways. The vast majority will make the right choice to repent, be forgiven, and follow how God wants humans to function. They will join the great Fall harvest as spirit beings.

There are many other events taking place I cannot expand here. The point is, God is a Just God. He judges every single human being by the *same standards* as set out in His Word, the Bible. This is practical Bible wisdom. Those norms are those of the 7 steps of how humans should function. It is the choice of EACH human to decide whether to follow the Tree of Life or the Tree of Death with the resultant justice.

The Sabbath summarizes this entire path of ceasing, refreshing, and resting in God's Kingdom. The Feast Days outline the key steps of the seasons and the seeding, growing, and harvesting of all of humankind. God is not a respecter of persons, He gives everyone the same opportunity for salvation, each in their time.

The Feast Days reveal how humans should function to prepare for the incredible eternal future God has planned for us.

2. Humankind's Place on Earth

Look closely at the moon, our closest astronomical body, desolate and pock-marked. It only gets worse as you distance yourself from Earth. Why is our planet so lush and livable? It's like our environment is there to nurture us. If so, what is our role in this vast arena of the Universe?

Fig Leaves or Clothing? Tinker or Build?

The first human solution applied by Adam and Eve was to dress themselves in fig leaves. God immediately came along and dressed them in clothes. Why?

I received two conflicting viewpoints on the Covid-19 pandemic this past week. One said, Coronavirus is a seasonal virus causing symptoms and there are treatments and there is no need for lockdown, no need for masks, and above all no need for fear. The other recounted, despite all the information about proper mask-wearing, distancing, etc. people just seem to be too cavalier in their approach. Many *contact* cases, not hospitalized, don't follow their isolation or quarantine according to the protocols they're given.

The consequence is we're seeing human behavior increasing the spread of the virus.

Which one is right? I wanted to reply to both these people who are close friends. I didn't want to rustle any feathers, not take sides, but give honest answers. Propose solid ideas that make sense, that hold up under scrutiny. What to do?

Well, I've been writing about Practical Bible Wisdom. How to apply it to this answer? *The Explanation* isn't some political or religious lobby trying to get followers or some police chief or pastor getting up on a pedestal telling people this is the finality of what they've got to do to make the problem go away. It just doesn't work like that.

After much thought and prayer, it came down to fig leaves and Proverbs. Now, there's a mixture for you. The link? Well, I already developed this subject in the seventh book of *The Explanation* series, *Agony of Humankind and the Antidote*. It could carry the sub-title *Fig leaves and Proverbs*. Let's see why.

God clothed Adam and Eve[1], for two reasons I'll mention here. First, fig leaves have a rather limited life span once removed from the plant. Second, God wanted to clothe them with not only something more permanent but also more solid and sound. The clothes were fitting (pun intended) and a long-term solution to the problem they'd caused. You can't tailor fig leaves they're a short-term, stopgap measure.

Both messages I received refer to fig leaves. In French, we have a lovely word, *rafistolage*. Rather difficult to translate. When I have such a task, I generally head over to Linguee[2]. They give the translation, but much more. They render genuine conversations

1. https://theexplanation.com/state-of-mind-understand-confused-human-psychology/

2. https://www.linguee.fr/francais-anglais/traduction/rafistolage.html

where speakers use these words in sentences. Here's what was displayed. I'm inserting the whole context because a pattern emerges beyond the translation. Figure it out.

> As a matter of fact, the scotch tape is starting to show. This entire process has been so flawed that...
>
> For these reasons, they consider that tinkering with the current system would not be the right solution and that a root cause should be dealt with.
>
> It patches things up, without doing anything to deal with the main problems and remove the main causes of the torment these animals undergo.
>
> A make do, buy some time agreement in 1999, was an opportunity to move forward, but no. What did we get?
>
> We have seen other pieces of legislation proposed in the House of Commons that we subsequently had to go in and fix because they were inadequate.
>
> It isn't broken just to the point where it needs tinkering; it needs a serious, long, hard look at what corner we've backed ourselves into that does not allow us to have openings.
>
> We believe the government needs to rethink and redesign the entire system rather than tinkering at the margins.
>
> This entails merely patching and reacting to problems instead of preventing them.
>
> It is broken and mere tinkering will not fix it.

> We have a few problems and we are tinkering.
>
> What's the point of talking about systemic crisis in the food system, when all you can really do is tinker at its margins?
>
> We cannot tinker with a system as large as drug addiction and just play with decriminalization of marijuana or drug impaired driving.
>
> I think it would be better for us to really rethink what we're doing with families in terms of the Divorce Act and to consider, first of all, an initial statement that it's recognized that the system is very much out of whack and that the change will come about, so that then we can work on it in a more positive way, rather than trying to just change a few things here and there.

Fig leaves represent *tinkering* and *patching-up*, possibly the best translations of *rafistolage*. Our society sits around discussing what other fig leaves we can apply to the fig leaves we're already wearing, hoping to repair our tattered and mangy garments.

I had you read several texts with *rafistolage*. They come mainly from members of the Canadian Parliament, where English and French are the two official languages. These are statements made by Congresspeople concerning major governmental issues affecting citizens individually and the country as a whole. Parliamentarians realize they are dealing with fig leaves, they know they can't mend them. They're saying, you've got to get back to basics and look at how we've dressed up society.

Let's look at solid, well-tailored clothes protecting us from the environment and not abusing the ground or animals. Clothing not irritating our skin, manufactured with taste and craftmanship by conscientious people who receive a fair wage.

I point you to this article to show Proverbs is one foundation on which we can build life[3]. It is a basis for the general population.

Male Gender

As you read these anti-fig leaves Proverbs, ask yourself the question, why is this written by a father addressing them to his son? Why not to his daughter? Why not the mother to her son or daughter? The answer to this question is basic knowledge our society has forgotten.

Who is responsible for most violence and sex crimes? Men or women?

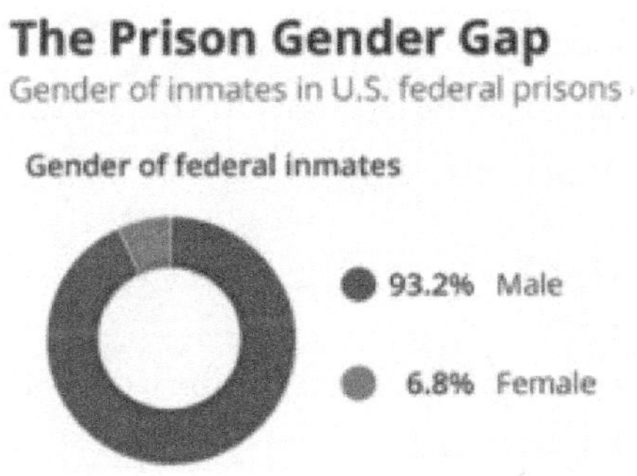

These are statistics for men and women in prison in the USA[4]. UK figures[5] reveal the same massive divergence, 77.400 men vs. 3.400

3. https://theexplanation.com/rules-for-life-wisdom-for-living-abundantly-in-the-world/

4. https://www.statista.com/chart/11573/gender-of-inmates-in-us-federal-prisons-and-general-population/#_853ae90f0351324bd73ea615e6487517__4c761f170e016836ff84498202b99827__853ae90f0351324bd73ea615e6487517_text_43ec3e5dee6e706af7766fffea512721_According_0bcef9c45bd8a48eda1b26eb0c61c869_20to_0bcef9c45bd8a48eda1b26eb0c61c8

women. I'd dare say we'd find similar proportions around the world. Men and women are not equal, men are much more difficult to guide in the right direction.

Who is better equipped to guide an adolescent toward the right way of life? Father or mother? This answer should be self-evident. It is in no way intended to put the mother down. On the contrary, motherhood is an essential role. Many single mothers have done excellent parenting, raising well-behaved, exceptional children. But regarding physical strength, no normal woman can control an adolescent physically. IF the boy has not already learned to respect and honor his mother by the time he becomes a teenager, it could very well be a lost cause.

Yes, I'm generalizing, but that's the state of affairs. When boys respect their mothers, they'll respect their sisters and other women as well. These concepts go hand-in-hand. And it all starts with the presence of loving and firm guidance from the father. That's why a father authors Proverbs for his son.

Proverbs 1:1-10

1 The proverbs of Solomon the son of David, king of Israel;

2 To know wisdom and instruction; to perceive the words of understanding;

69_20the_0bcef9c45bd8a48eda1b26eb0c61c869_20most_0bcef9c45bd8a48eda1b26eb0c61c869_20recent_c0cb5f0fcf239ab3d9c1fcd31fff1efc_makeup_0bcef9c45bd8a48eda1b26eb0c61c869_20of_0bcef9c45bd8a48eda1b26eb0c61c869_20the_0bcef9c45bd8a48eda1b26eb0c61c869_20general_0bcef9c45bd8a48eda1b26eb0c61c869_20population.

5. https://www.statista.com/statistics/283475/prison-population-and-capacity-of-united-kingdom-uk-by-gender/

3 To receive the instruction of wisdom, justice, and judgment, and equity;

4 To give subtilty to the simple, to the young man knowledge and discretion.

5 A wise man will hear, and will increase learning; and a man of understanding shall attain to wise counsels:

6 To understand a proverb, and the interpretation; the words of the wise, and their dark sayings.

7 The fear of the LORD is the beginning of knowledge: but fools despise wisdom and instruction.

8 My son, hear the instruction of your father, and forsake not the law of your mother:

9 For they shall be an ornament of grace to your head, and chains about your neck.

10 My son, if sinners entice you, consent you not.

These ten verses reveal the foundation for building society, and the principles apply worldwide. God removed the fig leaves and tailor-made clothing for Adam and Eve. Down through history humans, worldwide, have taken off and discarded God's clothing and fashioned their own fig leaves. In the 21st century, fig leaves are still in fashion. On the other hand, God has continuously made well-fitted, lasting rules available. So much so, the pattern is the most widespread best-selling book in the world, the Bible. We buy it, read it, don't understand the pattern, and do our own thing... with fig leaves! God gave Adam and Eve clothes they could wear permanently. The couple represents all of humankind.

Realize what this means. They have rejected God's rules, His way of life. We'd call them UNconverted people(s). This is the world population that has not partaken of the Tree of Life. Remember, God shooed them out of the Garden of Eden so they would not eat of this life-giving Tree. but, and this is all-important, God gave them rules to govern their UNconverted lives. These Proverbs remind us of those basic rules. Anything else is putting on fig leaves. Read verses 25-33 to see the result of not applying this basic information individually and collectively.

What do we have in these first ten verses of Proverbs?

1. A father instructing his son.
2. A mother who knows the law.
3. The origin of instruction and law is the fear/respect of the LORD.
4. A son who listens to his father and mother.
5. Wisdom is in the hearing of this teaching.
6. Fools despise this instruction.
7. This wisdom will crown your head and save your neck.
8. Real justice is in this wisdom.

You can add more points and much more wisdom to each of the above Biblical truths. I want to dwell on two events relating to two principles here.

What if Earth were Unique?

France 5, a national, more educational TV channel presented an amazing ninety-minute program recently entitled *What if Earth were Unique?* (Et si la Terre était unique?), produced by Laurent Lichtenstein. For the time being, I believe it's only available in French but I do hope someone will dub it into English, and why not, other languages. Here is the brief introduction, a must-read. In the context of this chapter, I ask you what you think? Does this have anything to do with fig leaves and fitted clothing? Does this link with any of God's principles in the first verses of Proverbs?

> What are the chances of one day discovering, somewhere in the universe, an ecosystem similar to ours? A planet on which the living would have taken forms as complex and diverse as those on Earth. Astronomers, biochemists and biologists take a trip to the heart of the solar system, discovering the incredible combination of circumstances allowing life to develop on Earth for nearly 4 billion years. Our ecosystem results from a dizzying series of hazards and catastrophes which should have destroyed life but which ultimately were beneficial to it. By scanning the sky for answers, researchers have discovered new worlds, distant planets, but none of them resemble Earth.

The program presented and explained the *dizzying series of hazards and catastrophes which should have destroyed life but which ultimately support life*. Extraordinary photography and filming. Eye-opening and revealing facts. It is impossible to get into the details of how Earth would *not* be habitable without the moon being *how* it is and *where* it is. Scientists have come up with an idea about its presence; read this article on the Giant-Impact Hypothesis[6].

In *Origin of the Universe, The Explanation* devoted a chapter to Big Bang and Stephen Hawking's ideas[7]. In a video at that link, he discusses the innumerable amount of IMperfections necessary to assemble a perfect life-giving and life-supporting Earth. How many hazards does it take for critical thinking[8] to realize *maybe* there's

6. https://en.wikipedia.org/wiki/Giant-impact_hypothesis

7. https://theexplanation.com/science-and-theology-agreement-on-real-evidence-for-big-bang/

some other origin to something as complex as Earth? And we can add Life itself.

The Bible book of Proverbs is *not* addressed to spiritually converted people. Solomon addressed it to a son who represents all of humankind. That might be a lot to digest. Please think about it. The instruction about *the incredible combination of circumstances* and *the dizzying series of hazards and catastrophes* should be a wake-up call to the realization there might be some Higher Power (Proverbs 1:7). Humankind has taken off God's clothing and dressed itself with fig leaves.

Romans 1:19-24

19 Because that which may be known of God is manifest in them; for God has shewed it to them.

20 For the invisible things of him from the creation of the world are clearly seen, being understood by the things that are made, even his eternal power and Godhead; so that they are without excuse:

21 Because that, when they knew God, they glorified him not as God, neither were thankful; but became vain in their imaginations, and their foolish heart was darkened.

22 Professing themselves to be wise, they became fools,

23 And changed the glory of the uncorruptible God into an image made like to corruptible man, and to birds, and fourfooted beasts, and creeping things.

---

8. https://theexplanation.com/critical-thinking-antidote-to-the-agony-of-humankind/

24 Wherefore God also gave them up to uncleanness through the lusts of their own hearts, to dishonour their own bodies between themselves:

25 Who changed the truth of God into a lie, and worshipped and served the creature more than the Creator, who is blessed for ever. Amen.

Samuel Paty, a teacher in France, decapitated

We had the most unfortunate of events last week here in France. An 18-year-old radical Islamist decapitated a 47-year-old teacher, Samuel Paty[9]. I do not want to dwell on that aspect and the polemic surrounding freedom of speech and caricatures; it is another subject that merits a lot of soul-searching to separate fig leaves from tailored clothing.

The Minister of education, Jean-Michel Blanquer, is launching a major political debate[10] (Grenelle de l'éducation) supposed to put teachers more "at the center of society." Certainly, teachers and schooling have a considerable role to play in the development of young minds. But here's the key.

> Proverbs says the preponderant, primary role falls to parents. This is a massive subject we cannot detail here but a child starting in school must arrive with a solid moral, ethical education. That education is during the formative years of a child[11] when their character and personality are in a malleable building stage.

---

9. https://en.wikipedia.org/wiki/Murder_of_Samuel_Paty

10. https://www.20minutes.fr/societe/2890899-20201022-salaires-profs-protection-jean-michel-blanquer-lance-grenelle-education

11. https://theexplanation.com/critical-periods-when-babies-and-children-learn/

It is much easier to construct suitably at the outset than *de*structure and *re*structure later in life. Grow, tutor, and prune a plant in the first years and it will yield fruit for many years to come. Likewise with children.

Parents are the center of society. The book of Proverbs is about a father teaching his son. It is the mother knowing the law and taking part 100% with the father in this education. That's parenting. It's not a teacher's role to REeducate a child in ethical behavior. Enough said you get the idea. It is up to the parents to clothe their children appropriately. That means no fig leaves. Here are some articles from *Audit of Humankind* in the section *How Humankind Socializes* regarding the central role of parents in child education.

- Family–The Cornerstone of Human Society[12].
- Parenting, Father & Mother have Essential Complementary Roles[13].

Get rid of the fig leaves. Put on well-tailored clothes. When we get back to teaching what a father and a mother's roles are and helping parents not just have babies but how to parent, we will be on our way to solving this issue. The question is, can we make such a societal u-turn?

I hesitated to include the following section of scripture to close out this chapter. It is very strong and to the point. These are words of practical Bible wisdom for the 21st century. "Wisdom cries without; she utters her voice in the streets:" (Proverbs 1:20). These are not the words of Sam Kneller. The end of Proverbs shows we can't blame anyone but ourselves when our tattered fig leaves disintegrate and we're standing there naked with no ground to grow linen and no

12. https://theexplanation.com/family-the-cornerstone-of-human-society/

13. https://theexplanation.com/parenting-father-mother-have-essential-complementary-roles/

animals for skins. It's a choice we have to make, individually and collectively.

Proverbs 1:22-33

22 How long, you simple ones, will you love simplicity (fig leaves)? and the scorners delight in their scorning, and fools hate knowledge (Godly-fitted clothing)?

23 Turn you at my reproof: behold, I will pour out my spirit to you, I will make known my words (clothing) to you.

24 Because I have called, and you refused; I have stretched out my hand, and no man regarded;

25 But you have set at nought all my counsel (clothing), and would none of my reproof:

26 I also will laugh at your calamity; I will mock when your fear comes;

27 When your fear comes as desolation, and your destruction comes as a whirlwind; when distress and anguish come upon you.

28 Then shall they call upon me, but I will not answer; they shall seek me early, but they shall not find me:

29 For that they hated knowledge, and did not choose the fear of the LORD:

30 They would none of my counsel: they despised all my reproof.

> 31 Therefore shall they eat of the fruit of their own way (fig leaves), and be filled with their own devices (fig leaves).
>
> 32 For the turning away (fig leaves) of the simple shall slay them, and the prosperity (fig leaves) of fools shall destroy them.
>
> 33 But whoso hearkens to me shall dwell safely, and shall be quiet from fear of evil.

Frayed and ripped jeans are in style, is that symptomatic? So many individuals and so many nations are wearing dried-up dilapidated fig leaves. Can we stop tinkering and build on a solid foundation? Are our own decisions going to destroy us, or will we choose practical Bible wisdom for our safety and tranquility?

How to Govern a Country Responsibly

Govern a country, there's a challenge. How to choose, train, then lead, guide, and prosper a country. Where's the instruction manual for that task?

Talk about how to govern a country. As I write, war just broke out in Karabakh between Armenian and Azerbaijan partisans. Two countries at loggerheads for decades over this forlorn territory. Such conflicts are more common around the world than we realize. Leaders are making belligerent statements regarding opposing forces, each one defending their own supposed territorial integrity. It's never-ending.

Is there a legitimate, not to say ideal, form of government? Is there a leadership assuring real unity and well-being to a nation? Not a semblance, but generalized peace and prosperity for an entire nation? Really govern a country equitably?

There are very few such leaderships and governments, they should serve as examples. But are there some guidelines, even directives to prepare and point future governors, at whatever level of government, toward *how to*? Where can we learn how to govern a country?

Philip Freeman wrote, "How to Run a Country: An Ancient Guide for Modern Leaders[1]." It summarizes the wisdom of Marcus Cicero, one of the greatest Roman statesmen, and one of the finest proponents of governance the world has known.

Here are ten principles to meditate on: how to govern a country.

1. There are universal laws governing the conduct of human affairs.
2. The best form of government embraces a balance of powers.
3. Leaders should be of exceptional character and integrity.
4. Keep your friends close — and your enemies closer.
5. Intelligence is not a dirty word.
6. Compromise is the key to getting things done.
7. Don't raise taxes — unless you absolutely must.
8. Immigration makes a country stronger.
9. Never start an unjust war.
10. Corruption destroys a nation.

Cicero influenced the American Founding Fathers[2] greatly, and his ideas found their way into the American constitution. Rome experienced three major models of government. *Kings* ran the first period of governance: the *Republic* followed their tyranny; *Emperors*

1. https://www.pdfdrive.com/how-to-run-a-country-an-ancient-guide-for-modern-leaders-e164455173.html

2. https://medium.com/s/story/romes-heroes-and-america-s-founding-fathers-6dada32a8885

ran the Empire from Rome. The transitions were bloody. Toward the end of the Republic, about 70 BCE, factions in the Senate were irreconcilable, leaving a vacuum of government. Cicero lived during this time; his *best form of government embraces a balance of powers* stating his staunch position in favor of a republic. The IMbalance of powers and infighting coupled with the rise of a military leader, Julius Caesar[3], lead to the Empire[4].

Cicero's pro-republic stance needs to be tempered by understanding his position in society. It's part of the fifth comment, by a reader, on the article about Cicero's influence on the U.S. founding fathers.[5] "They (Cicero and Cato) stood for the status quo and wealth and privilege. They were not interested in the status of the poor or of the slaves in what was very much a slave economy." This is a vital point they neglected in how to govern a country. Poverty, just making-ends-meet, living from month to month with no perspective of a better tomorrow is not propitious for a country's cohesiveness. *The Explanation* broached this subject in *Audit of Humankind*, Government for the People is Also Concern for the Poor[6]. When you govern a country, the leadership must take care of every faction of its population.

Unfortunately, the 21st century is not the epitome of such benevolent government. In fact, we could easily entitle a book, *How NOT to govern a country*. A prime example is what's happening in Lebanon, the Pearl of the Middle East, as we knew it. No more.

At the beginning of September 2020[7], during the visit of French President Emmanuel Macron, Lebanese political parties pledged to

3. https://en.wikipedia.org/wiki/Julius_Caesar

4. https://www.nationalgeographic.org/article/romes-transition-republic-empire

5. https://medium.com/s/story/romes-heroes-and-america-s-founding-fathers-6dada32a8885

6. https://theexplanation.com/government-for-people-concern-for-poor/

form a *mission* cabinet made up of *competent* and *independent* ministers within two weeks to lead the country out of the economic slump.

But the process is stalling, in this country where power is shared between the different religious communities, because of differences over the allocation of ministerial portfolios. The Prime Minister resigned and we're back to square one, no government. In the meantime, poverty and disaster reign following the massive explosion that devastated Beirut.

In an enlightened era of humankind, one of the biggest paradoxes is the peril in which we find government. This is true for practically every single nation around the world. Let's be realistic. What's going on? How do we govern a country?

Down through history, humankind has experimented with every single type of governance possible. Vestiges of these tentatives to govern a country still affect modern society. I include this labyrinth list of Basic forms of government[8] solely for you to see the sore need for instruction in how to govern a country.

Separation

- Associated state
- Chiefdom
- Dominion
- Protectorate

Federalism

7. https://www.bfmtv.com/international/liban-le-premier-ministre-renonce-a-former-un-nouveau-gouvernement_AD-202009260067.html#xtor_43ec3e5dee6e706af7766fffea512721_AL-68

8. https://en.wikipedia.org/wiki/List_of_forms_of_government

- Confederation
- Devolution
- Federation

Integration

- Empire
- Hegemony
- Unitary state

Power source

Democracy (rule by many)

- Demarchy
- Direct
- Liberal
- Representative
- Social
- Socialist
- Others

Oligarchy (rule by few)

- Anocracy
- Aristocracy
- Ergatocracy
- Gerontocracy
- Kleptocracy
- Kritarchy
- Noocracy
- Particracy

- Plutocracy
- Stratocracy
- Technocracy

Autocracy (rule by one)

- Despotism
- Dictatorship
- Military dictatorship
- Tyranny

Anarchism (rule by none)

- Anarchy
- Free association
- Stateless

Power ideology

Monarchy vs. republic (socio-political ideologies)

- Absolute
- Constitutional
- Directorial
- Legalist
- Parliamentary
- Presidential
- Semi-presidential
- Socialist

Authoritarian vs. libertarian (socio-economic ideologies)

- Anarchism
- Colonialism
- Communism
- Despotism
- Distributism
- Feudalism
- Socialism
- Totalitarianism
- Tribalism

Global vs. local (geo-cultural ideologies)

- Commune
- City-state
- Intergovernmental organization
- National government
- World government
- Nationalism
- Internationalism
- Globalism

The Explanation and how to govern a nation

To answer questions about government and leadership, you must first understand where *The Explanation* stands. Especially if you're reading this for the first time. The basis for the approach is Deut. 4:5-9, please study this in the article about critical thinking, antidote to the agony of humankind[9]. At the end of 40 years in the desert, God gave a new generation of Israelites and descendants of other peoples (Ex. 12:38 a mixed multitude) a set of rules, laws, and

9. https://theexplanation.com/critical-thinking-antidote-to-the-agony-of-humankind/

statutes; call them what you may. This code of ethics is a way of living, a way to ensure proper rulership and human relations for a nation.

This group of hundreds of thousands of people, men, women, and children, were about to cross into and occupy a land they'd never seen before. This nation had twelve tribes, and each one would receive a portion of the new territory. They had to set up everything from scratch. It was a clean slate on which they would write their own story.

The leader of this imposing group was Moses. God called him forty years earlier to lead His people out of Egypt into the desert, where they received a set of laws for their 40 years of residence in that hostile environment. Those laws are in Exodus. Now, just before crossing the Jordan river God, through Moses, promulgated a new set of laws to govern a country, their new home.

These laws cover all the primary areas to administer a nation. This book expounds on certain of these subjects. God gave the laws in Deuteronomy some 3500 years ago. Most people think it is a decrepit, outdated, anti-human, misogynist caricature. If you read it from a 21st century humanistic point-of-view I fully understand such a reaction.

That's the reason *The Explanation* has written, at length, about its value and necessity to update the code of ethics, to adapt the practices, not the intention, for our century. You will find, what I'd call, the *updating of the laws* of Deuteronomy in the book of Proverbs. God gave this wisdom to King Solomon, who governed the nation of Israel during its most prosperous time in the history of the Old Testament. His wisdom surpassed any human brain and mind power we've had until this day. The book of Proverbs is the distillation of that wisdom in tidbits of practical advice: how to govern a nation and how to govern our individual lives.

Proverbs reveals God's law should be updated without losing the basic purpose intended by God to govern a country and an individual. Times, culture, traditions, practices change with time. There was no pornography on the Internet nor accessibility and abuse of opioids, neither during Moses' nor Solomon's eras. There are no laws specific to those two areas. However, there is sufficient basic instruction to know exactly how to govern a nation and our individual lives regarding these two and many other domains.

It might surprise you *The Explanation* is not referring to New Testament instructions given by Christ and the Apostles. Here's the reason, and it's quite simple, although mostly overlooked by teachers and readers. The New Testament is for *converted, God-fearing, God-practicing* servants of God. The New Testament is not destined for the world. The world cannot possibly apply its spiritual instruction. This is not the time to elaborate, but meditate on this simple concept. God says the New Testament way of life will be in our hearts and minds (Col. 3:15, Heb. 10:16, 1 Pet. 3:15). Question: How many people have even opened their hearts and minds to this spiritual instruction? Enough said.

The Old Testament instruction was for *all* peoples everywhere. Those Israelites, accompanied by people from other origins, were *not* spiritually converted. They, like the vast majority of people today, partake of the Tree of Good and Evil, *not* the Tree of Life.

The updated laws of Deuteronomy and Proverbs apply in this case. They instruct us in all the basics to govern a country. Here are some contexts relative to how to govern a country. *The Explanation* comments on them to show how they apply in the 21st century.

Deuteronomy

Deuteronomy 17:14-20: How leadership should govern a country

> **14** When you are come to the land which the LORD your God gives you, and shall possess it, and shall dwell therein, and shall say, I will set a king over me, like as all the nations that are about me;

We cannot go into all the ramifications here. Just note God agreed to what the people wanted. Why did God consent when He knew it was against their best interests? The answer opens up an understanding of God's approach not only to Israel, but to all peoples and how to govern a country. That's the reason for the labyrinth list of ways to govern a county. Just as he did with the Israelites, God is letting all nations govern their country the way THEY want, regardless of what God says.

Today, some nations still have a King or Queen as head of state. In most cases, at least in the West, they are powerless to govern the country; rulership is in the hands of an elected President or Prime Minister. These principles apply to ALL national leaders today.

> **15** You shall in any wise set him king over you, whom the LORD your God shall choose: one from among your brethren shall you set king over you: you may not set a stranger over you, which is not your brother.

God chose the King in Israel, Saul. And the second, David, after whom came his descendants. In Joshua, leaders were called Judges and we find an awful lot of intrigue going on, including assassination. Not Godly at all, such is the nature of Old Testament Israel, like other nations.

This verse makes provision for *who* should govern a country. It should be someone from the populace, a *brother*, not a *stranger*. Someone who has empathy and understanding of their own people, who is part of the national fiber. A nation is a family, the leader is their father.

> **16** But he shall not multiply horses to himself, nor cause the people to return to Egypt, to the end that he should multiply horses: forasmuch as the LORD has said to you, You shall henceforth return no more that way.

No leader is breeding horses at that level today. Horses, often coupled with chariots, were weapons. Modern talk is army, air force, and navy. When you govern a country, you don't spend outlandish amounts on your military forces. The goal is not to take over other's territory, but to be satisfied with what you possess and develop the resources at your disposal. We could also understand a leader should not be militarily or commercially dependent on another nation.

> **17** Neither shall he multiply wives to himself, that his heart turn not away: neither shall he greatly multiply to himself silver and gold.

Leaders, by their position, yield power and influence. They can constrain the opposite sex and women can seduce a leader. There's great temptation to increase one's wealth, as attested by leaders now and in the past in many countries. This is an injunction on governors to lead decent family lives and live within the reasonable salary limits they receive for their service. A father takes care of his family, not his own desires at the expense of his wife and children. He does not accumulate wealth at the expense of the nation.

> **18** And it shall be, when he sits upon the throne of his kingdom, that he shall write him a copy of this law in a book out of that which is before the priests the Levites:

The previous verses discuss the external dos and don'ts of the President or Prime Minister. Now, we get to the nitty-gritty of how to govern a country. It is not test and experiment. The basics do not involve imagination and innovation; they are God-given and clear-cut principles to apply. They're in the Bible: Deuteronomy, Proverbs, and the other books are the *basics. Writing out* your *own copy* of the *rules* is the best way to *internalize* a way of life. As an aside, in school *writing* and *reading* (next verse) were the basis of education. Modern experimental schooling *rejects* this fundamental learning method. Just look at the results.

The leader must learn and know, inside out, God's way of life, God's message. He must wear God's clothes, not fig leaves. How to treat humankind, one's brothers, fathers, and mothers, young and old, rich and poor. There's no better way than to copy a manuscript for yourself. As you write by hand, you're obliged to think about the meaning of words, sentences, and paragraphs. You're filled with how to apply this information to govern a country. Learn the practical know-how.

> **19** And it shall be with him, and he shall read therein all the days of his life: that he may learn to fear the LORD his God, to *keep* (H8104) all the words of this law and these statutes, to *do* them:

Plainer I cannot be. Every day, without fail, a governor is to read and meditate on his hand-written copy of the Bible, at least the first five books. I'd add, at least, Proverbs. Note the foremost principle a non-converted leader is to retain. To respect God. To know there is a

Power over himself Who is giving him direction. The governor is to *keep and do* these words.

Keep *and do* reminds us of what God told Adam and Eve, *dress and* ***keep***[10]. Read this article for the explanation[11]. The injunction for the governor here is not identical, but it includes ***keep***. The point is, what God told Adam and Eve to *observe*, He tells all Governors the same. "You shall *diligently* (H8104) *keep* (H8104) the commandments of the Lord..." And you know what, God tells *all* the nation and humankind the same directive, "*write* out, *read* and *keep* God's laws and statutes." The same ones we find in the Old Testament.

> **20** That his heart be not lifted up above his brethren, and that he turn not aside from the commandment, to the right hand, or to the left: to the end that he may prolong his days in his kingdom, he, and his children, in the midst of Israel.

There are basic principles every human can learn; you do not have to be spiritually converted to oversee your *heart*. To point your mental attitude and mindset in the right direction. A normally constituted person with a working mind should learn basic self-control for a proper way of life identical to what we're seeing here. From birth, this is a lifelong endeavor. This verse tells the leader not to become arrogant, bossy, and cocky. We're all in the same boat, there's a captain, but we all progress together, with no one overboard. Maintain the right heading by keeping your mind on God's way of life as expressed through His teachings.

A leader is at the helm, behind the wheel for steering a ship. The wheel swings the *rudder* (*gouvernail* in French, from which we derive

---

10. https://theexplanation.com/dress-keep-garden-of-eden-man-destined-to-be-a-gardener/

11. https://theexplanation.com/dress-keep-garden-of-eden-man-destined-to-be-a-gardener/

govern, to govern a country) right or left to maintain the correct direction. Today, most ships don't have a wheel anymore, they have electronic equipment to maintain the right heading. Just as technology has adapted, so the principles of God's Old Testament commandments are adapted to our modern way of life.

But the basic principles of guiding a ship with a *gouvernail* and the basic principles of instructing a leader to govern a country are unchanged. That's practical Bible wisdom.

Further Study

Below you'll find a list of verses in Proverbs relevant to KINGship. Substitute Governor, Prime Minister, President or the title the head of government, or other leaders, have in your country. Why not replace it with your name, after all, you're a potential leader? Think about the underlying intention and principle of each verse. What is God telling the leader of the nation about how to govern a country?

This exercise will produce two results.

1. A revelation of the qualities the leader of a country should possess BEFORE they take office.
2. The realization of these principles is just as valid and worthwhile in the 21st century as it ever was in the past. And in a hundred years it'll still be the go-to instruction to know how to govern a country.

If a reader would like to comment on these verses, as I commented on the ones in Deuteronomy, I'd be happy to entertain the idea of adding the commentary, subject to editing, to the verses below. Pick up the gauntlet.

Proverbs 1:1 The proverbs of Solomon the son of David, king of Israel;

Pro. 14:28 In the multitude of people is the king's honour: but in the want of people is the destruction of the prince.

Pro. 14:35 The king's favour is toward a wise servant: but his wrath is against him that causes shame.

Pro. 16:10 A divine sentence is in the lips of the king: his mouth transgresses not in judgment.

Pro. 16:14 The wrath of a king is as messengers of death: but a wise man will pacify it.

Pro. 16:15 In the light of the king's countenance is life; and his favour is as a cloud of the latter rain.

Pro. 19:12 The king's wrath is as the roaring of a lion; but his favour is as dew upon the grass.

Pro. 20:2 The fear of a king is as the roaring of a lion: whoso provokes him to anger sins against his own soul.

Pro. 20:8 A king that sits in the throne of judgment scatters away all evil with his eyes.

Pro. 20:26 A wise king scatters the wicked, and brings the wheel over them.

Pro. 20:28 Mercy and truth preserve the king: and his throne is upheld by mercy.

Pro. 21:1 The king's heart is in the hand of the LORD, as the rivers of water: he turns it whithersoever he will.

Pro. 22:11 He that loves pureness of heart, for the grace of his lips the king shall be his friend.

Pro. 24:21 My son, fear you the LORD and the king: and meddle not with them that are given to change:

Pro. 25:1 These are also proverbs of Solomon, which the men of Hezekiah king of Judah copied out.

Pro. 25:5 Take away the wicked from before the king, and his throne shall be established in righteousness.

Pro. 25:6 Put not forth yourself in the presence of the king, and stand not in the place of great men:

Pro. 29:4 The king by judgment establishes the land: but he that receives gifts overthrows it.

Pro. 29:14 The king that faithfully judges the poor, his throne shall be established for ever.

Pro. 30:27 The locusts have no king, yet go they forth all of them by bands;

Pro. 30:31 A greyhound; an he goat also; and a king, against whom there is no rising up.

Pro. 31:1 The words of king Lemuel, the prophecy that his mother taught him.

A leader with the above qualities will know how to govern a country, and the citizens will benefit from peace and prosperity.

Leaders and Followers. Organization

Leaders and followers and their relationships. How to organize all levels of the population in a nation.

For any successful venture, leaders and followers must have a way to communicate and cooperate. Solve this dilemma. A bus is full of fifty tourists with one guide. They get off for a visit and the guide gives them 30 minutes of *free time* before leaving for the next destination. How does the guide verify all passengers are onboard before departure? The guide does this in ten seconds. How?

I once read a story of a scuba-diving tourist boat with about 70 people aboard spending an afternoon at sea. Everybody enjoyed exploring the marine flora and fauna, and the boat arrived back at port. The next day, as they were cleaning the boat, they found some clothing and ID under a seat. They'd left ONE diver out at sea!!! It has a happy ending because the story is about how the diver survived his night afloat in the middle of nowhere. There was a problem between leaders and followers on this excursion.

> Here's a Bible Proverb, "The king that faithfully judges the poor, his throne shall be established for ever," Pro. 29:14.
>
> How can a king judge a poor person? All nations have *many* poor. How can a king judge *many* poor?

Leaders and followers can be in different worlds. Certainly, a king and a pauper are. In a nation of one, fifty, two hundred million, or more subjects, how do you communicate and cooperate? A king and a pauper will NEVER meet. Palaces and slums don't mix.

The Explanation broaches this subject of communication between top leadership and street citizens in the organization of a country. How can the top be in touch with the bottom? By saying bottom, I do not intend to be pejorative, we all know the chasm between high-level administration and the person-on-the-street. Although, yesterday, French President Macron visited a few flood-devastated towns in South East France and talked directly with the victims.

Does the Bible say anything about such a complex, yet down-to-earth subject? Many consider the Bible an antiquated collection of folkloric fiction, a book written in the dinosaur age with no application for 21st century civilization. Nothing could be further from reality. We're going to see some practical wisdom about leaders and followers.

As we approach this subject, let's define some basic principles. What characterizes a leader? What are their proper goals and aspirations? If we don't establish genuine leadership qualities, then we're wasting our time. Our ruler must be a legitimate leader!

Wise Leader

With leaders and followers, a leader knows they'll have *all* types and classes of followers. Age differences, cultural, racial, backgrounds, intelligence, you name it. The chief-of-state must have a plan encompassing ALL strata under their leadership. In *Audit of Humankind*, there's a chapter entitled Government for the People is also Concern for the Poor[1]. We're not just referring to the monetarily poor, there are also poor education, poor health, and other poor areas. This is the relationship leaders and followers must develop, the King and the pauper.

> A leader has a sound plan and communicative conviction, including all people.

Here's an interview with Carlos Tavares,[2] who brought the automobile manufacturing company, Peugeot, in France, back from bankruptcy. I suggest you read the entire article about leadership. However, concentrate on the principles he highlights regarding relations and communication between leaders and followers. This quote reveals a given. *First*, you've got to have a competent leader.

> Head of a Car company (Tavares) who started at shop level and can discuss the inwards of motors!

> Tavares: A project should unite people and constitute an essential lever for attaining one or more objectives. Even the best plan will never reach its full potential if it is not put into perspective, patiently explained, and executed with discipline and focus at all times. A project rarely

1. https://theexplanation.com/government-for-people-concern-for-poor/

2. https://www.leadersleague.com/en/news/carlos-tavares-psa-peugeot-citroen-i-don-t-believe-in-the-concept-of-an-isolated-charismatic-leader

brings about the ultimate performance by itself, nor does it cement the group, unless a leader brings it to life.

Create the Team

Leaders and followers, two groups of people, both in the plural. A leader with a *big* idea cannot do it alone. S/he needs an organization, sometimes a vast organization. Many questions arise. How do you recruit? How do you develop? You can't do it alone. How do you grow the organization? And our key question today, how do you assemble and always maintain communication between the upper and lower echelons, all tiers of the organization?

The goal of this chapter points out practical Bible wisdom in Exodus with Moses. He was the leader of some 600,000 people (Ex. 12:37) whom he'd lead into the desert under God's guidance. Through him, God revealed the Ten Commandments (Exodus 20) and all the statutes (Ex. 21-23) permitting all these people to live harmoniously.

They were divided into 13 groups called tribes. The basis is the 12 sons of Jacob. However, there are 2 modifications. One son, Joseph, had his tribe divided in two: Manasseh and Ephraim. Which makes 13 tribes. However, one tribe, Levi, became the spiritual representatives of the nation. They did not receive a territory, but rather cities in the territories of the remaining 12 tribes. The narrative of the organization of Levi in relation to the other tribes is a story in itself. It also contains much practical Bible wisdom.

Moses was the leader of the leaders (Numbers 1) of these thirteen tribes of followers. How do you structure such a group?

Exodus 18 is the answer to top-down government. I hear you, in the West, we have democracy, which is bottom-up governance. True, but can you apply the principles of top-down leadership? Definitely.

Because once the elections are over, you have a top-down structure. It's a matter of placing the right people in the right governmental positions.

In Ex. 18, two points are obvious. God is in charge and He's appointed Moses as the human leader of the nation. Moses' father-in-law meets him in the desert.

Ex. 18:1, 6-7

1 When Jethro, the priest of Midian, Moses' father in law, heard of all that God had done for Moses, and for Israel his people, and that the LORD had brought Israel out of Egypt;

6 And he said to Moses, I your father in law Jethro am come to you, and your wife, and her two sons with her.

7 And Moses went out to meet his father in law, and did *obeisance* (H7812), and kissed him; and they asked each other of their welfare; and they came into the tent.

Moses' conduct is exemplary. His father-in-law, Jethro, is a priest of Midian. Go to UnlockBibleMeaning.com[3] and study *Midian*. You will see their religion has nothing to do with Old Testament Israel practices. Yet, the leader of a major nation, Moses, paid homage (obeisance - H7812) to this man. This reveals Moses' humility; these two men were close to one another with an excellent relationship. This difference of *religious* opinion did not cause a rift between them.

In fact, the Israelite Exodus experience opened the mind of Jethro because he came to see who the true God is. "Now I know that the LORD is greater than all gods: for in the thing wherein they

3. https://unlockbiblemeaning.com

(the Egyptians) dealt proudly he was above them" (verse 11). What transpired in this episode was beneficial to both men; their reciprocal relationship sets the stage for a change in the governing of a nation. Now for the leaders and followers.

Exodus 18:13-16

> 13 And it came to pass on the morrow, that Moses sat to judge the people: and the people stood by Moses from the morning to the evening.
>
> 14 And when Moses' father in law saw all that he did to the people, he said, What is this thing that you do to the people? why sit you yourself alone, and all the people stand by you from morning to even?
>
> 15 And Moses said to his father in law, Because the people come to me to inquire of God:
>
> 16 When they have a matter, they come to me; and I judge between one and another, and I do make them know the statutes of God, and his laws.

In one word, there was a problem with a long, long waiting line. It reminds me of lines outside stores when rationing of foodstuff was in effect, or now with Covid-19 with only so many people allowed in stores, while others form long lines outside. You know what it's like just to stand in a queue waiting for a cashier. Here was Moses teaching *and* judging 600,000 people, *alone.* Imagine how long EACH case must take. Jethro immediately saw the problem and proposed a leader's and followers' solution.

Exodus 18:18-23

> 18 You will surely wear away, both you, and this people that is with you: for this thing is too heavy for you; you are not able to perform it yourself alone.
>
> 19 Hearken now to my voice, I will give you counsel, and God shall be with you: Be you for the people to God-ward, that you may bring the causes to God:
>
> 20 And you shall teach them ordinances and laws, and shall shew them the way wherein they must walk, and the work that they must do.
>
> 21 Moreover you shall provide out of all the people able men, such as fear God, men of truth, hating covetousness; and place such over them, to be rulers of thousands, and rulers of hundreds, rulers of fifties, and rulers of tens:
>
> 22 And let them judge the people at all seasons: and it shall be, that every great matter they shall bring to you, but every small matter they shall judge: so shall it be easier for yourself, and they shall bear the burden with you.
>
> 23 If you shall do this thing, and God command you so, then you shall be able to endure, and all this people shall also go to their place in peace.

There is more common sense and wisdom in these six verses in the Old Testament than in a lot of leadership books. This is practical hands-on, how-to-do information. This has *nothing* to do with worshipping God or how Godly or not Godly a nation is. This is valid for *all* nations today. Why do you think the author devotes an entire chapter to this subject? For our instruction.

What's going on here?

Delegation down to street level. Rulers over ten

If you want to have a personal relationship with people, ten individuals are about the maximum. This responsibility is undoubtedly community service on top of your own social, professional, and family life. These people were not full-time. There were full-time leaders, the Levites, but that's another story.

This is a pyramidal structure. From 10 to 50, 100 and 1000. At the ground level, if we have a leader of ten, then the leader of 100 would work with only those first 10 leaders. Likewise, with the leader of 1000, they'd only work with the ten leaders over the 100. Continuing in a leadership structure you'd have 10, 100, 1000, 10000, 100000, 1000000, six levels to govern a million people, eight levels to rule a nation of one hundred million.

In this scenario, Moses with 600000 people = 100000 x 6, which means he'd have direct contact with only *six* governors. Totally realistic, and each of those leaders would only work with 10 people under them. Leaders are counselors and with 10 subordinates you can take the necessary time to give each one the attention they need. This is how the King is aware of the pauper. There's a responsible communication channel.

Here, we're talking about citizen's needs. We're not talking about national needs like military or infrastructure for transport or hospitals. Moses was handling citizen needs, and Jethro showed him how to relieve himself of this burden.

Note the benefits.

1. You shall endure. No burnout for Moses.
2. They shall bear the burden with you. Delegation via a leader development program.

3. People shall also go to their place in peace. The citizens know they are heard and cared for.

This is a win-win-win situation. A nation well-governed. Prospects of peace and prosperity. This is practical Bible wisdom.

The reputation of these leaders at ALL levels

Leaders are to fear God, people of truth, hating covetousness (verse 21). I wrote above, this concerns all nations, Godly and not Godly. Again, draw on the principle. Even if many people are not Godly inclined in our society, they can still have values and morals. It is those people who we seek as leaders.

Did you notice *truth*? A big five-letter word today. In an era of post-truth, in certain countries, we might have gone past the point of no return. Here's a definition of post-truth.

> Post-truth politics[4] is a political culture in which debate is framed largely by appeals to emotion disconnected from the details of policy, and by the repeated assertion of talking points to which factual rebuttals are ignored.

If there's no *truth* in leadership, it's a lost cause. This quality is fundamental. It goes hand-in-hand with *facts* and *hating covetousness*. Out with bribes, lobbies, influencers. In with facts and competent advisors. Here's practical Bible wisdom in three words; truth, hating covetousness.

Citizens would have a very favorable and appreciable approach to such benevolent oversight.

Moses, the Teacher

4. https://en.wikipedia.org/wiki/Post-truth_politics

Moses had a primordial role. He was not just a Head-of-State, in the sense of governing. His number one goal, as Jethro pointed out, "you shall teach them ordinances and laws, and shall shew them the way wherein they must walk, and the work that they must do"

Remember what Carlos Taveres said, "Even the best plan will never reach its full potential if it is not put into perspective, patiently explained, and executed with discipline and focus at all times. A project rarely brings about the ultimate performance by itself, nor does it cement the group, unless a leader brings it to life."

Jethro liberated Moses from the tasks other people could handle. He needed to get back to leadership, patiently explaining, bringing to life. We're talking about motivation and guidance, the lot of a genuine leader, to articulate the global project and handle the overriding issues, which the lower echelon leaders brought to him.

That's exactly what the Bible is, the story of humankind. It starts with the Creation of man and woman and ends with all humans transformed into spirit beings. The Bible covers God's project for humans, a venture lasting about 7000 years[5]. But it has implications for all of eternity. The role of God's delegated Ministers is *patiently preaching* His *project*, articulating *how* God's people are to conduct themselves. I leave you with that meditation.

Collective leadership

You prepare leadership, one by one, little by little. When you look at an overview of God's plan, that's exactly what's happening. The first key leader was Abraham, the father of the faithful. There were others before him like Enoch and Noah, but Abraham started the first leader-example nation (Deuteronomy 4). Christ founded the first Spiritual Leadership School, His Church of which He's the Founder

5. https://theexplanation.com/timeline-history-universe-earth-humans/

and Headmaster, the Foundation and the Capstone, the Alpha and the Omega.

Look at what Carlos Tavares, General Director of Peugeot Automobiles, has to say about collective leadership. It's a question of leaders and followers, plural.

You might think I'm mixing apples and oranges, commercial and spiritual. Yes, simply to show you how practical the Bible is. Leadership experts have discovered the working principles. God recorded them in His Word and puts them into action over millennia.

> Collective leadership provides the momentum that reinforces innate, sometimes unconscious self-confidence within each leader. It is the catalyst that creates systematically more space for everybody's potential. It also boosts performance, making it possible to deliver more than the sum of all the individual potentials.
>
> Collective leadership also allows a team to set ambitious objectives that make the company grow, even if these are only partially attained. However, this requires work. Everything needs to be just right, and you must create the conditions that will enable each player along the value chain to act as a leader instead of a follower. A leader's ultimate satisfaction comes from driving a group of individuals towards an ambitious, perhaps even seemingly unrealistic goal, and from experiencing the shared pleasure of reaching or even surpassing this goal.

The Father doesn't call people just for the people themselves. Christianity is not a private-personal-isolated endeavor. His Church is preparing Kings and Priests, in modern language, leaders, with followers to come.

God starts forming leaders from the top down. Christ came to train His top echelon leaders, the Apostles. They, in turn, enable those who work in the Ministry, Evangelists, Pastors, and then there are Elders in various places as well as deacons. The breadth and depth of leadership necessary to manage a Church, an organization, starts small and grows larger over time.

I'm sure you get the idea. First come leaders, then followers. This next passage is prophetic. It's after Christ's Return, during the Millenium when people will come out of probably the darkest moment of human history and begin to live in peace, real peace. Such quietude will exist because God's way of life will be present on Earth. In particular, because correctly trained teachers, who are the leaders, will be present to guide the people.

> **Isaiah 30:19-21**
>
> 19 For the people shall dwell in Zion at Jerusalem: you shall weep no more: he will be very gracious to you at the voice of your cry; when he shall hear it, he will answer you.
>
> 20 And though the Lord give you the bread of adversity, and the water of affliction, yet shall not your teachers be removed into a corner any more, but your eyes shall see your teachers:
>
> 21 And your ears shall hear a word behind you, saying, This is the way, walk you in it, when you turn to the right hand, and when you turn to the left.

As Jethro told Moses, "shew them the way wherein they must walk, and the work that they must do." So those prepared leaders and followers will cooperate personally, "this is the way, walk you in it."

From the way Moses and Christ, during His Ministry, and in the Millennium, develop and organize leaders, we know and learn the practical Bible relationship between leaders and followers.

How can the guide know everyone is onboard the bus in ten seconds? Well, the leader has delegated leaders and followers. The 50 passengers form groups of 3 (or 4, but not 2). The only stipulation is the group of 3 can *not* include someone you're traveling with (husband, wife, friend), it must be someone you don't know. When the bus is ready for departure, each person must look the other two in the eye, no guessing, thus knowing they're present. Each passenger is responsible for the presence of two others. Two glances in ten seconds and we're off to our next destination. The wisdom of leadership and followers.

History of Individuals and Nations

Bible history of Individuals and Nations. With whom does God work? Does YHVH work on a PERSONAL or NATIONAL scale? Individuals and/or groups?

History in the Bible tends to focus on individuals. It starts with Adam and Eve, Cain and Abel, Noah, Abraham and his sons, Moses, Joshua, and then the Kings. When we get to the New Testament, theology puts the accent on individuals. Repent and be baptized, references to faith are directives addressed to individuals. It would appear New Testament theology is less interested, not to say, NOT at all concerned with the history of countries. Spiritual conversion is an individual matter, not on a national level.

The fundamental question *The Explanation* asks is, how would you bring peace and prosperity to the entire world? The *entire world* includes all people and all nations. Individuals and countries. When we consider God alone, the Creator of humankind, can instigate worldwide peace, then our question *does God work with individuals and countries?* becomes very relevant. What does practical Bible wisdom say about this subject?

History of the nations and the Bible. Agreed, they are strange bedfellows. Why approach it? The Bible has much to say about the relationship between *individuals and collectivities*. In an era of individualism, which is the case now, we need to see the practical Bible perspective. To prepare for the next chapter, I want to develop the notion of collectivities in the Bible, notably of nations and empires. We'll especially see God's outlook toward *all* nations, which are large communities or collectivities. We need to see the other side of the coin.

The Bible starts with the Creation of the Universe and the world, narrating the history of humankind with the Creation of the first man and woman. That's *history*; whether you believe it is another matter. The Bible, among other things, is a history book. It references and names individual people, tribes, and countries. It gives geographical data allowing us to locate certain countries on a world map. Granted some, even a lot of the names are unknown, but this is because in the 21st century we lack knowledge. Most reject Bible history[1].

Many say this is fiction, these places, and people never existed. At the same time, there are many serious studies over decades, like the Biblical Archaeological Society, [2]witnessing to finds corroborating historic Bible events. Unfortunately, many original histories of such events are incomplete.

---

1. https://books.google.fr/books/about/The_Mythic_Past_Biblical_Archaeology_And.html?id=DXg4DgAAQBAJ

2. https://www.biblicalarchaeology.org/

These are very erudite subjects taking years to master, and additional evidence from archaeologic and other sources make this an ever-changing argument. The Biblical Archaeological Society, at the link above, brings new findings to the public. National Geographic[3], a reputed source, also broaches this subject[4].

Debates on the veracity or not of Bible narratives, archaeology, geography, history, etc. are *not* the goal of *The Explanation*. This book aims to reveal practical Bible wisdom applied to real living in the 21st century. Many see the Bible only through spiritual, faith-based eyes. Evidently, that is its primary purpose. But it is an *instruction manual for living in society harmoniously*. Most don't see how Bible wisdom, if understood and applied, would bring more peace and prosperity to people and nations today.

Abrahamic religions tend to be rather closed-minded regarding *their group*. Our relationship with God is one-on-one. Yes, we think about others, but it's generally about our local perspective. *Why can't they think and act as I do?* Like my Church does? This is a rather narrow-minded approach that needs to be expanded if we are to understand individuals (which you are) in respect to collectivities (beyond your Church and/or ethnic group).

God is not your exclusive God, nor is He exclusive to your Church. God is the God of every single human being, individually. Bible history shows us God is God of every single nation, collectively.

Here are the first verses referring to nations. This history follows Noah's flood and the survival of only eight people composing four couples, including his three sons and their wives. Today's worldwide population descends from these three families. Note God's action in

---

3. https://www.nationalgeographic.com/search?q=bible%20archaeology

4. https://www.youtube.com/watch?v=znKO_a72ft0

this sequence. True theology focuses on what *God accomplishes and why He does it*. the LORD confounded their language and scattered them to the four corners of the Earth.

Genesis 11:6-9

6 And the LORD said, Behold, the people is one, and they have all one language; and this they begin to do: and now nothing will be restrained from them, which they have imagined to do.

7 Go to, let us go down, and there confound their language, that they may not understand one another's speech.

8 So the LORD scattered them abroad from thence upon the face of all the earth: and they left off to build the city.

9 Therefore is the name of it called Babel; because the LORD did there confound the language of all the earth: and from thence did the LORD scatter them abroad upon the face of all the earth.

This could be considered a punishment, but it really is a means of preserving people alive. After the flood, humankind's population grew, but they were in a downward spiral. God promised not to wipe out humanity. Instead, He scattered them to prevent the pooling of resources.

In the previous chapter of Genesis, we have the descendants of the three sons and the narrative of their migrations. The three genealogies end with the same phrase, which I've included below. Four Biblical Hebrew words merit a closer study.

Genesis 10:1, 5, 20, 31

1 Now these are the generations of the sons of Noah, Shem, Ham, and Japheth: and to them were sons born after the flood.

Japheth

5 By these were the *isles* (H339) of the *Gentiles* (H1471) divided in their *lands* (H776); every one after his *tongue* (H3956), after their *families* (H4940), in their *nations* (H1471),

Ham

20 These are the sons of Ham, after their *families* (H4940), after their *tongues* (H3956), in their *countries*, (H776) and in their *nations* (H1471).

Shem

31 These are the sons of Shem, after their *families* (H4940), after their *tongues* (H3956), in their *lands* (H776), after their *nations* (H1471).

Go to UnlockBibleMeaning.com[5], look up, and study those words. Together they reveal God's implication in the history of ALL nations worldwide. Collectivities are a major focus for God.

H339

אִי ’îy ee; from H183 (אָוָה); properly, a habitable spot (as desirable); dry land, a coast, an island:

5. https://unlockbiblemeaning.com

KJV - country, isle, island.

H776

אֶרֶץ ’erets eh’-rets; from an unused root probably meaning to be firm; the earth (at large, or partitively a land):

KJV - × common, country, earth, field, ground, land, × nations, way, + wilderness, world.

H1471

גּוֹי gôwy go’-ee; rarely (shortened) גֹּי; apparently from the same root as H1465 (גֵּוָה) (in the sense of massing); a foreign nation; hence, a Gentile; also (figuratively) a troop of animals, or a flight of locusts:

KJV - Gentile, heathen, nation, people.

H3956

לָשׁוֹן lâshôwn law-shone’; or לָשֹׁן; also (in plural) feminine לְשֹׁנָה; from H3960 (לָשַׁן); the tongue (of man or animals), used literally (as the instrument of licking, eating, or speech), and figuratively (speech, an ingot, a fork of flame, a cove of water):

KJV - + babbler, bay, + evil speaker, language, talker, tongue, wedge.

H4940

מִשְׁפָּחָה mishpâchâh mish-paw-khaw’; from H8192 (שָׁפָה) compare H8198 (שִׁפְחָה) a family, i.e. circle of relatives; figuratively, a class (of persons), a species (of animals) or sort (of things); by extension a tribe or people:

KJV - family, kind(-red).

There are many points and lessons here. I will highlight only two. First, the world population starts with *two* unique individuals, a male and a female, just like Adam and Eve. It develops into a family and grows from there. *Audit of Humankind* devoted a section to *How Humankind Socializes*. Refresh your mind with these chapter titles and content. Only the human species develops from a couple into nations occupying specific land territories everywhere around the world. All the Biblical Hebrew words above culminate in *individuals* and *nations*. God separated people by *family* and gave each of them their *language* and *land* to establish their *country*.

- Human Society, the Only Global Social Species[6].
- You are a Unique Individual among 7 Billion on Earth[7].
- Gender Equality, Gender Inequality or Gender Compatibility?[8]
- Bride and Groom is a Cross-Cultural, Worldwide Phenomenon[9].
- Couple Relationship–Binding Husband and Wife in Marriage[10].
- Healthy Marriage, A Happy Twosome with Abundant Benefits[11].

6. https://theexplanation.com/human-society-the-only-global-social-species/

7. https://theexplanation.com/you-are-a-unique-individual-among-7-billion-on-earth/

8. https://theexplanation.com/gender-equality-gender-inequality-or-gender-compatibility/

9. https://theexplanation.com/bride-and-groom-is-a-cross-cultural-worldwide-phenomenon/

10. https://theexplanation.com/couple-relationship-binding-husband-and-wife-in-marriage/

11. https://theexplanation.com/healthy-marriage-a-happy-twosome-with-abundant-benefits/

- Family–The Cornerstone of Human Society[12].
- Parenting, Father & Mother have Essential Complementary Roles[13].
- Extended family. Many Generations = World Population[14].
- Ethnicity, Clans, Tribes, Where did They All Come From?[15]
- Nations Are Identified by Their Own Patriotic Ethnic Culture[16].
- Origin of Language, An Unsolvable Scientific Mystery[17].
- Globalization: Integration Versus Segregation of People[18].

Nation = Goy (H1471) in Biblical Hebrew

The second point to retain is more cultural. H1471 גּוֹי gôwy; The common pronunciation is *goy,* like *boy* with a hard *g*. You might be aware of this word. It is often used by Jews to refer to non-Jewish people as Gentiles. From the KJV renditions, the translators used *Gentile*. What needs clarification is nowadays Jews use this term to designate non-Jews. However, Biblically, the nation of Israel is *goy*; it is neither pejorative to Jews nor non-Jews. H1471 is simply a Biblical Hebrew word defining *all nations*. Here it refers to the descendants of Abraham.

Genesis 12:22

---

12. https://theexplanation.com/family-the-cornerstone-of-human-society/

13. https://theexplanation.com/parenting-father-mother-have-essential-complementary-roles/

14. https://theexplanation.com/extended-family-many-generations-world-population/

15. https://theexplanation.com/ethnicity-clans-tribes-where-did-they-all-come-from/

16. https://theexplanation.com/nations-identified-by-their-own-patriotic-ethnic-culture/

17. https://theexplanation.com/origin-of-language-an-unsolvable-scientific-mystery

18. https://theexplanation.com/globalization-integration-segregation/

And I will make of you a great *nation* (H1471), and I will bless you, and make your name great; and you shall be a blessing:

Genesis 18:18

Seeing that Abraham shall surely become a great and mighty *nation* (H1471). and all the *nations* (H1471) of the earth shall be blessed in him?

Exodus 19:6

And you shall be to me (God) a kingdom of priests, and an *holy nation* (H1471 goy kadosh). These are the words which you shall speak to the children of Israel.

Notice Gen. 18:18 God will bless both the Abrahamic nation and *all* the nations of Earth. Both references to nation use H1471, *goy*. Some might consider this unjust. Why the preeminence for the Abrahamic nation? Well, as many examples reveal, there has to be a first in any group or sequence. Christ is the first of the firstfruits, those who will be with Him at His Return. It's not possible to develop anything like a family, school, business, association, government unless you have a founder or founders. There are always those who come first to set the pace and show the way, as we saw in the last chapter about leaders and followers.

History shows us, these founders, in whatever venture, whether secular or Biblical, have the *most* trials and the *most* responsibility. It is *not* given to every person or every nation to be a leader. Much more can be said about this point, but that's another story.

Sam's Reflections

As I present this history of the beginning of nations to you, there's a gnawing thought going through my mind. Many Bible scholars, Christian preachers, even Jewish Rabbis reject the Bible as history. I don't feel like giving you any references, do a Google search using *scholars reject bible history*.

The Explanation devoted many pages of *Origin of the Universe*[19] to explain Biblical Hebrew as the basis of God's Word. It expounded scientific findings and shows how it all assembles with the Creation narrative in Genesis. Yes, I quote scripture about history, Noah, his sons, Abraham, Moses, Egypt, and the Exodus. No, I don't have proof, although there's evidence for some of these narratives as indicated by the Biblical Archaeological Society above.

We can ask, is God in touch with history? Is He a present God? Is He interested in His Creation? All the Universe, down to Earth and ALL its inhabitants and their doings? I believe the answer is yes to all those questions.

I read the other day, another writer's definition of theology, analyzing God's Word. *The Explanation* discussed true theology at length[20], studying to see what God says and how it applies to us. God's Word is God's Word and John 10:10 states it's the truth, including the history.

Please click on the links above regarding theology, science, and Genesis. I cannot go back each time and

19. https://theexplanation.com/read-content-origin-universe-online/

20. https://theexplanation.com/into-theology-a-fifth-approach-to-life-with-peace-and-prosperity/

REexplain these concepts. Among others, these are the reasons *The Explanation* takes God's Word at face value.

God and Goyim - Nations

God is not only interested in nations, but individuals in those nations. Abraham was the father of the faithful because God made a covenant with him. An important aspect of God's plan was to *include* non-Abrahamic people *in* His covenant.

> **Genesis 17:11-13**
>
> 11 And you shall circumcise the flesh of your foreskin; and it shall be a token of the covenant between me and you.
>
> 12 And he that is eight days old shall be circumcised among you, every man child in your generations, he that is born in the house, or bought with money of any stranger, which is not of your seed.
>
> 13 He that is born in your house, and he that is bought with your money, must needs be circumcised: and my covenant shall be in your flesh for an everlasting covenant.

This is not the place to discuss circumcision. Abraham had hundreds of servants who were all circumcised (Gen. 14:14 mentions 318). They had been in Abraham's service for some time and witnessed the presence of God in his life. God *included* these foreigners in the covenant. They are part of the faithful.

Another lesser-known of the Bible references about the Exodus from Egypt includes the same principle as Abraham. God takes care of His nation, but He also brings people from other nations along. God is preparing people from *all* nations for an incredible future. As we saw, *all* nations will be blessed in Abraham.

Exodus 12:37-38

37 And the children of Israel journeyed from Rameses to Succoth, about six hundred thousand on foot that were men, beside children.

38 And a mixed multitude went up also with them; and flocks, and herds, even very much cattle.

This *mixed multitude* refers to people in Egypt who were not descendants of Abraham. They witnessed the ten plagues and were well aware of God's power of intervention. It doesn't say whether they too were slaves or whether there were any Egyptians among this mixed multitude. God's concern for other nations is a theme running throughout the Bible.

Here is a verse *The Explanation* quotes a fair amount of times. For a reason. We need to understand the relationship between God's people and everyone else, including other nations.

Deuteronomy 4:5-8

5 Behold, I have taught you statutes and judgments, even as the LORD my God commanded me, that you should do so in the land where you go to possess it.

6 Keep therefore and do them; for this is your wisdom and your understanding in the sight of the nations, which shall hear all these statutes, and say, Surely this great nation is a wise and understanding people.

> 7 For what nation is there so great, who has God so near to them, as the LORD our God is in all things that we call upon him for?
>
> 8 And what nation is there so great, that has statutes and judgments so righteous as all this law, which I set before you this day?

Those verses reveal the statutes and judgments in the *Old* Testament are righteous. The other *nations* would come to see God through the peace and prosperity the application of these laws would bring the Israelites. To use *New* Testament terminology, remember these other nations were IN this world. The *Old* Testament laws were a witness to *un*converted *nations*. As *The Explanation* points out, these same laws should serve the *same purpose* today, but our nations, our leaders, even our religious leaders feel these laws are abrogated and of little or no value. Read these chapters about the laws in Exodus and Deuteronomy[21] as well as Proverbs[22]. These are needed today to provide stability for all nations.

Note verse 6, *this is your* ***wisdom*** *and your understanding in the sight of the nations*. The title of this book, *Evidence for Bible Wisdom*, comes from this source referring to the statutes and judgments in Deut. 4:5. I hope we realize these are in addition to the Ten Commandments. However, the wisdom is not simply the knowledge of these Words of God; the wisdom is in the *keeping* and *doing*. *Keep* in verse 6 is H8104 (shamar), identical to the injunction given to the nation's leader in Deuteronomy 16:19, we read in the chapter about *how to govern a country properly*. The same Bible wisdom is good for leaders, the Israelites, and non-Israelites, to bring peace and

21. https://theexplanation.com/critical-thinking-antidote-to-the-agony-of-humankind/

22. https://theexplanation.com/rules-for-life-wisdom-for-living-abundantly-in-the-world/

prosperity to all peoples worldwide. Spiritual conversion has nothing to do with this Old Testament wisdom.

The statutes, judgments, and law were and are beacons to the world and the nations. Here's a shortlist of God's servants who marked the history of non-Israelite *nations* and *empires*. Joseph > Egypt, Solomon > Queen of Sheba in Africa, Jonah > Nineveh, Nebuchadnezzar in Babylon, Daniel > Babylon, Cyrus in Persia. The Old Testament is the history of the descendants of Abraham but *not* to the exclusion of other peoples' history. I leave you to dig for more Bible meaning by reading these narratives.

New Testament countries and nations

God is the God of *all* individuals and *all* countries and nations. Today bordering countries fight over land and religion. Religious minorities within countries suffer at the hand of religious majorities. They are fractured countries and God allows it so they learn lessons. *Agony of Humankind* explained WHY God lets people and nations follow their own ways[23], which is eating of the Tree of Good and Evil.

Acts 14:16

> Who in times past suffered all nations to walk in their own ways.

Acts 17:26

> And has made of one blood all nations of men for to dwell on all the face of the earth, and has determined the times before appointed, and the bounds of their habitation;

23. https://theexplanation.com/get-out-of-my-garden-god-told-adam-and-eve-why/

God isn't some distant, uninterested Entity. He knows exactly what He's doing. Yes, it may appear God has withdrawn Himself, but no, His plan calls for letting nations and individuals do their own thing (Acts 14:16). Notice, He's appointed a *timeframe* and *location* for each *nation*. As we move into our second confinement here in France and as miserable as the European scene and worldwide countries appear, God knows it is in their best interest to experience these trials for a *time*. The World's nations need to learn lessons; they haven't yet. God cannot intervene too soon or He'll defeat His purpose. The following verses make it abundantly clear the history of nations is in God's hands.

> **Romans 16:26**
>
> But now is made manifest, and by the scriptures of the prophets, according to the commandment of the everlasting God, made known to all nations for the obedience of faith:
>
> **Galatians 3:8** And the scripture, foreseeing that God would justify the heathen through faith, preached before the gospel to Abraham, saying, In you shall all nations be blessed.
>
> **Revelation 2:26** And he that overcomes, and keeps my works to the end, to him will I give power over the nations:
>
> **Revelation 7:9** After this I beheld, and, lo, a great multitude, which no man could number, of all nations, and kindreds, and people, and tongues, stood before the throne, and before the Lamb, clothed with white robes, and palms in their hands;

That last verse in Revelation indicates the future of all the goyim - nations. They too will benefit from all the blessings of salvation. God is well aware of all individuals and all nations. The Bible, God's Word, is both their history and their future.

Individual Rights vs Collective Rights

People's and human rights are major issues today. Regarding individual and collective rights, where should the balance be? Why?

The question of whose rights come first, personal or community, colors the debate of many subjects. Today, Covid-19 is front and center for wearing masks and social distancing. Electric scooters on sidewalks and loud parties in quiet neighborhoods are genuine issues. Can individuals do whatever they want in exercising their rights? Or, for the good of the community, are there collective rights to which individuals should adhere, not to say, submit?

Citizen rights. In the 21st century, we have two primary blocks of nations when we look at this subject. We have a block of nations, in the minority, where individual rights have the upper hand and most nations where collective rights take the lead.

The Explanation broaches this subject because it relates to How Humans Socialize[1]. The book *Audit of Humankind* devoted a Section to this subject. In the context of human relationships in an appeased society, we need principles to guide inter-relational associations. We can call it etiquette or ethics, we need valid and applicable guidelines. It is no mystery; *The Explanation* looks for the guidance code in the Bible and theology[2]. I've devoted much space to show the value of the Bible teaching in Exodus, Deuteronomy[3], and Proverbs[4] for today's society. Yes, we must *adapt* the principles to the 21st century with spiritual wisdom, but they are the basis for harmonious living. And they reveal the relationship between individual and collective rights.

Rights extend into every field of living

One of the fundamental issues is individual freedom vs group freedom. There's the other side to this subject, responsibility; meaning somewhere, somehow, one or both parties needs to restrain its freedom, not an easy equation to establish. How much? Why me and not the other guy? Who decides? How do you apply restraints? Who enforces them? These are real questions we face in handling the Covid-19 pandemic. Here's a partial list of rights disturbing practically every society and country around the world. Many are major issues, affecting millions of people. We do not have accepted practices of how to handle these situations, only adding to the confusion society finds itself in.

1. https://theexplanation.com/read-all-the-content-of-audit-of-humankind-online/

2. https://theexplanation.com/deity-and-sound-reasoned-words-are-the-crux-of-theology/

3. https://theexplanation.com/critical-thinking-antidote-to-the-agony-of-humankind/

4. https://theexplanation.com/rules-for-life-wisdom-for-living-abundantly-in-the-world/

- Freedom of religion[5], speech, [6]press[7].
- Right to food[8], housing, [9]water[10].
- Right to an adequate standard of living, [11]health, [12]social security[13], disability[14].
- Environmental racism[15], gay rights[16], identity politics[17], indigenous[18], intersex[19].
- Institutionalized discrimination[20], minority[21], racial[22], special rights[23].

Society's definition of Rights

But first, we need to define what rights are. Here's what Wikipedia has to say[24].

5. https://en.wikipedia.org/wiki/Freedom_of_religion
6. https://en.wikipedia.org/wiki/Freedom_of_speech
7. https://en.wikipedia.org/wiki/Freedom_of_the_press
8. https://en.wikipedia.org/wiki/Right_to_food
9. https://en.wikipedia.org/wiki/Right_to_housing
10. https://en.wikipedia.org/wiki/Right_to_water
11. https://en.wikipedia.org/wiki/Right_to_an_adequate_standard_of_living
12. https://en.wikipedia.org/wiki/Right_to_health
13. https://en.wikipedia.org/wiki/Right_to_social_security
14. https://en.wikipedia.org/wiki/Disability_rights_movement
15. https://en.wikipedia.org/wiki/Environmental_racism
16. https://en.wikipedia.org/wiki/Gay_rights
17. https://en.wikipedia.org/wiki/Identity_politics
18. https://en.wikipedia.org/wiki/Indigenous_rights
19. https://en.wikipedia.org/wiki/Intersex_human_rights
20. https://en.wikipedia.org/wiki/Institutionalized_discrimination
21. https://en.wikipedia.org/wiki/Minority_rights
22. https://en.wikipedia.org/wiki/Racial_segregation
23. https://en.wikipedia.org/wiki/Special_rights
24. https://en.wikipedia.org/wiki/Rights

> Rights are legal, social, or ethical principles of freedom or entitlement; that is, rights are the fundamental normative rules about what is allowed of people or owed to people according to some legal system, social convention, or ethical theory. Rights are of essential importance in such disciplines as law and ethics, especially theories of justice and deontology.
>
> Rights are often considered fundamental to civilization, for they are regarded as established pillars of society and culture, and the history of social conflicts can be found in the history of each right and its development. According to the Stanford Encyclopedia of Philosophy, "rights structure the form of governments, the content of laws, and the shape of morality as it is currently perceived".

Please retain, "rights structure ... the content of laws." In this definition, rights have the upper hand. They come first and they define the law. Laws develop AS people, social conflicts, and revolutions recognize rights.

The Explanation's ground-rule definition of Rights

To discuss this tricky and touchy subject, *The Explanation* must first establish a basis for its presentation. Given the existence of rights, the foremost question is: *who* has the *right* to establish *rights*? Alternately, we could ask *who* has the *authority* to decide what rights are? To codify them? To promulgate them? And especially to enforce them?

From reading this book you know *The Explanation's* answer to all those questions. God, Elohim, Yahveh Elohim are our point of departure. Any contestation is another subject.

Each person has free will[25] and the right to exercise it. Decisions are the basis of our resultant behavior[26], but we also have the responsibility to exercise free will within the confines of a code of ethics[27] summed up by *love God and your neighbor.*

This is where *individualism* meets *collectivism.* As an individual, we have *both* rights and responsibilities, which we can call *obligations*, to God and our entourage.

Above in the list of *rights,* we saw: Freedom of religion, speech, press.

The keyword is *freedom.* In the West we consider *freedom* to be a *right.* In France, where I am, the national motto of the country is *Liberté, Egalité, Fraternité.* It starts with freedom!

In 2020, events in France crystallized and focused worldwide attention on *freedom of the press*; revolving around the caricatures of Mohammed. One cannot talk about freedom without addressing the question of responsibility to one's neighbor. They go hand-in-hand. This is where wisdom enters the picture, whether or not you are God-fearing. One side is defending its right to freedom of the press, the other its right to how its religion is presented. Terrorism, demonstrations, open conflict result from non-agreement of freedom and obligations.

We are discussing rights in the context of *people, all* people. We're broaching practical Bible wisdom for individuals and collectivities worldwide, regardless of their beliefs in a superior power. Did God set in motion rules applying to these circumstances? He did.

---

25. https://theexplanation.com/free-will-we-all-possess-it-but-we-cant-always-utilize-it/
26. https://theexplanation.com/social-behavior-an-audit-of-human-nature-coupled-with-free-will/
27. https://theexplanation.com/ethics-are-the-blueprint-for-behavior-how-humanity-should-function/

We have discussed these at length in the realm of *relationships* and *rulership* in Genesis 1[28]. The first institution God established was a married couple[29] to procreate and engender a family[30]. *The Explanation* has already developed the theme of humans made in the image of God[31]. As well as human institutions in the image of God's institutions, in the upcoming chapter on family ties.

Family is a collectivity

Many wonder why *family* is a worldwide institution. No matter the culture, race, religion, or ethics, family is the fundamental configuration of humans living together; a group of *individuals* living as a *collectivity*.

> The relationships between father, mother, children; husband, wife; parents, offspring; brothers and sisters are the foundation for individual and collective living.

This is part of How Humans Socialize because these rights determine how we live as individuals within a community[32]. Which is what we are from the family to a nation, to a family of nations[33].

This is the reason individuals are to be beacons for the collectivity. And the collectivity, likewise, to be a beacon for the individuals.

Regarding evil-doers, they too become a lesson for the collectivity, a negative one. Here's an example of freedom of speech and the obligation of justice.

---

28. https://theexplanation.com/genesis-1-reveals-basics-social-relations-rulership/

29. https://theexplanation.com/couple-relationship-binding-husband-and-wife-in-marriage/

30. https://theexplanation.com/family-the-cornerstone-of-human-society/

31. https://theexplanation.com/made-in-the-image-of-god-the-definition/

32. https://theexplanation.com/marriage-relationship-man-woman-in-front-beside-or-behind/

33. https://theexplanation.com/history-of-individuals-and-nations-practical-bible-wisdom/

Deuteronomy 19:16-20

16 If a false witness rise up against any man to testify against him that which is wrong;

17 Then both the men, between whom the controversy is, shall stand before the Lord, before the priests and the judges, which shall be in those days;

18 And the judges shall make diligent inquisition: and, behold, if the witness be a false witness, and has testified falsely against his brother;

19 Then shall you do to him, as he had thought to have done to his brother: so shall you put the evil away from among you.

20 And those which remain shall hear, and fear, and shall henceforth commit no more any such evil among you.

In the Old Testament, with UNconverted people, God was concerned with the welfare of the *entire community*. He did not hesitate to make an example of the individual for the benefit of the community. People choose to speak whatever they want, they have freedom of speech. But with freedom comes responsibility. The responsibility of loving your neighbor. If they do not meet the obligation, then the person must accept the consequences of their acts.

Those who remain (Deut. 19:20). Of course, this was a group of individuals, the community. God considers the importance of the coherence and understanding of the group. Everyone should behave ethically as a group. The individual has free will, but only within the limits of the rules applying to the community. Through the illicit acts of an individual, God teaches the nation an important lesson about lying. Individuals in a community must know lying doesn't pay.

Why God allows people BACK into the Garden of Eden.

We discussed why God expelled Adam and Eve[34], and hence, all humankind, from the Garden of Eden. Subsequently, we also explained how Christ opened the *way* back *into* the Garden[35].

The question is, *who* does God let back into the Garden and *why*? Can anybody enter under any circumstances? Adam and Eve were put out because of non-conformity to rules God established. God put in motion those rules for an excellent reason.

> So the community can live in harmony. So individuals can know how to live in a community. Love God and neighbor.

God's people are going to be together for all eternity. We've got to *get along* with ALL the other Eternal beings. On a worldly level, there must be rules applying to living in harmony with ALL others; each person has their free will, but it must be within the community rules. The following verse sums up that relationship.

> **Deuteronomy 17:13**
>
> And all the people shall hear, and fear, and do no more presumptuously.

Practical Bible wisdom does not dilly dally around with aimless, innocuous sayings. Bible advice is clear and straightforward. It is for

---

34. https://theexplanation.com/get-out-of-my-garden-god-told-adam-and-eve-why/

35. https://theexplanation.com/the-antidote-ultimate-solution-to-agony-of-humankind/

individuals, like those hundreds of thousands of people preparing to go into a new country, and establish a new *functioning society*, to live in harmony in a community. It is for *all* the people (the community) to benefit from the freedom by assuming their obligations (hear and fear) and adjusting their behavior in accordance with the code of ethics (do no more presumptuously). Freedom and responsibility go hand-in-hand.

Sound Bible wisdom counsels its observance *and* its enforcement by the competent authorities. We should bring a controversy before the priests and the judges (Deut. 19:17). I hear you, there are no priests; however, there are pastors and judges. Unfortunately, they do not necessarily match the qualifications indicated by Bible wisdom. *The Explanation* broaches this in a forthcoming chapter *True Justice in the Old Testament*. Everything said, there is an authoritative body to handle controversy, which must assume its role for individuals to live in a community where freedom and obligations give rise to harmony.

Extremes don't work

"Individual rights are absolute." "Collective rights are absolute." Such statements fly in the face of reality. Individuals together make a collectivity and a collectivity is a group of individuals. Both have rights. No rights are exclusive, the rights of one cannot infringe on the rights of the other.

Today, some people, communities, groups have become polarized and can't see beyond their own rights. Obviously, that's problematic, especially when you can no longer reason with them. This is where fanaticism and absolutism take over.

In the context of How Humans Function[36], one singularity[37] is rising to the challenge[38]. This takes imagination and innovation[39], which

36. https://theexplanation.com/focus-on-human-behavior-study-how-humans-function/

are extremely positive qualities. Collectivism should not put brakes on these characteristics. The inventive mind[40] describes what humans are. Removing that opportunity is like extracting a part of their brain: there is nothing wrong with personal growth, goals, and success, to the contrary. However, it must not come by oppressing or cheating others; at this point, collective limits and rights put boundaries on imagination. Some might think it's unfair to limit imagination. Well, do they also think unlimited innovation *is ok* to harm others?

The key is relationships[41]. Relations with God, relations with neighbor. One word, relations, summarizes the two great commandments. Individuals need to consider their personal identity in relational terms.

> I want to be *me*, but I must fit into the *we*. Indeed, you have the right to be you, but you also have the obligation to not impede others from being themselves.

Proverbs 18:24

> A man that has friends must show himself friendly: and there is a friend that sticks closer than a brother.

Here is the reciprocity of the individual within the collective. As the Three Musketeers say, "one for all (a friend must show himself friendly), all for one (has friends, plural)." This is an individual who has integrated a group. In Proverbs, it is a group animated by the

37. https://theexplanation.com/rule-life-responsibly-the-key-human-singularity/

38. https://theexplanation.com/challenge-accompanied-courage-needed-face-new-struggles-another-human-singularity/

39. https://theexplanation.com/imagination-another-singularity-of-humankind-in-your-mind/

40. https://theexplanation.com/two-greatest-gifts-mankind-mind-hands/

41. https://theexplanation.com/genesis-1-reveals-basics-social-relations-rulership/

principles of God. It's a unified group, or family, enjoying and applying the same ethics.

Here's a quote from Agony of Humankind[42]. Societal rights are a serious matter.

> For society to function there must be a semblance of order. Should a population live in fear because a rapist or killer is on the prowl? That's the question of the Rights of Society versus Individual Rights. From a Biblical perspective, societal rights have the priority. It is the responsibility of the individual to conform to the laws of the land. For God's society and the laws He's promulgated, He knows what's best for living in peace and prosperity. Respect for that way of life in that society is a necessity. The individual still has a choice, but they must be ready to pay the consequences for a wrong one.

The individual in a God-respecting society blends into the collective while maintaining their freedom WITH responsibility. They work in tandem.

Look at a wider angle of this subject; individuals compose a collective nation. Does God promote the individual over the nation or the nation over the individual?[43] This becomes a vital subject when we talk about human rights, in particular *individual* rights. Which has the upper hand? We've seen the practical Bible wisdom regarding deciding between individual and collective rights. The community respects the freedom of the individual, where the individual respects the harmony of the community.

---

42. https://theexplanation.com/what-is-death-rest-in-peace-or-dust-which-why/

43. https://theexplanation.com/history-of-individuals-and-nations-practical-bible-wisdom/

Lies are Damaging. Stop Them

Lies are nauseous. Like cancer, it starts with one cell, then 2, 4, 8, multiplying. Soon you can't stop it. Lies kill individuals, nations, and the world.

Lies destroy truth, that's the bottom line. Today, it goes even further because many question the definition of truth, and whether such a virtue exists. We're hitting rock-bottom. Practical Bible wisdom reveals there is truth and an antidote to lies.

I had the strangest dream a few days ago. Maybe it was preparing this chapter by working at an unconscious level. I was flying around at tree-height level (don't get rational; I don't remember the mechanism). Somebody else flew past me slightly higher, and I purposely raised my hand and touched their sled. It caused a crash. The driver got up and ran after me, throwing a purse, which I caught. The question is, what to do with that purse? My first thought was to throw it away, drop it into the ocean. Then I realized, since I caught it, there are probably fingerprints or fibers on it identifying me! And the surmisings, excuses, options multiplied from there. *All* that justification to *avoid admitting* my mistake. Crazy dream right! The point?

Lies twist your mind.

Trying to cover up a lie forces you into telling more and more lies. It affects your conscience, the deepest part of your being. I couldn't get out of my dream. I realized I'd done wrong and wanted to correct it without getting myself caught. *No* consequences for me! The purse owner's ID was in the purse. I thought about sending it back with money to cover repairs and make amends. But *how* to do this without having the package traced back to me? *One act, one lie,* starts a *never-ending chain reaction.*

The Bible confirms how deep lies reach. Proverbs 18:8, "The words of a talebearer are as wounds, and they go down into the innermost parts of the belly."

Inveterate Liars are very intelligent people

Lies must be believable, but they must have a story. As someone said, a liar needs an excellent memory. They must remember their lies and be capable of fabricating a story where all the pieces fit together around that lie. Police spend hours interrogating a suspect, going over and over all the details until the suspect trips up. During such a grueling interrogation, a guilty person, trying to weave a story by blaming someone else, or denying their deeds, gets caught up in the web of their reasoning and words. They have no choice but to admit their guilt.

But people don't always have the acumen veteran police do, and fall for lies. They believe in traditions, folklore, myth, or what society has wrongly taught them with so much conviction. To the extent of myriad beliefs about anything and everything.

Kasparov from Russia was the former world chess champion. He now lives in Croatia and founded the Renew Democracy Initiative to defend and promote liberal democracy in the USA and around the world. He is also an author. Regarding lies, called propaganda, he tweeted[1].

"The point of modern propaganda isn't only to misinform or push an agenda. It is to exhaust your critical thinking, to annihilate truth."

I wrote about critical thinking[2] as an antidote to confusion. Certainly, misinformation fits into the categories of both chaos and lies. When you begin to realize the extent of psychological manipulation[3] and its vast array of practices, you realize just how devastating it is. Here's another article elaborating on how lies undermine truth[4], specifically oriented to the state of politics in the USA in a pre-election period.

Lies kill critical thinking, being so rampant, people are lost in a sea of opposing nuances and debates. Add fake news in a post-truth age we call the information age, and we've got a potent mess of facts and fiction. There's so much shredded confetti nobody can sort it out or make heads or tails of what to believe or not believe. People are giving up in despair.

Lies for Manipulation

1. https://twitter.com/kasparov63/status/808750564284702720?lang=en

2. https://theexplanation.com/critical-thinking-antidote-to-the-agony-of-humankind

3. https://en.wikipedia.org/wiki/Psychological_manipulation

4. https://medium.com/@tswriting/why-trump-lies-7489e35997e6

There are various reasons people tell lies. A key one is they don't want anyone catching them for something they've done wrong, like theft or murder. This is egotistical and concerns the person or their partners in crime.

You also get manipulation on a major scale when lies are told affecting dozens, hundreds, and thousands of people. We've seen this down through history. Read this National Geographic article[5] to see some of the biggest lies in politics, sports, finance, entertainment... These are swindlers, corruptors, fraud on a large scale.

One of the major areas of lies to manipulate is in the field of *un*provable phenomena. Specifically, the spiritual or religious fields. It's a vast area involving the immaterial or intangible world; the opposite of science which handles measurable, material matters. But even science can lead you up the garden path. John Horgan wrote "The End of Science[6]," in which he refers to *ironic science*, the imaginary speculation scientists add to what's proven. When one has established their reputation, they can advance ideas listeners will swallow hook, line, and sinker, with no supporting evidence.

One vivid example of this is to answer the question of what preceded the Big Bang. Where did the first piece of *physical matter* that developed into our Cosmos come from? Some scientists put forth the idea *something can come from nothing* and many believe it, or the idea asteroids deposited all the water we have on Earth. There's no proof, but *authority manipulates*. Lies are powerful influences.

The Bible points to a liar par excellence. When you talk about the reality of a talking, wise, manipulating Serpent, most will smile and think you're a little naïve or weird. The key verse is in this lengthy

5. https://www.nationalgeographic.com/magazine/2017/06/famous-liars/

6. https://blogs.scientificamerican.com/cross-check/was-i-wrong-about-8220-the-end-of-science-8221/

context in the book of John below. I've included it because it reveals the delusion the religious leaders were under to maintain their status in front of the people. Christ cuts to the core issue in verse 44. Here, He points out *why* and *who* their real influence is. There's a short phrase in this verse, *When he speaks a lie, he speaks of his own*; it's worth understanding. *Of his own* points to how deeply ingrained in its character lying is.

Read this article[7] to see the origin of the devil's lies. They started way before the Creation in Genesis 1:1. By that time it was already an inveterate liar with a cohort of one-third of the spirit beings as demons. Christ states *from the beginning* (vs. 44) referring to when our world was established. The devil is a pathological liar and can no longer help itself.

John 8:32-59

32 And you shall know the truth, and the truth shall make you free.

33 They answered him, We be Abraham's seed, and were never in bondage to any man: how say you, You shall be made free?

34 Jesus answered them, Verily, verily, I say to you, Whosoever commits sin is the servant of sin.

35 And the servant abides not in the house for ever: but the Son abides ever.

36 If the Son therefore shall make you free, you shall be free indeed.

7. https://theexplanation.com/the-bible-serpent-liar-and-influencer-par-excellence/

37 I know that you are Abraham's seed; but you seek to kill me, because my word has no place in you.

38 I speak that which I have seen with my Father: and you do that which you have seen with your father.

39 They answered and said to him, Abraham is our father. Jesus said to them, If you were Abraham's children, you would do the works of Abraham.

40 But now you seek to kill me, a man that has told you the truth, which I have heard of God: this did not Abraham.

41 You do the deeds of your father. Then said they to him, We be not born of fornication; we have one Father, even God.

42 Jesus said to them, If God were your Father, you would love me: for I proceeded forth and came from God; neither came I of myself, but he sent me.

43 Why do you not understand my speech? even because you cannot hear my word.

44 You are of your father the devil, and the lusts of your father you will do. He was a murderer from the beginning, and abode not in the truth, because there is no truth in him. When he speaks a lie, he speaks of his own: for he is a liar, and the father of it.

45 And because I tell you the truth, you believe me not.

46 Which of you convinces me of sin? And if I say the truth, why do you not believe me?

47 He that is of God hears God's words: you therefore hear them not, because you are not of God.

48 Then answered the Jews, and said to him, Say we not well that you are a Samaritan, and have a devil?

49 Jesus answered, I have not a devil; but I honour my Father, and you do dishonour me.

50 And I seek not mine own glory: there is one that seeks and judges.

51 Verily, verily, I say to you, If a man keep my saying, he shall never see death.

52 Then said the Jews to him, Now we know that you have a devil. Abraham is dead, and the prophets; and you say, If a man keep my saying, he shall never taste of death.

53 Are you greater than our father Abraham, which is dead? and the prophets are dead: whom makes you yourself?

54 Jesus answered, If I honour myself, my honour is nothing: it is my Father that honours me; of whom you say, that he is your God:

55 Yet you have not known him; but I know him: and if I should say, I know him not, I shall be a liar like you: but I know him, and keep his saying.

> 56 Your father Abraham rejoiced to see my day: and he saw it, and was glad.
>
> 57 Then said the Jews to him, you are not yet fifty years old, and have you seen Abraham?
>
> 58 Jesus said to them, Verily, verily, I say to you, Before Abraham was, I am.
>
> 59 Then took they up stones to cast at him: but Jesus hid himself, and went out of the temple, going through the midst of them, and so passed by.

These religious leaders were manipulating scripture. It could be said they misunderstood the scope of the Hebrew Bible contexts. However, Christ points out they are liars, meaning they're manipulating scripture, outright lies, to remain the wise of the day, when the Wisest was on the scene.

Deuteronomy Antidote

Right from the start, in Genesis 3, and down through history, God condemns lies. God judged the father of lies and the final sentence will be carried out in due course. In the Old Testament, there is a clear condemnation of lies. The ninth commandment, part of the Ten Commandments, the ultimate ethical code, says "You shall not bear false witness against your neighbour" (Ex. 20:16). It is followed by umpteen verses and allusions to not distorting the truth.

> **Leviticus 19:16** You shall not go up and down as a talebearer among thy people: neither shall you stand against the blood of your neighbour: I am the LORD.

Lev. 19:11 You shall not steal, neither deal falsely, neither lie one to another.

In a Court of Law, the sentence, when the Judges caught someone lying, was very stiff. It could be capital punishment.

Deuteronomy 19:15-20

15 One witness shall not rise up against a man for any iniquity, or for any sin, in any sin that he sins: at the mouth of two witnesses, or at the mouth of three witnesses, shall the matter be established.

16 If a false witness rise up against any man to testify against him that which is wrong;

17 Then both the men, between whom the controversy is, shall stand before the LORD, before the priests and the judges, which shall be in those days;

18 And the judges shall make diligent inquisition: and, behold, if the witness be a false witness, and has testified falsely against his brother;

19 Then shall you do to him, as he had thought to have done to his brother: so shall you put the evil away from among you.

20 And those which remain shall hear, and fear, and shall henceforth commit no more any such evil among you.

Note verse 20, everybody in the community should deeply comprehend lying would *not be tolerated*. Imagine if people had such apprehension toward lies today! You decide whether this is practical Bible wisdom, whether it leads to more civil society.

Many are surprised and even upset to find a *God of love* advocate the death sentence in the Bible. In our liberal fake news, post-truth society we don't understand the havoc lies cause, although I think a lot are realizing we've gone way too far. God doesn't take this lightly. He nips it in the bud. Before the infection gets a stronghold and the epidemic is out of control. With Covid-19 we see just how fast an infectious disease can spread; how difficult it is to bring it to an end. The best approach is to take strict measures to eradicate it at the outset; God adopts this method, even if you think it's brutal. The more it causes damage, the swifter you must intervene and take stiff action to curb its spread.

Later Problem and Antidote

Later in the Bible, as society and social outlooks changed, we continue to find strong injunctions against lies, although we don't find such stiff penalties. However, telling lies still has a stiff penalty for those who make it a practice. This is a study needing meditation.

> **Proverbs 13:5** A righteous man hates lying: but a wicked man is loathsome, and comes to shame.

> **Pro. 20:19** He that goes about as a talebearer reveals secrets: therefore meddle not with him that flatters with his lips.

King Solomon addresses the Book of Proverbs to his son, representative of all individuals. Here, self-control is advised Bible wisdom.

Proverbs 11:13 A talebearer reveals secrets: but he that is of a faithful spirit conceals the matter.

Proverbs 26:20 Where no wood is, there the fire goes out: so where there is no talebearer, the strife ceases.

New Testament Antidote

When we get to the New Testament era we still see lies, even in the Church. Pastors are to catch them in the bud, otherwise, they become ingrained.

1 Timothy 5:13

13 And withal they learn to be idle, wandering about from house to house; and not only idle, but tattlers also and busybodies, speaking things which they ought not.

James 3:10-17

10 Out of the same mouth proceeds blessing and cursing. My brethren, these things ought not so to be.

11 Does a fountain send forth at the same place sweet water and bitter?

12 Can the fig tree, my brethren, bear olive berries? either a vine, figs? so can no fountain both yield salt water and fresh.

13 Who is a wise man and endued with knowledge among you? let him shew out of a good conversation his works with meekness of wisdom.

14 But if you have bitter envying and strife in your hearts, glory not, and **lie not against the truth**.

15 This wisdom descends not from above, but is earthly, sensual, devilish.

16 For where envying and strife is, there is **confusion** and every evil work.

17 But the **wisdom that is from above** is first pure, then peaceable, gentle, and easy to be intreated, full of mercy and good fruits, without partiality, and without hypocrisy.

18 And the fruit of righteousness is sown in peace of them that make peace.

Truth - the Ultimate Antidote

John 8:32 And you shall know the truth, and the truth shall make you free.

The ONLY WAY to end a lie is to TELL THE TRUTH.

If you make a mistake, the best remedy is to *admit* the mistake *immediately*. Then, hopefully, the offended person will accord forgiveness, certainly God will. Help is there if need be, maybe even a sanction if it's warranted, and a lesson learned by the person, necessary to gain wisdom.

Bible, for your consideration

One aspect of the Bible is the narrative tells it forthrightly, as it took place. There's no camouflage, filter, toning down of violence or sex. It states outright what you can do and what you can't do.

Whether you'll live or die. You can disagree all you want with the Bible, but one thing you can say is the narrative is direct. It doesn't hide behind any censorship. It tells you God killed all humans and saved only eight people during Noah's flood. It tells you Abraham tried to assassinate his son Isaac. It tells you Judah committed adultery with a woman who prostituted herself to trap him.

Many of these events turn people against God and His Word. It is understandable. However, there are valid reasons God allowed or even commanded these episodes. *Evidence for Bible Wisdom* is an effort to bring Godly reasoning to answer such queries and doubts.

The Bible doesn't pretend to be something it isn't. It states it's the Word of God. There's no manipulation. The Word of God is not trying to manipulate you. One could even say it pushes many people *away* by its content and frankness.

And after all is said and done, Christ, referring to the Father, said, "Sanctify them through your truth: your word is truth."

God's Word is Truth

How do you know if someone is telling you lies?

> **Pro. 2:6, 1:7**
>
> 6 For the LORD gives wisdom, and from his mouth come knowledge and understanding
>
> 1:7 The fear of the LORD is the beginning of knowledge: but fools despise wisdom and instruction.
>
> **Isa 8:20**

> To the law and to the testimony: if they speak not according to this word, it is because there is no light in them.

Let's go to the core of the matter. When you listen to the first five minutes or read the first pages of a narrative, you can tell *where* the story comes from. God's Word, His law, and testimony is the rule of comparison; if it's not the basis, then the knowledge is non-truth, equivalent to lies.

God forces nothing on you, it's your free will choice.

3. Social Relations

Love your neighbor encompasses all social relations, including your enemies (Matthew 5:44). Let's see *Evidence for Bible Wisdom* in the vast field of human relationships. Proper interaction with people from all walks of life, near and far, is the mainstay of a solid and durable society.

Family Ties, Gender, Sex, Marriage

Family ties are the foundation of a stable society. The Bible clearly states their composition and responsibilities.

Relationships between people have come to a head in today's society. It's a free-for-all. Anything can have sex with anything goes. There are no governing rules other than what society sets, and even then, individuals justify anything. Science, philosophy, and observation or experience cannot answer. There's no solid base for society establishing the ethics it does for family ties.

When it comes to the Bible, only religion has a say. And today, religion is so fragmented it too has conflicting views of social relations. Its voice is a whisper when explaining what is Biblical and what is not.

The result from all sides is confusion. Opposing points of view, whether secular or biblical, are supported by expert *opinions* or scholarly *interpretations* and *commentaries* on Bible passages.

We are going to approach this subject from the perspective of Godview. How and when did God establish people and procreation relationships? Why did He establish interpersonal rapport this way? What configuration did God give to humans for family ties? For God-given knowledge and understanding, we start with the examples and rules He set in motion; the root and trunk. We do not start by analyzing what a particular verse or word means, those are the twigs. This paragraph is the foundation for investigating social relationships and any other Bible-related subject. We want a Godview, not a worldview, and certainly not a personalview[1].

Here's what God unequivocally established in the beginning. This is the trunk of family ties.

Genesis 2:24

> Therefore shall a man leave his father and his mother, and shall cleave to his wife: and they shall be one flesh.

This verse is the tale of three families. First, a father and a mother with a son. Second, the family of the wife. Third, the son leaves the family home, and with his bride, inaugurates a new family with a husband and wife, and kids to come; the root of family ties.

Here are two, what might be strange questions: What genders were the father and mother? Is this original family configuration still valid?

Matthew 19:3-8

1. https://theexplanation.com/can-you-build-true-worldview-on-savvy-opinions-experience/

> 3 The Pharisees also came to him [Jesus Christ], tempting him, and saying to him, Is it lawful for a man to put away his wife for every cause?
>
> 4 And he answered and said to them, Have you not read, that he which made them at the beginning made them male and female,
>
> 5 And said, For this cause shall a man leave father and mother, and shall cleave to his wife: and they twain shall be one flesh?
>
> 6 Wherefore they are no more twain, but one flesh. What therefore God has joined together, let not man put asunder.
>
> 7 They say to him, Why did Moses then command to give a writing of divorcement, and to put her away?
>
> 8 He said to them, Moses because of the hardness of your hearts suffered you to put away your wives: but from the beginning it was not so.

First answer: The father and mother are male and female (vs. 4). *The Explanation* and Sam's personalview are not saying this. Godview, through Christ, states this, quoting Genesis.

Second answer: The marriage-family configuration of a male and female, husband and wife, is still valid today (vs. 5-6). Christ Himself said it, pointing the Pharisees right back to Creation. If you believe in Christ, His Existence, His Words, then you believe in a family composed of a male and female. We can add God's injunction to this couple, they were to procreate. Giving birth to children is the prerogative of a male and female in a marriage union; Biblical family ties.

This is Godview. In Genesis, according to Christ's Word, this male-female couple makes up a family. In a moment, I'll explain *why* this configuration is so important to God.

But first, let's answer the objections. Or rather, let Christ answer the Pharisees' objection. They invoked Moses' writing of divorcement. They're telling Christ, what God said in Genesis 1 is not valid anymore! Christ answers. Because of the hardness of *your* hearts, Christ permitted (see G2010 in Matthew 19:8 at UnlockBibleMeaning.com[2] for the full meaning), but it was not so from the start.

Do you see Christ answering by going to the trunk of the tree *...at the beginning...*? He is directing the Pharisees to Genesis and the context of marriage; Godview. In verse 6, ... *what God has joined together* is the equivalent of *God blessed them*[3] (Gen. 1:22), *let no man put asunder*. That's as inseparable as it gets.

After establishing the Godview, Christ confirms there is a command about divorce in the Old Testament law (Deuteronomy 24.1), because of the HARDNESS of YOUR HEARTS, BUT in the beginning, it was NOT intended. God gave a command concerning the ending of a marriage, nothing to do with the composition of the couple or the original family ties. Only because of the state of the couple's hardened hearts. We expanded *hardness of heart*[4] in Chapter 1.5.

---

2. https://unlockbiblemeaning.com

3. *https://theexplanation.com/god-blessed-the-male-and-the-female-heres-the-meaning/*

4. https://theexplanation.com/hardness-of-heart-how-to-deal-with-it-practical-bible-wisdom/

What is interesting in this passage is God established commandments *because* of the *hardness* of their *hearts*. Not because God wanted to. This is another subject, here's the resume. Christ said there are only two great commandments: Love God, love neighbor, all the other commandments elaborate on those two. *Why* are there only two and not 200 or 2000? Because when *hardness of heart* is replaced with putting those commandments *in your heart*, no other commandments will be necessary for Godly family ties.

When we understand that loving God and neighbor is a male and female forming a married couple with children creating family ties, then we won't need any other commandments. Until then, we need other laws, and God gave them at Mount Sinai.

I hope we all agree the Ten Commandments came from God. Various commandments refer to marriage and family.

- Visiting the iniquity of the fathers upon the children to the third and fourth generation of them that hate me.
- You shall not do any work, you, nor your son, nor your daughter.
- Honor your father and your mother.
- You shall not commit adultery.
- You shall not covet your neighbor's wife.

Five of the ten commandments point directly to maintaining the integrity of the family. All the elements of a family, husband, wife, and children are clearly indicated in the Ten Commandments. Think about it, yes, devotion to God is the number one theme, but number two is the honorability of the family unit.

Does the Bible support this? In every way. On an animal level, sex coupling is necessary to grow the population. Yes, there is some mating, but it is rare and is no comparison to family ties. On a human level, it's the only way to grow the population, but sex is a pleasurable binding force and healthy as well. Read about the benefits of marriage here[5]. Not only do parents benefit but the parental example sets the right family ties for children who likewise benefit.

The Old Testament is full of commands to preserve gender, sexual relations, marriage, and family ties. They are unmistakable because of the hardness of their and *our* hearts. We are going to look at just a few and draw out the practical Bible wisdom for us in our 21st century.

SINGLES

Before marriage, there is a fundamental axiom which a lot of young people miss. This example refers to war; go beyond and see what it's telling us.

> **Deuteronomy 21:10-14**
>
> 10 When you go forth to war against your enemies, and the LORD your God has delivered them into your hands, and you have taken them captive,
>
> 11 And see among the captives a beautiful woman, and have a desire to her, that you would have her to your wife;
>
> 12 Then you shall bring her home to your house; and she shall shave her head, and pare her nails;
>
> 13 And she shall put the raiment of her captivity from off her, and shall remain in your house, and bewail her father

5. https://theexplanation.com/healthy-marriage-a-happy-twosome-with-abundant-benefits/

> and her mother a full month: and after that you shall go in to her, and be her husband, and she shall be your wife.
>
> 14 And it shall be, if you have no delight in her, then you shall let her go whither she will; but you shall not sell her at all for money, you shall not make merchandise of her, because you have humbled her.

Outwardly, this sounds horrible, but keep in mind the hardness of their heart. The point of this example is the need for reflection *before* you marry. Her hair, make-up (nails), and dressy clothing are not the focus of attention, they enhance outward beauty. Thirty days with a person living in close quarters gives you a serious chance to know what the woman is like on the inside, what's on her mind, and whether you are compatible; the principle evoked here.

How many couples *talk* and *exchange ideas, converse, disagree*, even *bicker* intimately and maintain their closeness and love? Then it was a matter of 30 days, now it's a matter of taking the time, however long, before marriage to get to know your future partner. Practice the art and heart of dating without sex, developing lasting family ties, *not be put asunder.*

Old Testament: Marriage, Divorce, Gender, Sex

Here are some commands from Leviticus 18 focused on maintaining proper family ties. When you understand Godview, the Genesis 1 and 2 approach to family ties, you do not need this list of do nots. This list is for those with hard hearts.

In France, as in all nations, cases of rape, the killing of wives, and particularly incest are being revealed. "One in three-to-four girls and one in five-to-seven boys are sexually abused before they turn 18[6]." Family ties are being ruined, the younger generations are traumatized and we play the fiddle while Rome burns. It is sad to say, but today activating hardness of heart, instead of suppressing it, seems to be the name of the game.

God's commands are to preserve family ties from wrong sexual interplay of any type other than between the husband and wife. Leviticus 18 is very explicit.

- No philandering between children and their mother or father (6-7). No incest.
- Sister, stepmother, and stepsister (8-9, 11).
- Grandchildren (10).
- Uncles and aunts (13-14).
- Daughter-in-law and sister-in-law (15-16).
- A kinswoman or any of their family (17-18).
- The neighbor's wife is repeated (20).
- Man and man (22).
- Man or woman and an animal (23, the verse adds, *this is confusion*).

None of the above practices reflect family ties as God established them from the beginning to this day, as we'll see below. Please read about proper sexual relations in marriage[7] and the role of women and feminism in Bible times[8].

New Testament upholds everything in the Old Testament

6. https://www.theatlantic.com/national/archive/2013/01/america-has-an-incest-problem/272459/

7. https://theexplanation.com/song-of-solomon-friends-and-lovers-love-and-sex/

8. https://theexplanation.com/proverbs-31-feminism-and-womens-rights-what-mix/

Christ's Apostles did not go into the details simply because when you're spiritually minded, the hardness of heart lessens and you understand and apply what God's original intent is.

Ephesians 5:21-28

21 Submitting yourselves one to another in the fear of God.

22 Wives, submit yourselves to your own husbands, as to the Lord.

23 For the husband is the head of the wife, even as Christ is the head of the church: and he is the saviour of the body.

24 Therefore as the church is subject to Christ, so let the wives be to their own husbands in every thing.

25 Husbands, love your wives, even as Christ also loved the church, and gave himself for it;

26 That he might sanctify and cleanse it with the washing of water by the word,

27 That he might present it to himself a glorious church, not having spot, or wrinkle, or any such thing; but that it should be holy and without blemish.

28 So ought men to love their wives as their own bodies. He that loves his wife loves himself.

The Apostle Paul reinforces Old Testament family ties for parents and children.

Ephesians 6:1-4

1 Children, obey your parents in the Lord: for this is right.

2 Honour your father and mother; (which is the first commandment with promise;)

3 That it may be well with you, and you may live long on the earth.

4 And, you fathers, provoke not your children to wrath: but bring them up in the nurture and admonition of the Lord.

Nobody is perfect. Christians then and now sin and make mistakes. Hopefully, we all repent and turn to God for forgiveness and a more upright way of life. Regardless of religion, all humans everywhere have a command to respect parents, children, and family ties.

The theme of family ties runs from the beginning in Genesis to the last book of Revelation, where we still find *hardness* raging and warring in some people's hearts.

Revelation 22:15

For without are dogs, and sorcerers, and *whoremongers* (G4205), and murderers, and idolaters, and whosoever loves and makes a lie.

The meaning of *whoremongers* reveals alignment with opponents to God's way, animated by the unchanging hardness of heart toward proper family ties.

G4205

> πόρνος pornos por'-nos; From πέρνημι pernēmi (to sell; akin to the base of G4097); a (male) prostitute (as venal) that is (by analogy) a debauchee (libertine):
>
> KJV - fornicator whoremonger.

All inter-gender relationships are addressed in the past, present 21st century, and future; that is Godview. Any other view is worldview or personalview.

Spiritual level

Unfortunately, the spiritual relationship between human marriage, the family institution, and God is practically unknown. One reason is, these family ties reveal not only the future of Christians but also the way to reach that goal.

The Explanation has expounded on this relationship enormously because it is fundamental in comprehending why humans are on Earth (to develop relationships[9]) and why God instituted the marriage union and family ties relationship. In four words, *God is a family*. If you're reading this for the first time, I understand both your amazement and especially your skepticism.

If there's one point to take away from this chapter, it's **God is a Family**. God gave humankind the family institution because He created us in His image. He's a family, so are we.

> **Ephesians 3:14-15**
>
> 14 For this cause I bow my knees to the Father of our Lord Jesus Christ,

9. https://theexplanation.com/genesis-1-reveals-basics-social-relations-rulership/

> 15 Of whom the whole family in heaven and earth is named,

John 1 reveals the bond we humans can have with God. It, too, is a family relationship. Deepen your comprehension of father-son (which is also a generic statement including all family members) family ties by reading this article[10].

John 1:12-13

> 12 But as many as received him, to them gave he power to **become the sons of God**, even to them that believe on his name:
>
> 13 Which were **born**, not of blood, nor of the will of the flesh, nor of the will of man, but of God.
>
> 14 And the Word was made flesh, and dwelt among us, (and we beheld his glory, the glory as of the only **begotten** of the Father,) full of grace and truth.

Sons of God, *born*—by the will of God, *begotten*—referring to Yahweh Elohim[11], *these are all family terms*. Are there any other such expressions to corroborate this? Let's look at some fundamental descriptions of God and His environment to better define What and Who this plural God (Elohim) Who has a singular verb is. Here's how humans relate to Yahweh Elohim and Elohim.

- God is called our *Father* (Matt. 6:8-9).
- Jesus, Who is also God, is presently the only spirit composed *Son* (Mat. 11:27).
- His Church is described as our *Mother* (Gal. 4:26).

10. https://theexplanation.com/yahweh-elohim-inseparable-relationship/

11. https://theexplanation.com/yahweh-elohim-inseparable-relationship/

- We are called His *children* (Rom. 8:16).
- In other words, His *sons* and *daughters* (2 Cor. 6:18).
- We are to be *brothers* of Christ, who is the *Firstborn* (Rom. 8:29).
- He called those who do the will of God, *brothers*, *sisters*, and *mothers* (Mark 3:35).
- The Apostle Paul refers to Jesus Christ and the Church as *husband* and *wife* (Eph. 5:22-23), who will be *married* at the Messiah's Return (Rev. 19:7).
- The terms *begotten* (1 Peter 1:3) and *born* (John 1:13-14) are employed, referring to Christians.

Here we have the origin of the family institution; this explains one of the critical pieces of the puzzle turned over and put in its rightful position. And you know what, in some ways, you're not surprised. Humankind knows very well the family is the base of society. The Bible is filled with references to the family and its functioning. No other book contains more pertinent information about this basic building block of society.

This chapter is but a brief presentation of practical Bible wisdom revealing the importance of marriage, couples, and family ties in God's eyes. It's a short incursion into the God family and the relationship with human family ties. It is the foundational understanding of the two great commandments. Loving God, our Heavenly Father, and loving neighbor, our spouse, and our children. Family ties are the foundation of a well-functioning society.

Family and social relations are the keys to handling other people-related issues shackling society today; like the elderly, subject of the next chapter.

The Elderly in our 21st Century Society

What's the role of older people in today's world? Often, we've shunted them into a corner as useless reminders of another age. Not Good.

A more fundamental question might be, should older people have a role in society? As baby boomers (born 1946-1964) transform into retirees alongside Generation Z (born after 2000) the rift between generations has never been greater. As the world population transitions into a more bi-polar, more young people, more old people configuration, this social issue takes on major proportions.

In a more affluent society of The Glorious Thirty (1945-1975), there was stable employment and a burgeoning economy, growing personal wealth, education, and culture. Everything wasn't right. There was the Cold War and Vietnam, but it was a time of emancipation and development. Older people from that generation retiring in the early 21st century years were in better shape, physically and financially. They were the motors of travel, leisure, discovery, and globalization.

As the working market got shakier in the 80s, that generation, now in their sixties, became more prone to degrading conditions[1]. The information in that article is for the USA but similar issues face other countries with bleaker outlooks for the future[2]. Today, as birth rates drop and we see a swing to an aging population, older people find their place in society diminishing. Out with the older people, in with the younger. Out with the experienced top wages, in with the younger job-jumping, smartphone-savvy generation.

What's the value of older people? In old-school countries, mainly non-anglophone, older people still have a preponderant role in the family. The extended family[3] is a more tight-knit unit; they live, eat and counsel together. We in the West are more dispersed, dependent on old people's homes, units, fenced communities, hospice care, and geriatrics.

What does the Bible say about the role of older people? In particular, the Old Testament? Why? Because the adapted regulations promulgated were for all societies[4]. Have humans developed in the last three thousand years? Yes, we've acquired more knowledge, gadgets, and technology. Yes, we communicate and travel faster and further than ever, but has human nature changed? Are humans fundamentally the same today as in Bible times? Yes. *The Explanation* has written extensively why the words of Exodus,

---

1. https://endhomelessness.org/building-a-conversation-aged-homelessness-on-the-rise/

2. https://nhchc.org/clinical-practice/homeless-services/special-populations/older-adults/

3. https://theexplanation.com/extended-family-many-generations-world-population/

4. https://theexplanation.com/rules-for-life-wisdom-for-living-abundantly-in-the-world/

Deuteronomy, and Proverbs are relevant today[5]. Please refresh your minds if need be.

Remember, the application of Old Testament principles is not a word-for-word interpretation. There's adaptability depending on the society, not situation ethics, always based on the underlying Biblical foundation. Families, husband, wife, father, mother, children, older people involving relationships and rulership[6]. All these fundamentals apply to all peoples worldwide, regardless of culture and epoch. Hence a set of regulations to help humans know how to live abundantly[7].

We base practical Bible wisdom on a solid base; a functional, balanced society. The basis of which is the family[8], discussed in the last chapter and at length in *Audit of Humankind*. Given the instability in this field, today we can only adapt Bible wisdom to the best of our ability. As you will recognize, many of the following precepts only work IF parents have assumed their responsibility within a stable couple of father and mother toward their children. Even the way we talk about the older people[9] in our society shows respect or contempt for this gray-haired age group.

---

5. https://theexplanation.com/fig-leaves-or-clothing-tinker-or-build-practical-bible-wisdom/
6. https://theexplanation.com/genesis-1-reveals-basics-social-relations-rulership/
7. https://theexplanation.com/rules-for-life-wisdom-for-living-abundantly-in-the-world/
8. https://theexplanation.com/family-the-cornerstone-of-human-society/
9. https://www.bcli.org/
older-adult-older-person#_853ae90f0351324bd73ea615e6487517__4c761f170e016836ff8
4498202b99827__853ae90f0351324bd73ea615e6487517_text_43ec3e5dee6e706af7766fff
ea512721__0bcef9c45bd8a48eda1b26eb0c61c869_E2_0bcef9c45bd8a48eda1b26eb0c61c8
69_80_0bcef9c45bd8a48eda1b26eb0c61c869_9CElderly_0bcef9c45bd8a48eda1b26eb0c6
1c869_E2_0bcef9c45bd8a48eda1b26eb0c61c869_80_0bcef9c45bd8a48eda1b26eb0c61c8
69_9D_0bcef9c45bd8a48eda1b26eb0c61c869_20connotes_0bcef9c45bd8a48eda1b26eb0c
61c869_20frailty._c0cb5f0fcf239ab3d9c1fcd31fff1efc_associated_0bcef9c45bd8a48eda1b2

Here is durable practical Bible wisdom, whatever the era, nation, culture, or language. The Bible is the story of humankind, all humans everywhere. No other book encompasses and disseminates such factual, constructive advice.

Physical strength diminishes, but the individual remains a person

The aging process is inexorable, today's young will be tomorrow's old. It's the cycle of physical life. Young and old need instruction about this life and life to come.[10] Recognition of the state of older people is an important part of child-rearing.

Abraham lived a long satisfying life and Job recognizes age brings wisdom, counsel, and understanding.

> **Psalm 71:9**
>
> Cast me not off in the time of old age; forsake me not when my strength fails.
>
> **Genesis 25:7-8**
>
> 7 And these are the days of the years of Abraham's life which he lived, an hundred threescore and fifteen years.
>
> 8 Then Abraham gave up the ghost, and died in a good old age, an old man, and full of years; and was gathered to his people.
>
> **Job 12:12-13**

6eb0c61c869_20with_0bcef9c45bd8a48eda1b26eb0c61c869_20this_0bcef9c45bd8a48eda1b26eb0c61c869_20benchmark_0bcef9c45bd8a48eda1b26eb0c61c869_20age.

10. https://theexplanation.com/life-and-death-major-issues/

> 12 With the ancient is wisdom; and in length of days understanding.
>
> 13 With him is wisdom and strength, he has counsel and understanding.

God takes us through the stages of life

The first verse in Isaiah refers to the nation of Israel, but the principle applies to how God works with the elderly and carries them.

> **Isaiah 46:3-4**
>
> 3 Hearken to me, O house of Jacob, and all the remnant of the house of Israel, which are borne by me from the belly, which are carried from the womb:
>
> 4 And even to your old age I am he; and even to hoar hairs will I carry you: I have made, and I will bear; even I will carry, and will deliver you.

Footprints in the Sand, a poem reminds us of God's presence.

> One night I dreamed a dream.
>
> As I was walking along the beach with my Lord.
>
> Across the dark sky flashed scenes from my life.
>
> For each scene, I noticed two sets of footprints in the sand,
>
> One belonging to me and one to my Lord.
>
> After the last scene of my life flashed before me,

I looked back at the footprints in the sand.

I noticed that at many times along the path of my life,

especially at the very lowest and saddest times,

there was only one set of footprints.

This really troubled me, so I asked the Lord about it.

"Lord, you said once I decided to follow you,

You'd walk with me all the way.

But I noticed that during the saddest and most troublesome times of my life,

there was only one set of footprints.

I don't understand why, when I needed You the most, You would leave me."

He whispered, "My precious child, I love you and will never leave you

Never, ever, during your trials and testings.

When you saw only one set of footprints,

It was then that I carried you."

We do not leave older people out of the picture in activities or for travel. Here's an example of the entire extended family traveling together. When the Israelites left Egypt, they could only go as fast as the slowest person in their massive group of hundreds of thousands.

The young people must've been of great aid to the older people during this journey. The words of Moses are clear.

Exodus 10:9

And Moses said, We will go with our young and with our old, with our sons and with our daughters, with our flocks and with our herds will we go; for we must hold a feast to the LORD.

Respect for older people

Here are 9 ways to honor older people[11]. They go from being polite to asking for advice and listening to them. They have plenty of stories about their lives, history, heritage to share. I would've loved to know more about my ancestors, but my parents didn't open up about it, and I didn't ask.

Here are a couple of verses that stand the test of time and modes of transport. Are the young respectful, standing up on public transport? Helping older people across the street when there's a need?

Leviticus 29:32

You shall stand up before the gray head and honor the face of an old man, and you shall fear your God: I am the Lord.

The younger are blessed with vigor, strength and endurance. Let them put it to appropriate use.

Proverbs 20:29

11. https://www.bayviewhealthcare.org/9-ways-honor-respect-elders/

> The glory of young men is their strength: and the beauty of old men is the gray head.

Here's an example of a younger man who patiently waited. In Biblical terms, it's a conversation lasting some thirty chapters, over a few hours, or maybe even days. When the younger person, Elihu, speaks up, he points out how he waited, despite his consuming inner impatience, bursting with words he had to express. What an example of patience, respect, and courage to wait and then face these older gentlemen. Older people aren't always right, but they should at least be given an ear.

> **Job 32:4**
>
> 2 Then was kindled the wrath of Elihu the son of Barachel the Buzite, of the kindred of Ram: against Job was his wrath kindled, because he justified himself rather than God.
>
> 3 Also against his three friends was his wrath kindled, because they had found no answer, and yet had condemned Job.
>
> 4 Now Elihu had waited till Job had spoken, because they were elder than he.

The whole idea of practical Bible wisdom is to show the Old Testament rules apply to all peoples at all times if we want a properly running society. This part of the Bible addresses people with hardened hearts (Matthew 19:8); they were not spiritually converted. They may know of God, even be religious, but still filled with worldliness. The New Testament is for people with hearts opened by the Holy Spirit. No more details now, but there is a continuity between the Old and the New. Respect for older people continues and is even intensified. Look at the Apostle Peter's recommendation.

1 Peter 5:5

Likewise, you younger, submit yourselves to the elder. Yea, all of you be subject one to another, and be clothed with humility: for God resists the proud, and gives grace to the humble.

We learn from each other, regardless of age, both young and old recognize this. Notwithstanding, the young should know their place regarding older people.

Taking care of one's parents

The human life cycle is unique. Not from the point of view of birth and death, all animals have those benchmarks. Human babies take about 20 years to reach maturity, during which their parents are ever-present to diaper, educate, help, and guide them to independence. When their parents reach a good old age, they, in turn, become physically dependent for various needs, be it shopping or dressing. Under the right conditions, it's the children's role to help their parents. Even grandchildren step in and learn to serve. Not sure if we should call this *payback time*, after all, it's the normal continuity of life. We do have a responsibility toward the older generation.

Proverbs 23:22

Hearken to your father that begat you, and despise not your mother when she is old.

1 Timothy 5:16

> If any man or woman that believes have widows, let them relieve them, and let not the church be charged; that it may relieve them that are widows indeed.

Here are two Old Testament examples of this interaction between the generations revealing care for older people.

> **Gen. 45:17**
>
> 17 And Pharaoh said to Joseph, Say to your brethren, This do you; lade your beasts, and go, get you to the land of Canaan;
>
> 18 And take your father and your households, and come to me: and I will give you the good of the land of Egypt, and you shall eat the fat of the land.

Joseph reunited with his father, and during the time of famine could care for him. Many years later, Moses took their bones back to Canaan, another sign of respect. Ruth is a touching story of a daughter-in-law's devotion to her mother-in-law. The younger woman would not abandon the older under any circumstances.

> **Ruth 1:16-17, 4:13-15**
>
> 16 And Ruth said, Intreat me not to leave you, or to return from following after you: for whither you go, I will go; and where you lodge, I will lodge: your people shall be my people, and your God my God:
>
> 17 Where you die, will I die, and there will I be buried: the LORD do so to me, and more also, if ought but death part you and me.

> 4:13 So Boaz took Ruth, and she was his wife: and when he went in to her, the LORD gave her conception, and she bare a son.
>
> 14 And the women said to Naomi, Blessed be the LORD, which has not left you this day without a kinsman, that his name may be famous in Israel.
>
> 15 And he shall be to you a restorer of your life, and a nourisher of your old age: for your daughter in law, which loves you, which is better to you than seven sons, has born him.

Care at home

Where the elderly live in the 21st century is a major question. Everyone is more comfortable and at home in familiar surroundings. The needs of today's employed caregivers and elders who want to *age in place*[12] need to be considered.

For information, read this report[13] under the auspices of the United Nations. *Ageing in the Twenty-First Century: A Celebration and A Challenge* analyzes the current situation of older persons and reviews progress in policies and actions taken by governments and other stakeholders since the Second World Assembly on Ageing.

Unfortunately, when organizations like the UN step in, it means we've stepped away from the family fundamentals of practical Bible wisdom. In my twenties, I lived and did an apprenticeship in Antwerp, Belgium. For two years I had a room with a 70-year-old widow who needed company and someone to help occasionally. It

12. *https://www.researchgate.net/publication/51733612_Families_and_Elder_Care_in_the_Twenty-First_Century*

13. https://www.unfpa.org/sites/default/files/pub-pdf/UNFPA-Exec-Summary.pdf

was a symbiotic relationship giving her some peace of mind, and me a roof over my head at a reasonable cost. In France, where there's a shortage of housing, university students from afar often find lodging with an older person in just such a beneficial relationship.

The older generation has much to offer the upcoming younger.

My father never retired. Work was an ingrained part of his daily existence. As he grew older, he reduced his workload but, believe it or not, he went into work the day he died in his 80s. Older people have a treasure of experience in many fields in their minds and hands. Young people should understand this and grasp the opportunity to search out and store up this precious resource, often dying and unattainable in books. What's more, experienced people are often more than willing to transmit their know-how, they're looking for an attentive ear.

Psalm 92:12-14

12 The righteous shall flourish like the palm tree: he shall grow like a cedar in Lebanon.

13 Those that be planted in the house of the LORD shall flourish in the courts of our God.

14 They shall still bring forth fruit in old age; they shall be fat and flourishing;

Physical

In our 21st century, the term *apprenticeship* is under-used. The transmission of know-how from the older to the younger. This is especially true regarding manual arts. This Bible example takes place in the desert with the building of the Tabernacle.

Exodus 35:30-35

30 And Moses said to the children of Israel, See, the LORD has called by name Bezaleel the son of Uri, the son of Hur, of the tribe of Judah;

31 And he has filled him with the spirit of God, in wisdom, in understanding, and in knowledge, and in all manner of workmanship;

32 And to devise curious works, to work in gold, and in silver, and in brass,

33 And in the cutting of stones, to set them, and in carving of wood, to make any manner of cunning work.

34 And he has put in his heart that he may *teach* (H3384), both he, and Aholiab, the son of Ahisamach, of the tribe of Dan.

35 Them has he filled with wisdom of heart, to work all manner of work, of the engraver, and of the cunning workman, and of the embroiderer, in blue, and in purple, in scarlet, and in fine linen, and of the weaver, even of them that do any work, and of those that devise cunning work.

As they built this place of worship, which was a work-of-art, they taught others the various trades needed. This invokes the fourth rule to master Biblical Hebrew, the figurative meaning of words[14]. Here, *teach* (H3384) derives from the flowing of water. An apprenticeship is the flowing of know-how from the older to the younger generation for its perpetuation.

> **H3384**
>
> יָרָה yârâh yaw-raw'; or (2 Chronicles 26:15) יָרָא; a primitive root; properly, to flow as water (i.e. to rain); transitively, to lay or throw (especially an arrow, i.e. to shoot); figuratively, to point out (as if by aiming the finger), to teach:
>
> KJV - ([phrase]) archer, cast, direct, inform, instruct, lay, shew, shoot, teach(-er,-ing), through.

Leadership

Leading people doesn't come automatically. It is an attribute one learns, often by attending to a prominent person. It, too, is an apprenticeship.

Here are a couple of examples. Moses apprenticed Joshua and Elijah apprenticed Elisha. In the New Testament, we have Paul, who apprenticed Timothy.

> **Deuteronomy 32:7**
>
> Remember the days of old, consider the years of many generations: ask your father, and he will shew you; your elders, and they will tell you.

One of the poorer examples of not taking advice from the older generation caused King Rehoboam and the nation much grief.

---

14. https://theexplanation.com/key-4-literal-and-figurative-meanings-for-biblical-hebrew-words/

1 Kings 12:6-8

6 And king Rehoboam consulted with the old men, that stood before Solomon his father while he yet lived, and said, How do you advise that I may answer this people?

7 And they spake to him, saying, If you will be a servant to this people this day, and will serve them, and answer them, and speak good words to them, then they will be your servants for ever.

8 But he forsook the counsel of the old men, which they had given him, and consulted with the young men that were grown up with him, and which stood before him:

Older people possess wisdom. The younger men gave him dreadful advice. Rehoboam faced an insurrection, causing the division of the 12 tribes of Israel into two separate states. He lost big.

Judges

One of the least known responsibilities of older people is their role as judges. Today we rely on an official system of justice with lawyers and judges. In Old Testament times, the nation called on older people to occupy this role. These people were known for their integrity and wisdom. Often, the latter comes with years and the experience of life. Some circumstances in the examples below are difficult to understand, explanations will be forthcoming. For now, please focus on the role of older people as judges, referred to here as elders.

Deuteronomy 21:2

> Then your elders and your judges shall come forth, and they shall measure to the cities which are round about him that is slain:
>
> **Deuteronomy 16:18**
>
> Judges and officers shall you make you in all your gates, which the LORD your God gives you, throughout your tribes: and they shall judge the people with just judgment.
>
> **Deuteronomy 21:19**
>
> Then shall his father and his mother lay hold on him, and bring him out to the elders of his city, and to the gate of his place;

There's no doubt. We are to respect older people. They are not only the memory of the nation, but its wealth. They have the experience which the younger generation sorely needs to learn from. They have leadership roles to fill where they render great service to their communities and nation. Practical Bible wisdom reveals the role of older people in all societies during all eras.

Another plague addresses society today. The rift between rich and poor. Here's how to help the poor get up, or back on their feet, a major milestone for the welfare of a nation.

Poor, widows, orphans, homeless, unemployed

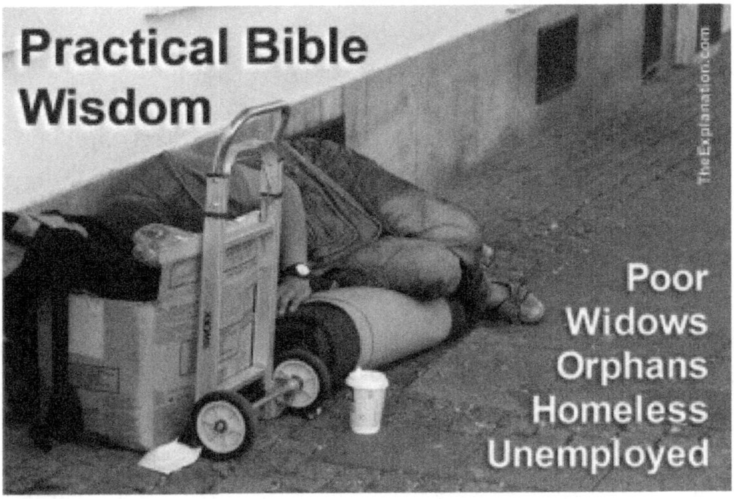

You will always have the poor with you. *The Explanation* does not affirm this. Jesus does in Matthew 26:11 with these same words.

Being poor is not a simple matter of economics or economic systems. There are a million and one reasons any person can become poor, a widow, an orphan, homeless or unemployed. Especially in today's turbulent society.

Life is unpredictable, and anyone can be in the wrong place at the wrong time. Depending on how we define the word *poor*, we could say a majority of the world population is in this category. You can be born into poverty, you can rise out or fall into being poor.

Sometimes, hopefully, you can make choices to change your life, but often people are captive to their non-existent choices.

Above I quoted Matthew 26:11, but Deuteronomy 15:11 says the same, "For the poor shall never cease out of the land: therefore I command you, saying, You shall open your hand wide to your brother, to your poor, and to your needy, in your land."

The Old Testament expounds practical Bible wisdom applying to all people in all nations. Reread the meaning of Deut. 4 to understand this all-important concept; God is Creator of all human beings. Yes, He chose an example nation, just as we'd choose one student as class representative. That person is both a leader and example; identical to Old Testament Israel. God gave them, and through them, to us, principles about our relationship with the poor.

Then, it was mainly an agricultural society, so we have to garner principles and apply them today. We will see how God wanted the poor cared for. But we also want to realize it was not a support state, not an encouragement for the poor to squat a stream of pedestrian traffic and expect people's generosity. On the contrary, there's a responsibility on behalf of the giver and receiver.

The poor were *not* to stay in a state of poverty. They had obligations, as we shall see, the key is to escape their misery with the help afforded them; assistance could take on various forms.

Educating the poor

The poor are just as intelligent as anyone else. We all grow up in different circumstances, and the goal here is not illustrations of impoverished situations. Many excellent books bring such a subject to life with poignant examples. Helping educate and train the poor is vital. Apprenticeships, which we've minimized, are an important part of a vibrant economy.

One of the misunderstood concepts of the Old Testament is *purchasing a brother*. In this chapter, I'll explain this concept from the perspective of poverty. In the next chapter, we'll expand the theme encompassing labor conditions.

Deuteronomy 15:12

> And if your brother, an Hebrew man, or an Hebrew woman, be sold to you, and serve you six years; then in the seventh year you shall let him go free from you.

Yes, this could happen because of misfortune, mismanagement, wrong decisions, and debt or bankruptcy. There weren't prisons or labor camps, there was a system of justice and rehabilitation. If a person was in trouble, they could be put in the hands of an overseer. Someone rich could even *purchase* a poor person; sounds terrible, let's understand the meaning.

Here's the question. Would you rather be out in the street *or* housed with an apprenticeship? I think and hope the answer is clear. Please, this is vital understanding to keep in mind, unconsidered by most detractors, Leviticus 25:35, "And if your brother be waxen poor, and fallen in decay with you; then you shall *relieve* (H2388) him: yea, though he be a stranger, or a sojourner; that he may live with you."

The meaning of the word *relieve* (*chazak* in Hebrew) is to *make strong*. This law is a promoter of socialization. It not only keeps people together, but it confers a mission on the strong to help the weak. Whether your compatriot has come from across the border (stranger) or is a local (sojourner) they join a home. Nobody on the street, nobody begging on the corner in this scenario. Making the person stronger entails giving them the mental, professional and physical help necessary to restore and put them back on their feet. To make them a contributing part of society.

Not everyone is equipped to assure such an aim; become a role model. Just like in any society, some are more successful than others, they need extra hands. They can invest financially in the acquisition of such a person. This is the meaning of *buying*. It is not a *slave* market in the sense the word portrays nowadays. We are not talking about a serf or captive doing toiling labor. Yes, the weak struggle to raise themselves up, but under proper working conditions.

When I was in my late teens, I was taken into hand by a couple of partners for an apprenticeship in diamond cutting. I was with them for over 2 years, during which I earned a minimum, enough to cover the basics with a little extra which went for bowling and travel. In the end, I had a trade that I intended to use, except I was sidetracked and went back to study in College. The point is, during those 2 years I was tied to that apprenticeship, earning from my work, acquiring a trade to start a career. I was the weaker, and they were the stronger helping me to progress.

Considering the loss of know-how in certain basic trades like plumbing and electricity, certain artistic trades like iron forging or stain glass windows, such apprenticeships would be worthwhile for society. Yes, it means two parties assuming their responsibilities and their obligations. Unfortunately for society, those are traits difficult to find now, especially with manual work. But the Old Testament gives practical Bible wisdom for the poor, and how to shepherd them properly.

Note Deut. 15:12 immediately talks about letting this poor person go free. The maximum time would be seven years, and it could be less. To top it off, on departure, the person hits the jackpot. Deut.

15:13-14, "And when you send him out free from you, you shall not let him go away empty: You shall furnish him liberally out of your flock, and out of your floor, and out of your winepress: of that wherewith the LORD your God has blessed you, you shall give to him." Wow!

This apprentice worked for his master-trainer for years, helping his overseer build his fortune. The apprentice also benefits from this joint venture at the *end* of his apprenticeship. Why? Because he came in poor, maybe because of some error on his part. Now, he's learned from his mistakes, he's watched his trainer, developed a system, know-how, for managing his welfare, now he is given the capital to set up and manage his own household.

Old Testament Bible wisdom is a win-win situation for both the master-trainer and the apprentice; a practical application of loving your neighbor. It helps reintegrate the poor into society, making it stable, peaceful, and prosperous.

Lending to the poor

Today we have banks and other financial institutions loaning money. We also have *credit ratings,* disastrous for someone who has made mistakes. The paradox of the system is those who need credit are the least likely candidates for loaning institutions. These people are too poor and have no collateral. Our society has it backward.

Deuteronomy. 15:7-9

> 7 If there be among you a poor man of one of your brethren within any of your gates in thy land which the LORD your God gives you, you shall not harden your heart, nor shut your hand from your poor brother:

8 But you shall open your hand wide to him, and shall surely lend him sufficient for his need, in that which he wants.

9 Beware that there be not a thought in your wicked heart, saying, The seventh year, the year of release, is at hand; and your eye be evil against your poor brother, and you give him nought; and he cry to the LORD against you, and it be sin to you.

10 You shall surely give him, and your heart shall not be grieved when you give to him: because that for this thing the LORD your God shall bless you in all your works, and in all that you put your hand to.

Notice the end of verse 8 below, "lend him sufficient for his need, in that which he wants." This is not talking about handouts or free lunches. It's someone with a valid proposition and business plan. Probably someone who needs guidance, which, if we are competent, we can offer.

No usury

Here's the follow-up to lending. A warning, even a law, to avoid pushing people into hardship. One of the biggest, if not the colossal cause of poverty; interest on loans, the cause of the 2008 subprime financial crisis.

Deuteronomy. 23:19-20

19 You shall not lend upon usury to your brother; usury of money, usury of victuals, usury of any thing that is lent upon usury:

> 20 To a stranger you may lend upon usury; but to your brother you shall not lend upon usury: that the LORD your God may bless you in all that you set your hand to in the land where you go to possess it.

God is aware of the destitute and He treats them with dignity. Tell me there are no reliable how-to laws in the Bible, specifically the Old Testament, to assure a stable society for *all* nations around the world.

In certain areas, the basic concept of the above is in practice. Micro-lending is now an accepted form of helping the poor financially. Here's a paper on Micro-lending in the Third World[1].

Despite these setbacks in public opinion, microfinance institutions around the world continue to operate. The potential bad is outweighed by the perceived good of the program and its capacity to curb poverty. Unlike charity, microfinance has the potential to teach people to be self-sufficient, instead of waiting for a handout. It is one of the chief reasons this type of support has gained popularity; it is perceived as equipping rather than giving.

This paper talks about micro-lending to help families grow their income, helping with the equality of women, dignity, and welfare. One interesting aspect of this type of financing is the closeness of the lender and the borrower. It is done locally with the lender following, advising, and helping the businessperson with their venture. There's an accompanied apprenticeship, beneficial to both parties with the exchange of know-how, trust, and partnership.

Supply essential needs

Education and loans are the keys to helping the poor develop a sustainable future. But what about the present? Some are poor and

1. https://core.ac.uk/download/pdf/58826651.pdf

need help right now, this instant. Practical Bible wisdom makes provision for them too. Food and clothing are on the list.

Deuteronomy 10:17-18

17 For the LORD your God is God of gods, and Lord of lords, a great God, a mighty, and a terrible, which regards not persons, nor takes reward:

18 He does execute the judgment of the fatherless and widow, and loves the stranger, in giving him food and raiment.

In France, we have the *Restos du Coeur*, an incredible organization distributing millions of free meals each year to the homeless and destitute. There are similar accomplishments for clothing and household necessities.

Deuteronomy 24:19-20, Leviticus 19:9-10, Deut. 14:19

19 When you cut down your harvest in your field, and have forgot a sheaf in the field, you shall not go again to fetch it:

20 it shall be for the stranger, for the fatherless, and for the widow: that the LORD your God may bless you in all the work of your hands.

Lev. 19:9 And when you reap the harvest of your land, you shall not wholly reap the corners of thy field, neither shall you gather the gleanings of your harvest.

> 10 And you shall not glean your vineyard, neither shall you gather every grape of your vineyard; you shall leave them for the poor and stranger: I am the LORD your God.
>
> **Deut. 14:19** And the Levite, (because he has no part nor inheritance with you,) and the stranger, and the fatherless, and the widow, which are within your gates, shall come, and shall eat and be satisfied; that the LORD your God may bless you in all the work of your hand which you do.

We're finding more and more working people in the poor lines. They work, but their salaries are simply not enough to make ends meet. Their labor doesn't feed the mouths of their family. This reveals a problem with the economy, which is another subject. A Bible principle states the salary should be worthy of a laborer's work; they should have enough to live on decently.

> **Ezekiel 16:49**
>
> Behold, this was the iniquity of your sister Sodom, pride, fulness of bread, and abundance of idleness was in her and in her daughters, neither did she strengthen the hand of the needy.

The rich, or at least, those *having the fulness of bread* are hoarding excess food and other goods rather than putting them to good use; including wastage. It is estimated 22% of nutritious food ends up in the garbage. In opulent nations, the well-off could improve management of their resources to provide for the poor.

Note the reference to gleaning, in Leviticus 19, is NOT a process of handouts, a paycheck, or stand in line to get what you need; there's a mutual effort. The poor, orphans, homeless, unemployed should strive and accomplish something worthwhile. They need help to maintain a work ethic and socialization. This is all part of participating in society.

Participation in spiritual life

This should be clear, but God wants people to socialize and progress with their mental activities. This means a *spiritual workout*. The Old Testament Assembly prefigured the New Testament Church. Attendance of the poor is more than recommended. It was up to the prosperous to assure the poor were present.

> **Deuteronomy 16:11, 14**
>
> 11 And you shall rejoice before the LORD your God, you, and your son, and your daughter, and your manservant, and your maidservant, and the Levite that is within your gates, and the stranger, and the fatherless, and the widow, that are among you, in the place which the LORD your God has chosen to place his name there.
>
> 14 And you shall rejoice in thy feast, you, and your son, and your daughter, and your manservant, and your maidservant, and the Levite, the stranger, and the fatherless, and the widow, that are within your gates.

Not to be taken advantage of

The poor are the most vulnerable to scams and the least likely to have the means to contest and fight back. It is an unscrupulous crime to take advantage of the poor and weak. There are clear rules regarding such heinous activity. In today's age of the Internet, we find too much fraud and deception.

Deuteronomy 24:17

> You shall not pervert the judgment of the stranger, nor of the fatherless; nor take a widow's raiment to pledge:

Times have not changed human nature. It's just as positive and negative now as it has been down through human history. It's the reason these Old Testament injunctions are just as valid today as they were in the past.

Future for the no longer poor

Muhammad Yunus and his bank set up the initial micro-lending program in Bangladesh in 1976; he hoped for a positive impact on the borrowers. The Grameen Bank website states their mission "to enable the poor, especially the poorest, to create a world without poverty." A noble quest, certainly in line with practical Bible wisdom, as is the conclusion of the report on micro-lending.

It is important to remember the basic premise behind microloan availability and the economic freedom it delivers to those with no available capital. Micro-lending in the third world is the only option and chance they get at economic opportunity. Aiding those who are in desperate need can help ensure a better world for everyone.

We started this chapter with, "the poor shall never cease out of the land." We end with a promise; there will come a time when poverty will be an issue of the past.

Deuteronomy. 15:4

> Save when there shall be no poor among you; for the LORD shall greatly bless you in the land which the

> LORD your God gives you for an inheritance to possess it:

The time will come when the entire population will enact these practical Bible rules for life, and the blessings for all peoples will be abundant. In the meantime, let's do our part to serve the needs of the poor.

What about working conditions, a worldwide sustainability issue?

Slavery, Labor, Working conditions

Labor and working conditions, maybe we think they're slavery, are our lot for eight hours a day. Sometimes much more. What does the Bible say?

When you put slavery in the same sentence with employment, you know ears will prick up. Definition of slavery: A condition in which individuals are owned by others who control where they live and at what they work. This includes sex slavery, child and forced labor under the most atrocious conditions.

Regarding God, Who is love (1 John 4:8), immediately slavery takes on a very unsavory taste. It appears to be at the antipodes of Godly principles. And indeed, as the dictionary defines it and as it's practiced, it's about as far from Godly as we can imagine.

So, why do we find God condoning slavery in the Old Testament? Why do we find rules to govern *forced labor*? Why do we even find references to it in the New Testament? What does the Bible really say?

First, keep in mind *hardness of heart*. A subject I dealt with at length in Chapter 1.5[1]. Please revise it. In essence, God gave laws for *non*-law-abiding people to maintain peace and order in an unconverted society. A society ignoring God, even if outwardly it talks about or even exercises supposedly godly practices.

Second, we must look at this from God's point of view. Not from ours, neither from the state nor national laws of any country trying to control or abolish slavery or establish proper labor laws. We must broach this subject theologically; revise the meaning of theological[2]. In one phrase, it means from God's perspective, not our interpretation.

Godview does not exist in the dictionary because the world is limited to *worldview*. Well, a worldview is much too limited to God. The world and its reasoning are wayward regarding God. The Bible is not a worldview; it presents Godview. Unfortunately, many approach the Bible from a worldview, resulting in so many interpretations and confusing viewpoints, the origin of so many religions.

Here's the Godview of Whom we work for, to Whom we owe allegiance. It goes right back to Genesis 2, in the Garden of Eden.

Genesis 2:15

---

1. https://theexplanation.com/hardness-of-heart-how-to-deal-with-it-practical-bible-wisdom/
2. https://theexplanation.com/into-theology-a-fifth-approach-to-life-with-peace-and-prosperity/

> And the LORD God took the man, and put him into the garden of Eden to *dress* (H5647) it and to keep it.

I wrote a chapter in *Origin of Woman*[3] devoted to these words *dress* and *keep*. Please read this online for fuller meaning Dress and Keep Garden of Eden. Man Destined to be a Gardener?[4] The Biblical Hebrew meaning of *dress* is *worship*; God put Adam and Eve in the Garden to worship, not *it*, but Him.

Keep in mind how to unlock Bible meaning by mastering Biblical Hebrew. Key 1, one Biblical Hebrew word can have multiple meanings[5], and Key 2, it can also have contradictory meanings[6]. Therefore, understand a fuller meaning of *dress*, H5647, directly related to *hard labor* and *slavery*.

> **H5647**
>
> עָבַד ‘âbad aw-bad’; a primitive root; to work (in any sense); by implication, to serve, till, (causatively) enslave, etc.:
>
> KJV - × be, keep in bondage, be bondmen, bond-service, compel, do, dress, ear, execute, + husbandman, keep, labour(-ing man, bring to pass, (cause to, make to) serve(-ing, self), (be, become) servant(-s), do (use) service, till(-er), transgress (from margin), (set a) work, be wrought, worshipper.

---

3. *https://theexplanation.com/read-all-the-content-of-origin-of-woman-online*
4. https://theexplanation.com/dress-keep-garden-of-eden-man-destined-to-be-a-gardener/?swcfpc=1
5. https://theexplanation.com/key-1-multiple-meanings-for-one-biblical-hebrew-word/
6. https://theexplanation.com/contradictory-meanings-for-biblical-hebrew-word/

Strong's annotation uses the word *enslave*, the KJV translators used old English *keep in bondage, bondmen, bond-service, compel.* They too use *labour*, so we can easily say it's *compelled labor,* which is tantamount to forced labor.

Yes, quite amazing, the Biblical Hebrew connects bondage and slavery to worship! When you can explain this association, you've come a very long way to understanding the relationship between the Old and New Testaments. Especially God's plan and the relation of a human being to God Himself. We will return to this point at the end of the chapter.

Note the various translations of *abad* (H5647). They are correct and include *all* these notions, including *slave*. There is ample evidence, as we shall see. Here's the implication; this is one of those *hard sayings* stated in the *Hardness of heart* chapter.

Adam was to be God's servant, he was to worship God alone. As such, Adam was to be God's slave.

Sounds awful, but why wouldn't you want to be the slave of a loving God? It's exactly what our destiny is!

If this is true, which it is, trying to prove God is *against* slavery is nonsense. God is absolutely against the *wrong* type of slavery. This is a key principle. There are abominable practices everywhere on this planet[7]. They include forced labour,[8] bonded labour,[9] child slavery,[10] child marriage[11], descent-based slavery[12], domestic slavery[13], slavery

7. https://www.antislavery.org/slavery-today/forced-labour/

8. https://www.antislavery.org/slavery-today/forced-labour/

9. https://www.antislavery.org/slavery-today/bonded-labour/

10. https://www.antislavery.org/slavery-today/child-slavery/

11. https://www.antislavery.org/slavery-today/child-marriage/

12. https://www.antislavery.org/slavery-today/descent-based-slavery/

in supply chains[14], slavery in the UK[15] and every country around the world[16], including yours. This practice takes many forms called unfree labor[17], but it ends up being slavery.

Please, please realize God is 1000%, totally against such forms of slavery. He condemns and abhors shackling human beings, period. The Bible has no tolerance for such behavior.

People have practiced the wrong type of slavery since time immemorial. In Old and New Testament times and today, around the world. The Bible condemns such practices.

It is because of this abhorrent slavery, because the hardness of the human heart goes to extremes in how it treats fellow humans, God instituted laws to govern *how* slavery is to be practiced.

Again, this might sound horrible but sometimes, for a human being, it is better to be in a *legitimate* (please bore that into your mind) master-slave relationship than to be homeless and destitute out in the cold hostile streets who knows where. Or to be treated like dirt and even worse.

The principles we will survey here apply equally to employers and employees. Hired workers, maybe more than we realize, feel they're treated like slaves, with wages, but slaves nonetheless. Employees are hassled, over-worked, underpaid, taken advantage of, forced to do abominable things, or threatened with losing their jobs. They're working under *slave* conditions, even if we don't call them slaves.

---

13. https://www.antislavery.org/slavery-today/domestic-work-and-slavery/

14. https://www.antislavery.org/slavery-today/slavery-in-global-supply-chains/

15. https://www.antislavery.org/slavery-today/slavery-uk/

16. https://www.theguardian.com/news/2019/feb/25/modern-slavery-trafficking-persons-one-in-200

17. https://en.wikipedia.org/wiki/Unfree_labour

Here's a summary of what the Bible says, there's too much material to go into all the details, but by grasping the Godview you can understand the rest.

> **Exodus 21:1-6**
>
> 1 Now these are the judgments which you shall set before them.
>
> 2 If thou buy an Hebrew *servant* (H5650 directly related to H5647 we saw above, this is a *slave*), six years he shall serve: and in the seventh he shall go out free for nothing.
>
> 3 If he came in by himself, he shall go out by himself: if he were married, then his wife shall go out with him.
>
> 4 If his master have given him a wife, and she have born him sons or daughters; the wife and her children shall be her master's and he shall go out by himself.
>
> 5 And if the servant shall plainly say, I love my master, my wife, and my children; I will not go out free:
>
> 6 Then his master shall bring him to the judges; he shall also bring him to the door, or to the door post; and his master shall bore his ear through with an aul; and he shall serve him for ever.

Ouch! Bore his ear with an awl. Straightaway this reads barbaric. First, interestingly, slavery is the very first judgment given by God following the Ten Commandments, and the above 6 verses are the very first verses about slavery. How is it possible for a loving God to give such wisdom as the Ten Commandments and immediately follow up with slavery? Again, when you can answer this question, you've come a long way to understanding Godview, the theology of the Old and New Testaments.

Remember, *hardness of heart*. These Israelites and the people who accompanied them during the Exodus are anything but *converted*. This episode is just a few weeks after the Exodus when they witnessed countless miracles of God Almighty. Yet, look at the people's reaction, "And all the people saw the thunderings, and the lightnings, and the noise of the trumpet, and the mountain smoking: and when the people saw it, they removed, and stood afar off. And they said to Moses, Speak you with us, and we will hear: but let not God speak with us, lest we die" (Exodus 20:18-19).

The people thought God would kill them! Amazing! God had just performed incredible miracles to save them. Hardness of heart is an understatement regarding their attitude. That's why God gave them worldly, physical judgments, nothing spiritual at all, hoping they'd follow them at a minimum; even those they transgressed.

But the *physical* practices have *spiritual* overtones. Here's a brief spiritual, figurative explanation of Exodus 21 about the Hebrew slave. This physical slavery is the counterpart of a Christian's spiritual slavery to God. In the case of a Hebrew, if they are *bought* it's because they're in dire straights, they've lost everything (remember, each Hebrew has a family and a land inheritance). For whatever reason, criminal, bankruptcy, personal problems, this Hebrew is destitute.

The spiritual parallel is God *bought* and paid for Christians with the blood of Jesus Christ. An unconverted person is spiritually destitute. If the slave decides to leave after marriage, the family stays. One, the man loves his family less than his own freedom. Two, it assures stability for the wife and children. Staying with his master is a free-will decision, just as a Christian makes with their calling by God.

Now the awl; it is the sign he belongs to his master. Just as circumcision is a similar sign in the flesh. The Christian has a spiritual seal, "And it was commanded them that they should not hurt the grass of the earth, neither any green thing, neither any tree; but only those men which have not the seal of God in their foreheads" (Revelation 19:4). The *seal of God* is the *Holy Spirit* coupled with *the spirit in man*[18] (Ephesians 1:13). Like the slave, those with the seal have decided to stay forever with their Master, God, and their family, the faithful Church.

This is the fulfillment of the two great commandments, love God your Master, love your neighbor, which will be all those in God's family, His Church. And it will be forever. Why is slavery broached immediately after the Commandments? Because It is the *physical* application of the *First* Commandment. I brought you out of the land of Egypt, the house of *worldly* bondage (Ex. 20:2). The slave master buys the slave out of destitution and gives him a home. The slave then had to show allegiance to his new owner. You shall have no other gods before me (Ex. 20:3).

When one understands a slave master has the position of a loving father to the slave, then it becomes easier to comprehend the whole concept of slavery and employer-employee working conditions in the Bible.

In the surrounding nations then, and with today's nations, slave masters know nothing of God's spiritual and physical practices. Here's what God told the unconverted Israelites regarding their worship and civil practices.

Deuteronomy 18:9

---

18. https://theexplanation.com/two-spirits-gods-spirit-spirit-in-humans/

> When you are come into the land which the LORD your God gives you, you shall not learn to do after the abominations of those nations.

God condemns their abominable way of life, including their horrendous ways of treating slaves. He gave them better ways. Never forget what Paul wrote about the commandments in Romans 7:12 "Wherefore the law is holy, and the commandment holy, and just, and good." Look how *good* they are toward the slave in Deuteronomy. These are the laws the Israelites were to apply on settlement in the Promised Land.

Deuteronomy 15:12-18

> 12 And if your brother, an Hebrew man, or an Hebrew woman, be sold to you, and serve you six years; then in the seventh year you shall let him go free from you.
>
> 13 And when you send him out free from you, you shall not let him go away empty:
>
> 14 You shall furnish him liberally out of your flock, and out of your floor, and out of your winepress: of that wherewith the LORD your God has blessed you you shall give to him.
>
> 15 And you shall remember that you were a bondman in the land of Egypt, and the LORD your God redeemed you: therefore I command you this thing to day.
>
> 16 And it shall be, if he say to you, I will not go away from you; because he loves you and your house, because he is well with you;

> 17 Then you shall take an aul, and thrust it through his ear to the door, and he shall be your servant for ever. And also to your maidservant you shall do likewise.
>
> 18 It shall not seem hard to you, when you send him away free from you; for he has been worth a double hired servant to you, in serving you six years: and the LORD your God shall bless you in all that you do.

The forlorn slave had up to six years of instructive supervision to prepare for a new start in life. During that time, he or she received nourishing food, a comfortable bed, and a home for their family. They became proficient in a trade after following an apprenticeship. They developed a professional skill, maybe more than one, along with the ethics of working hard and efficiently. When they left, they were not cast out on the street; they had enough goods and capital to start their new life without being indebted to some loan shark or bank. More favorable conditions would be scarce, even today.

Non-Hebrew workers did not benefit from all these advantages, but their lot was far better and fairer than anything in the surrounding nations. Here are just a few laws to consider.

- Canaanite slaves must work forever unless injured in one of their limbs — Lev. 25:46.
- Not to extradite a slave who fled to Biblical Israel — Deut. 23:16.
- Not to wrong a slave who has come to Israel for refuge — Deut. 23:16.

Workers had legal rights enforced by Judges

- Courts were to carry out the laws of a hired worker and hired guard — Ex. 22:9.

- Employers must pay wages at the end of the day's work — Deut. 24:15.
- If there was an *agreed negotiated* time for payment, there is to be no delay — Lev. 19:13.
- No allowance to oppress workers — Lev. 25:53.
- While employed, the hired worker could eat from the employer's unharvested crops — Deut. 23:25.
- But the worker could not eat during hired time — Deut. 23:26.
- The worker should not take more than they can eat from the unharvested field — Deut. 23:25.
- Even treatment of animals was in the law. Don't muzzle an ox while it's plowing — Deut. 25:4.

There's a negotiation and an absence of oppression. Both employers and employees have rights and one is to respect the other. An agreement is mutual, even with a slave.

The meaning of slavery in the New Testament

In the New Testament, we find Christians involved with vestiges of slavery. We're in Roman times when slavery existed, and God called both slaves and masters who became Christians. The single chapter book of Philemon, the name of a Christian who hosted God's assemblies in his house, was also a slave master. His slave, Onesimus, had escaped and gone to the Apostle Paul.

Onesimus is a Christian convert, so both the slave master and slave are in the Church. Paul writes, "For perhaps he (Onesimus) therefore departed for a season, that you (Philemon) should receive him for ever; Not now as a *servant* (G1401), but above a servant, a brother beloved, specially to me, but how much more to you, both in the flesh, and in the Lord?" Paul tells Philemon about Onesimus, but it's up to him to decide the future of his slave.

Paul requests the slave's release. On what grounds? Yes, there's the seventh year release in the Old Testament, but there's especially Christian mercy. It doesn't say what the outcome was. However, the key here is although the New Testament talks about slavery, by its sheer existence, in no case does it prone nor condone it, To the contrary, from Philemon, we learn to treat them as a Christian should, including letting them go free.

Spiritual meaning of slave

Let's return to the spiritual meaning of a slave. Here's the ultimate example, one we are to follow.

> **Matthew 20:25-28**
>
> 25 But Jesus called them (His disciples) to him, and said, You know that the princes of the Gentiles exercise dominion over them, and they that are great exercise authority on them.
>
> 26 But it shall not be so among you: but whosoever will be great among you, let him be your minister;
>
> 27 And whosoever will be chief among you, let him be your *servant* (G1401):
>
> 28 Even as the Son of man came not to be ministered to, but to minister, and to give his life a ransom for many.

Jesus came to be a servant, the Servant of servants. Look at the meaning of the Greek.

G1401

δοῦλος doulos doo'-los; From G1210; a slave (literally or figuratively involuntarily or voluntarily; frequently therefore in a qualified sense of subjection or subserviency):

KJV - bond (-man) servant.

G1210

δέω deō deh'-o; a primary verb; to bind (in various applications literally or figuratively):

KJV - bind be in bonds knit tie wind. See also G1163 G118.

In Romans 1:1 Paul calls himself "a servant of Christ Jesus." He uses the Greek *doulos* (H1401) which means *slave*. Peter and James do the same in the first verses of their Epistles. In Rom. 1:9 Paul adds, for God is my witness, whom I serve (G3000) with my spirit in the gospel of his Son. Look it up at UnlockBibleMeaning.com[19]. Strong indicates λατρεύω from λάτρις latris (a hired *menial*); to minister (to God) that is render religious homage: The KJV translations: serve, do the service, worship (-per).

A *slave* doing God's *service* is a *worshipper*. Interestingly, it takes us back to the reason God created Adam and placed him in His Garden, to serve and worship. That kind of slavery is spiritual excellence.

Slavery with its atrocities is an abomination to God, it is at the antipodes of *loving your neighbor*. The Old Testament laws, because

19. https://unlockbiblemeaning.com

of hardness of their hearts, were for a humane employer-employee relationship with everyone's rights protected. It could develop into a lifetime working relationship for both parties. In the new Testament, Christians become willing slaves of God's righteousness. Their goal is to be a worshipper or slave of God in His Garden of Eden, the Kingdom of God, forever.

True Justice in Old Testament. Savage or Salutary?

We can have ethical justice for all. How it was in former times and how we could apply it today.

True justice in the Old Testament is a major point of contention because of its apparent cruelty. I say *apparently,* because from a humanistic point-of-view, which we, in the West have, harsh application of punishment is a sore issue.

Before discussing true justice[1], we must consider the framework. Why does a loving God treat people this way? And to add fuel to the fire, why does God treat His own chosen nation this way? Assimilate the overview first, then we can discuss individual laws.

First Principle: God's People are Holy Morally Clean

1. https://en.wikipedia.org/wiki/Justice

That's quite a dogmatic affirmation. *How can The Explanation* support such a statement, especially the first one? The Bible says so, as you see in the verse below. We are talking about major principles here and there has to be some sort of order in their presentation. Here are a couple of connecting lines. First, the Bible confirms this holiness in the Old Testament for UNconverted people. God's chosen nation was not a God-respecting, accommodating people, to the contrary.

In the New Testament, I hope it goes without saying God's people, H's Assembly is a holy one. We'll see the meaning in just a minute. Second, we could ask, why does God want His people to be holy? The quick answer is God is Holy, and we are created in His image. So, we should be holy, too. But there's an even more important reason we discussed it in the *Family Ties* chapter regarding the nature of God and His people as sons and daughters, a family relationship. Suffice to say, God's people is a holy people.

Deuteronomy 7:6, 9

> 6 For you are an *holy* (H6918) people to the LORD your God: the LORD your God has chosen you to be a special people to himself, above all people that are upon the face of the earth.
>
> 9 Know therefore that the LORD your God, he is God, the faithful God, which keeps covenant and mercy with them that love him and keep his commandments to a thousand generations;

A *holy* nation. A *religious* word used frequently which has lost much of its meaning. Here is the Biblical Hebrew.

H6918

קָדוֹשׁ qâdôwsh kaw-doshe'; or קָדֹשׁ from H6942 (קָדַשׁ); sacred (ceremonially or morally); (as noun) God (by eminence), an angel, a saint, a sanctuary:

KJV - holy (One), saint.

H6942

קָדַשׁ qâdash kaw-dash'; a primitive root; to be (causatively, make, pronounce or observe as) clean (ceremonially or morally):

KJV - appoint, bid, consecrate, dedicate, defile, hallow, (be, keep) holy(-er, place), keep, prepare, proclaim, purify, sanctify(-ied one, self), × wholly.

The key to retain is *purify* and *sanctify* which Strong sums up as *clean morally.* God wants His people to be clean in the conduct of their lives. A verse in Ephesians says the same thing. "That he (Christ) might present it to himself a glorious church, not having spot, or wrinkle, or any such thing; but that it should be holy and without blemish" (Eph. 5:27). God's Church with no moral spot, holy, and pristine.

Morally clean is just as valid in the Old Testament era. Strong's comment is *ceremonially* clean. Yes, there's a lot of ceremony with the washings and clothing but it goes much further. God wants the lifestyle of his nation to be decent. In particular, the behavior of each citizen of His nation. And I remind you we're talking about an unconverted nation. As an aside, if you think you're living in a Godly nation, ask yourself the question, does my nation possess a clean moral lifestyle?

This is a fundamental Godly principle, throughout God's Word, Old and New Testaments. God's people are holy, pure, and clean. We cannot go into details without this clarification. This does not mean God's people are perfect, no human can be. It means God's converted people are leading their lives God's way and have accepted the death of Christ to pay for their sins. Only God's forgiveness makes us clean and holy. It means that even those who don't believe in God lead decent lives. God wants His nation(s) to be a special people (Deut. 7:6) examples of clean living. That's why there must be true **justice**.

Second Principle: Definition of clean. Keeping God's way

What does it mean to lead our lives God's way? Deut. 7:9 already answered that "love Him and keep His Commandments." It doesn't end there, "to a thousand generations." Many think it's an exaggeration to emphasize how much Old Testament Israel was to keep the commandments. But the New Testament, Bible-wide corroboration confirms believers must still keep the New Testament commandments (John 14:15, 15:10). At 20 years per generation, that's 20,000 years. We're well within those 20k years[2], we're still to be clean, as a nation of God and as God respecting individuals.

We can sum up *keeping God's commandments* by citing the Two Great Commandments. But remember, "on them hang ALL the law." These are the principles of the law of the Old Testament[3].

You could arrange ALL the hundreds of verses about God's laws, statutes, judgments into two groups. The way to love God and the way to love your neighbor. These two principles have never changed and never will.

2. https://theexplanation.com/timeline-history-universe-earth-humans/

3. https://theexplanation.com/critical-thinking-antidote-to-the-agony-of-humankind/

To be holy is to keep God's commandments. Be careful with this statement. Remember, being holy is not the same as being saved. Being holy does not *get you saved*. Keeping God's commandments is not what saves anyone. We are saved by Christ and only by Christ; I hope that's 'lear.

But are we to be holy? The Bible says yes. So, regardless of salvation, we are to keep the commandments, love God and love our neighbor, on these hang all the law. This applies in Old Testament and New Testament times, then and now.

Third Principle: Free choice in Old Testament and New Testament

We ALL, every human being, have free choice. In the Old and New Testaments, everybody has alternatives. The decision is between two Trees. The Tree of Life and the Tree of Death.

- We can choose God's way, His cleanliness, holiness, and Christ's sacrifice. In other words, the Tree of Life.

OR

- We can choose to do it our way, according to our definition of good and evil. In other words, the Tree of Death.

These are not always straightforward choices. In fact, they are very difficult ones in real life. I realize we are bound by certain situations depending on our position in life and we don't have the freedom we need. Nonetheless, there are two ways in front of us, all our lives, and each moment, and each of us has free will to make our own decisions.

Fourth Principle: Physical precedes Spiritual

There is, however, one radically changed aspect between these two dispensations, the fulcrum point being Christ's First Coming. *Before,* God dealt with the *physical* nation of Israel. *After,* God works with the *spiritual* nation of His Church.

The physical precedes *and* prefigures the spiritual. The implications of what *The Explanation* expounds here are vital to understand. They are foundational regarding God's plan for humankind.

> **In the Old Testament,** they had to keep the letter of the law in their bodies. If not, true justice is applied. For the innocent, the Tree of Life. For the guilty, the Tree of Death. it was a literal application of the appropriate punishment to fit the crime. Necessary to maintain true Justice and peace in a physical, unconverted nation. Sounds harsh, but it's exactly what justice in all nations does today, with more or less success.
>
> **In the New Testament,** we keep the spirit of the law in our minds (which expresses itself by loving God and neighbor through our material actions). Otherwise, God's true justice will be applied. Under the New Testament dispensation, the ultimate punishment is the Tree of the second death (Revelation 21:8). The ultimate blessing is the Tree of Eternal Life; escaping the second death (Revelation 20:6) to be the kings and priests (rulers and teachers) with God for eternity.

Fifth Principle: Death in the Old Testament is the First Death, then comes a Resurrection

We don't have space to elaborate here; read Life Prevails[4] for details. The bottom line is the death penalty existed; God and the Israelites practiced it under the Old Covenant. However, those who died, during Noah's flood, the entry into Canaan, from any sickness, war, old age, accidents, or any other cause whatsoever, are not condemned eternally. There is a first death followed by a resurrection according to God's plan. Death is sorrowful, but there's hope for all the dead in the future.

Most people are aware of the horrific death penalty both in our world and especially in the Old Testament with a loving God, which they cannot explain. Even theologians deny it was ever applied or avoid answering the question. It's there in black and white, so to speak. On the other hand, the resurrection is also there in black and white and few comprehend this applies to giving life to ALL dead, including the worst sinners and those who were punished by the death penalty under the Old Covenant. True justice maintains peace, it is God's goal, then, now, and in the future.

When the time comes for the resurrection of all people, there will be enough rulers and priests to teach and nurture them properly. The resurrected will live in a Godly society, and witness first-hand the benefits of living according to Godly principles. The priests and teachers will healthily use their spiritual tools, and wisely help those who were the most depraved during their first life.

When this fifth principle is understood and integrated into one's knowledge base, one's mind, then it becomes easier to understand God's true justice, including the why and how of its workings.

God chose a nation and gave them land and leaders

Here's 'n overview of how true justice worked in ancient Israel. Again, these principles can apply to modern justice to maintain law and order, or put another way, peace for individuals and the general

4. https://theexplanation.com/what-is-death-rest-in-peace-or-dust-which-why/

population. God set up the nation in a territory and He says who to establish as rulers. Notice verse 15, the leadership comprises sufficient responsible people throughout the tribes.

Deut. 1:1-15

1 These be the words which Moses spoke to all Israel on this side Jordan in the wilderness,

3 And it came to pass in the fortieth year, in the eleventh month,

8 Behold, I have **set the land before you**: go in and possess the land which the LORD sware to your fathers, Abraham, Isaac, and Jacob, to give to them and to their seed after them.

13 Take you **wise men**, and **understanding**, and **known** among your tribes, and I will make them **rulers over you**.

14 And you answered me, and said, The thing which you have spoken is good for us to do.

15 So I took the chief of your tribes, wise men, and known, and **made them heads over you**, captains over thousands, and captains over hundreds, and captains over fifties, and captains over tens, and officers among your tribes.

He appoints judges, judging fairly in the gates

In the same way, the nation established officers for the cause of true justice. From the local to the tribal to the national level, there were competent judges to apply genuine justice. Notice court sessions took place at the gates; everyone passed by this location, these are public hearings. Note how in few words the law defines the demeanor of judges.

Deut. 16:18-19

> Judges and officers shall you make you in all your gates, which the LORD your God gives you, throughout your tribes: and they shall judge the people with just judgment.
>
> 19 You shall not wrest judgment; you shall not respect persons, neither take a gift: for a gift does blind the eyes of the wise, and pervert the words of the righteous.

The following verses show the extent and the equity of true justice. The foreigner had the same rights and obligations as the Israelites, there was equity between the rich and poor. Judges were not to be intimidated, and they could admit they were not competent if the case was beyond them. There was a Supreme or Higher Court.

Deut. 1:16-17

> 16 And I charged your judges at that time, saying, Hear the causes between your brethren, and judge righteously between every man and his brother, and the stranger that is with him.
>
> 17 You shall not respect persons in judgment; but you shall hear the small as well as the great; you shall not be afraid of the face of man; for the judgment is God's: and the cause that is too hard for you, bring it to me, and I will hear it.

God gives humans the obligation to apply true justice

Immediately after Noah's flood, God passed the responsibility of judging humans to humans (Gen. 9:5-6). That injunction was still in effect in Paul's time, some 2000 years ago after the First Coming of Christ. It is still in effect today. Society, governorship, countries, and people change, but the principles applying to true justice remain in human hands for application. Please note I said the principles of the law. *The Explanation* has expounded on the development and application of the law from the time of Moses to Solomon, notably in the book of Proverbs[5].

Genesis 9:5-6

5 And surely your blood of your lives will I require; at the hand of every beast will I require it, and at the hand of man; at the hand of every man's brother will I require the life of man.

6 Whoso sheds man's blood, by man shall his blood be shed: for in the image of God made he man.

Romans 13:1

Let every soul be subject to the higher powers. For there is no power but of God: the powers that be are ordained of God.

Psalm 82:3-4

2 How long will you judge unjustly, and accept the persons of the wicked? Selah.

3 Defend the poor and fatherless: do justice to the afflicted and needy.

5. https://theexplanation.com/how-to-govern-a-country-responsibly-practical-bible-advice/

4 Deliver the poor and needy: rid them out of the hand of the wicked.

Proverbs 21:3, 29:4

3 To do justice and judgment is more acceptable to the LORD than sacrifice.

4 The king by judgment establishes the land: but he that receives gifts overthrows it.

God has always set in motion the principles for equitable justice. This Bible wisdom should be the basis and application of worldwide courts of justice in the 21st century.

Here are different categories of judiciary litigation. Space lacks to give many verses both in Proverbs, Exodus, Leviticus, and Deuteronomy. An interesting study is finding the same offense in different books and seeing how God and His servants apply true justice. How there is modification, but the principle of true justice remains unchanged.

Property

Proverbs 23:10 Remove not the old landmark; and enter not into the fields of the fatherless:

Bribes

Amos 2:6 Thus says the LORD; For three transgressions of Israel, and for four, I will not turn away the punishment thereof; because they sold the righteous for silver, and the poor for a pair of shoes;

Fraud

This reminds me of a grocery store in a poor country using scales with a bowl. Under the bowl, a small fish was caught in the mechanism and added to the weight each time the bowl was placed on the scales. Not heavy, true, but it's like stealing cents from thousands of people. It adds up, even with paltry amounts, the intent is there, it's fraud.

Amos 8:5 Saying, When will the new moon be gone, that we may sell corn? and the sabbath, that we may set forth wheat, making the ephah small, and the shekel great, and falsifying the balances by deceit?

The new moon and Sabbath were special days. On the latter, no commerce took place, but these people had their minds focused on business and tricking their customers instead of devotion to God.

There are so many Bible verses on this matter: Deut. 25:13-16, Lev. 19:35-37. Note below how bona fide justice is a national subject for the well-being of all citizens.

> **Deuteronomy 27:17-19**
>
> 17 Cursed be he that removes his neighbour's landmark. And *all the people shall say, Amen.*
>
> 18 Cursed be he that makes the blind to wander out of the way. And *all the people shall say, Amen.*
>
> 19 Cursed be he that perverts the judgment of the stranger, fatherless, and widow. And *all the people shall say, Amen.*

There are many other categories of offenses and true justice; study Proverbs for dishonesty, violence, etc. Make categories and find verses.

True justice as a dissuasion

True justice has the role of keeping peace and order when someone commits a crime. But there's another primary purpose we have forgotten today, and it's causing much sorrow. True justice should be a source of dissuasion for those thinking about doing wrong. In the Old Testament, you find the people of Israel, the man and woman in the street, as we'd say, taking part in true justice not just as a spectator, often as a participator. Read the verses below, notably verse 20.

This *hear and fear* is an external motivation to put them in the offender's seat, participate in the criminal's crime, feel what would happen to them if they committed such a felony. In a world of liberalism, this sounds harsh, but God knows he's dealing with a definite trait characterizing His people. They are hard-hearted as we've seen. They are not open-minded to doing what's right, to the contrary, they are prone to sidestepping the law. Taking part in the punishment is a deterrent. So it should be with true justice.

Today death is so common on TV, in movies, and especially in violent video games, we've become accustomed to seeing killing and maiming. Many sports have raised the ante from aggressive to brutal. People are apathetic to death or crave watching it; nothing is dissuading them from committing crime.

> **Deut. 19:15-21**
>
> 15 One witness shall not rise up against a man for any iniquity, or for any sin, in any sin that he sins: at the mouth of two witnesses, or at the mouth of three witnesses, shall the matter be established.

> 16 If a false witness rise up against any man to testify against him that which is wrong;
>
> 17 Then both the men, between whom the controversy is, shall stand before the LORD, before the priests and the judges, which shall be in those days;
>
> 18 And the judges shall make diligent inquisition: and, behold, if the witness be a false witness, and has testified falsely against his brother;
>
> 19 Then shall you do to him, as he had thought to have done to his brother: so shall you put the evil away from among you.
>
> 20 And **those which remain shall hear, and fear, and shall henceforth commit no more any such evil among you.**
>
> 21 And your eye shall not pity; but life shall go for life, eye for eye, tooth for tooth, hand for hand, foot for foot.

Verse 21 includes the famous *eye for an eye* punishment that has Bible detractors up-in-arms. I agree it sounds and must be horrific. There's no example of it being carried out in the Bible, so I don't know if it ever happened. Regarding capital punishment, there are examples (in Joshua 7, they stoned Achan for stealing. 2 Samuel 1, an Amalekite is slain for saying he killed King Saul). There's even an example in the New Testament with Ananias and Sapphira, who lied and died suddenly (Acts 5). These are serious matters God has recorded for our benefit. This is where you have to keep in mind the various principles above, in particular the fifth, regarding the first death.

The Bible concludes the entire story of humankind with a blessing and a very stern warning.

Revelation 22:14-15

> 14 Blessed are they that do his commandments, that they may have right to the tree of life, and may enter in through the gates into the city.
>
> 15 For without are dogs, and sorcerers, and whoremongers, and murderers, and idolaters, and whosoever loves and makes a lie.

These are the two Trees I referred to above. The Tree of Life for those who do God's will, and in verse 15, those without, who ultimately rebel and reject God's way. Notice they love wrong-doing, they're set in their ways. Theirs is the Tree of Death, the Second Death. There are deterrents in the New Testament we are to heed.

Old Testament law represents but a few pages of text, a few chapters compared to the library of books and interpretations of law-makers' efforts to cover every possible criminal situation. This in itself is a masterpiece, it covers individual and community law for:

- Property (theft, damage).
- Health (quarantine and Covid-19).
- Injury and murder (cities of refuge, capital punishment, reparation).
- Religion (false gods and preachers, Priests, and Levites).
- Family (marriage, sexual practices, parenting).
- Rulership, the King.

Very concise and clear; judgment was fair and swift. Oh, that we have such Godly justice in our countries today.

4. Rulership

Let's just call it management. Whether it's government or you and me, we all have people, activities, possessions, and time to whom and for which we have a responsibility. How do we know the rules for handling major and minor fields of our own lives and those in our sphere of influence?

Education. Teach & Learn to Reach Wisdom

We sorely need a definition of education. Is it the dissemination of data, facts to fill students' heads? Or should it be wise information to learn how to live?

Why do we need to define education? Because we are discussing practical Bible wisdom. Simply put, those three words, plus *moral*, summarize the essence of education. I suppose I could end this chapter right here, but we need to give some corroboration for the term *practical moral Bible wisdom* as a definition of education.

After all, isn't the Bible, at worst, just an archaic collection of imaginative myths, and, at best, an outdated record of a few historical nations and people? Let's put both those ideas to rest and reveal how and why the Bible elaborates on education and is 21st century up-to-date. We need both facts for a prosperous professional life and wisdom for a peaceful social and spiritual existence. If you don't care for the term *spiritual*, then substitute *peace of mind*; I believe everyone can live with that.

We're giving this definition of education[1] in a specific context. Practical Bible wisdom for all people worldwide, regardless of nationality, language, gender, age, religion, or any other nomenclature we use to divide and group humans. Humanity is one race with the same modus operandi worldwide. We differ in traditions, beliefs, customs, and many other areas, just as you can have huge political or religious differences splitting any family. Nonetheless, it's still one family.

Today, the state of moral education is in shambles, particularly in the West where we've abdicated our appropriate, purposeful role as parents. We've handed the responsibility to other authorities, namely schools, which are ill-equipped to instill morals after children reach class-attending age. Here's a definition of education and it's in tight straights[2].

We find the practical instructions of education God gave the first man and woman from the start, in Genesis, throughout the Old Testament, and into the New Testament.

God's Education to Adam and Eve

Genesis 1:28

Be fruitful, and multiply, and replenish the earth, and subdue it:

---

1. https://theexplanation.com/will-education-lead-the-world-in-the-right-direction/

2. https://link.springer.com/referenceworkentry/10.1007%2F978-0-387-71799-9_260

He told them what their occupations would be. First, develop socially in the family of humankind. Second, subdue Earth encompasses their professional lives; they are managers of Earth's resources. Think about it. Those two activities are identical to our 21st century vocations: family and profession. We do not differ from Adam and Eve; those are our occupations. Are there any guidelines for education? Yes, there are.

Gen. 2:15-17

15 And the LORD God took the man, and put him into the garden of Eden to dress it and to keep it.

16 And the LORD God commanded the man, saying, Of every tree of the garden you may freely eat:

17 But of the tree of the knowledge of good and evil, you shall not eat of it: for in the day that you eat thereof you shall surely die.

The definition of education is twofold.

1. God is the basis and focal point of education.
2. Moral choices come first for our own and other people's well-being.

1. God is the foundation and all-in-all definition of education

This chapter cannot develop the meaning of Gen. 2:15. At first reading, it appears God named Adam chief landscaper, grass-cutter, and gardener in the Garden of Eden. Not so. Read this chapter to understand, *dress it and keep it* means *worship and observe*[3]; *it* points to *God*. These words are the foundation of the definition of education; King Solomon's introduction to Proverbs corroborates this basis for education. *Worship* God and *observe* proper instruction.

> **Proverbs 1:7-8**
>
> 7 The fear of the LORD is the beginning of knowledge: but fools despise wisdom and instruction.
>
> 8 My son, hear the instruction of your father, and forsake not the law of your mother:

Fear refers to the deep respect all humans should have toward God. Of course, such *worship* is not the case today, humankind does not know their true origin and their definition of education is askew. Instead of God being the foundation, it is scholarly knowledge to obtain degrees. Certainly, there is a place for diplomas, but they are not the basis of beneficial education.

2. Moral choices to guide us toward life and away from despair

The two Trees in the Garden of Eden symbolize our options. We can eat from a virtuous Tree tending to an abundant life, or the noxious Tree of knowledge of good and evil pointing to anguished misery. Parents are the first to feed their children, physically and morally. Both choices are permanently on the menu, which are we serving?

The full definition of education is teaching and learning how to make life-giving moral choices to progress in our family (social) and professional (subdue the Earth) lives, based on the respect of God, the beginning of all knowledge. Father and mother are front and

---

3. https://theexplanation.com/dress-keep-garden-of-eden-man-destined-to-be-a-gardener/

center to instill in their children respect, *observing* proper moral instruction.

To press home this Bible definition of wise education, let's follow the lives of some key Bible personalities to witness the primary role Godly guidance played in their lives.

Noah practiced Godly education

Noah's life, hopefully via his parents, certainly via his choices, was one of respect for God and the appropriate upbringing of his children. They followed their father on this perilous adventure, despite the pressure society exercised against them.

Gen. 6:13-14, 22, 7:1

13-14 And God said to Noah... Make you an ark of gopher wood; rooms shall you make in the ark, and shall pitch it within and without with pitch.

22 Thus did Noah; according to all that God commanded him, so did he.

7:1 And the LORD said to Noah, Come you and all your house into the ark; for you have I seen *righteous* (H6662) before me in this generation.

H6662

צַדִּיק tsaddîyq tsad-deek'; from H6663 (צָדַק); just:

KJV - just, lawful, righteous (man).

H6663

צָדַק tsâdaq tsaw-dak'; a primitive root; to be (causatively, make) right (in a moral or forensic sense):

KJV - cleanse, clear self, (be, do) just(-ice, -ify, -ify self), (be turn to) righteous(-ness).

The definition of education includes both teaching and learning. An identifying sign of God's servants is their preaching in conformity with the Tree of Life. God's moral code in social and professional affairs leads to peace and prosperity; an abundant life now and in the future.

2 Peter 2:5

5 And spared not the old world, but saved Noah the eighth person, a *preacher* (G2783) of righteousness, bringing in the flood upon the world of the ungodly;

G2783

κήρυξ kērux kay'-roox; From G2784; a herald that is of divine truth (especially of the gospel):

KJV - preacher.

A herald is an instructor with a message. A righteous herald is someone who knows, practices, and teaches the Godly definition of education.

God's Education to Abraham

Following Noah, the next milestone servant of God is Abraham. He is a key figure in God's plan, being the *father of the faithful.* The profoundness of this phrase needs expansion, but one quality included in the *faith* of *faithful* is understanding the necessity to teach God's moral code of ethics. In the next two contexts, we see God preaching to/teaching Abraham, who then transmits God's knowledge to his family.

Galatians 3:6-8

6 Even as Abraham believed God, and it was accounted to him for righteousness.

7 Know you therefore that they which are of faith, the same are the children of Abraham.

8 And the scripture, foreseeing that God would justify the heathen through faith, **preached before the gospel to Abraham**, saying, In you shall all nations be blessed.

Gen. 18:17-19

17 And the LORD said, Shall I hide from Abraham that thing which I do;

18 Seeing that Abraham shall surely become a great and mighty nation, and all the nations of the earth shall be blessed in him?

19 For I know him, that he will command his children and his household after him, and they shall keep the way of the LORD, to do justice and judgment; that the LORD may bring upon Abraham that which he has spoken of him.

By definition, education is an educator, father, and mother, passing on honorable instruction, in continuity, to the next generation. All the nations will be blessed in Abraham; these peoples obtain this blessing because they accept the same gospel preached to Abraham. This is prophetic. God's definition of education is regardless of gender, nation, culture, traditions, creed, and beliefs. It is the same Godly education for everyone at all times.

Abraham carbon-copied the Gospel message of justice and judgment to his household; some of his immediate children did the same. God's Bible wisdom, from generation to generation, is the same for peoples today as it was in the time of Abraham and Moses.

God's Education to Moses

After educating Abraham and his family, that instruction carried on until Joseph became a prominent leader in Egypt. However, with a change of Pharaoh, Israel's fate shifted radically. After 430 years of captivity (Exodus 12:40-41) God's education was lost. With the preparation and calling of Moses, the definition of divine education could again be broadcast. This time, not to an individual and his family (Abraham), but to the entirety of his descendants, a nation.

> **Deuteronomy 6:7-9**
>
> 4 Hear, O Israel: The LORD our God is one LORD:
>
> 5 And you shall love the LORD your God with all your heart, and with all your soul, and with all your might.
>
> 6 And these words, which I command you this day, shall be in your heart:
>
> 7 And you shall teach them diligently to your children, and shall talk of them when you sit in your house, and when you walk by the way, and when you lie down, and when you rise up.

> 8 And you shall bind them for a sign on your hand, and they shall be as frontlets between your eyes.
>
> 9 And you shall write them on the posts of your house, and on your gates.

Israel's education comprises the same content as Adam, Noah, and Abraham. *Love the Lord* is the beginning of practical Bible wisdom. The presence and continuity of God's education are assured by its teaching to future generations and its presence as frontlets and on doorposts. Jewish people still practice this today with Tefillin[4] and the Mezuzah[5]. According to the New Covenant definition of education, God's way is now written and active in our minds. As with them, God's education is permanently with us and transmitted to our children. Clearly, the responsibility falls to the parents first, not schools nor any other authorities.

God's education disseminated by the Priests (Kohanim) and Levites

God set aside an entire tribe, the descendants of Levi, to be the teachers of Israel. The Levites had various professions and tasks, but one of their primary roles was education. It was their responsibility, alongside the Priests, to give Israel God's instructions, His education.

Studying this aspect of the Levites, their role as educators is a stimulating dive into the definition of education in the Old Testament. I leave this study up to you. Remember UnlockBibleMeaning.com with an online concordance helps you easily locate verses and context to bolster this study.

---

4. https://en.wikipedia.org/wiki/Tefillin

5. https://en.wikipedia.org/wiki/Mezuzah

The point to emphasize here goes beyond just God's education. It is the choice of an entire tribe, about one-twelfth of the population, for God's service, primarily to make sure His education was available throughout the nation. From North to South and from East to West.

If you want a vast number of people to follow edifying education, you must have sufficient qualified teachers versed in God's definition of education. The high ratio of one in twelve being a national servant should tell us something. Bible wisdom points out much fell to the Levites; among other responsibilities, they taught fathers and mothers who then could assume their roles.

God's Education to Kings David and Solomon

We cannot omit them, for at least two reasons.

- First, they are the authors, inspired by God, of Psalms and Proverbs. These books are the epitome of the practical definition of education under the Old Covenant. These words define God's lifestyle for His people, and even more, God's lifestyle for ALL peoples EVERYWHERE on planet Earth. It is in Proverbs we find the verses I quoted earlier, "the fear of the LORD is the beginning of knowledge: but fools despise wisdom and instruction. My son, hear the instruction of your father, and forsake not the law of your mother.

Fools despise this practical wisdom and instruction, with the catastrophic results we have in our 21st century society in the social family, and environmental management fields. *The Explanation* has written extensively about the content of Proverbs[6]; it carries practical wisdom for all

6. https://theexplanation.com/rules-for-life-wisdom-for-living-abundantly-in-the-world/

peoples. It is God's definition of education to clothe all of humankind in peace and prosperity if only humanity would apply it.

Proverbs 1:6

To understand a proverb, and the interpretation; the words of the wise, and their *dark sayings* (H2420).

Note the meaning of dark sayings translated elsewhere, *hard questions.*

H2420

חִידָה chîydâh khee-daw'; from H2330 (חוּד); a puzzle, hence, a trick, conundrum, sententious maxim:

KJV - dark saying (sentence, speech), hard question, proverb, riddle.

There are many hard questions in life. We'd also call them *the big questions of life*. Science, Philosophy, and Religion are in confusion regarding many issues. Practical wisdom is not in those disciplines; it is in the Theology of the Bible, God's Word, His definition of education.

- Second, the reason for including these servants of God and their books relates to the management of Earth's resources. Both were men animated by God's will. Solomon was extremely rich, maybe the richest man to have ever lived. God gave him the wisdom to write about how to manage such riches. Proverbs gives abundant council for the rich to govern their approach to money and possessions.

Christ's definition of education

The teachings of Christ are innumerable. He is the Word who taught the Word. Not only by the spoken word but by His living example. He is The Teacher.

Matthew 4:23

> And Jesus went about all Galilee, teaching in their synagogues, and preaching the gospel of the kingdom, and healing all manner of sickness and all manner of disease among the people.

He is the Teacher of universal education to ALL peoples of all languages and origins. I'd have to verify this more closely, but I don't think any other religious or spiritual leader destined their teachings for a worldwide audience. Jesus Christ did. He gave the definitions of education, the example of education for each person who has ever walked the face of this Earth.

But there is another aspect to Christ's teaching experience. He specially chose and trained twelve apostles. He spent 3 1/2 years with them, day and night. It impregnated them with His approach, answers, analysis, and awe. Why did Jesus put so much effort into creating this tight group of followers?

Matthew 28:18-20

> 18 And Jesus came and spake to them, saying, All power is given to me in heaven and in earth.
>
> 19 Go you therefore, and teach all nations, baptizing them in the name of the Father, and of the Son, and of the Holy Ghost:

> 20 Teaching them to observe all things whatsoever I have commanded you: and, lo, I am with you alway, even to the end of the world. Amen.

The twelve Apostles represent the core of teachers who will set the stage for a future worldwide teaching program. The basis of this education is "Teach them to observe all things whatsoever I have commanded you." These are the two great commandments. Love God and love your neighbor and the entire way of life, in the form of all the law resulting from the knowledge of God.

Verse 20 sets the standard for the definition of a worldwide education system, God's way.

God's education to the Apostles and His Church

In the Old Testament, when God preached the Gospel to Abraham (Gal. 3:8 above) his symbol of acceptance was the circumcision of himself and the males in his household. God taught the Gospel to Abraham. It is the same as the Apostle's teaching, "repent and be baptized for the forgiveness of your sins." Repent is the equivalent of saying, "there's a moral code you've transgressed, it's now time to turn your life around. Observe the things I've commanded you." Baptism symbolizes the burial or death of one's past sinful life and the rising out of the watery grave to a new righteous life, accepting God's definition of education.

God's education to His Church Today

We've gone from Adam and Eve to the 21st century with God's education. In essence, it has not changed. It's always been for all peoples everywhere; it's always been *teach and do* what I, God, command you.

Unfortunately, many teacher-pastors are teaching the *wrong* way, leading the flock astray. Peter gives a stern warning about false teachers and teachings.

> **2 Peter 2:1-3**
>
> 1 But there were false prophets also among the people, even as there shall be false teachers among you, who privily shall bring in damnable heresies, even denying the Lord that bought them, and bring upon themselves swift destruction.
>
> 2 And many shall follow their pernicious ways; by reason of whom the way of truth shall be evil spoken of.
>
> 3 And through covetousness shall they with feigned words make merchandise of you: whose judgment now of a long time lingers not, and their damnation slumbers not.

We are to study to show ourselves approved, rightly dividing the word of truth (2 Timothy 2:15). We are to hold fast to the word (1 Cor 15:1-3). This is the definition of education. Why is it so important? Because it has an immense impact on the future, and for all eternity.

God's education in the future

Some wonder, why doesn't God Return NOW?! When Christ returns, there will be millions and millions of people of all nations on Earth who do not know Him or anything about Him. Each one is going to need personalized support in the form of teaching. Not just any instruction, but the Godly definition of teaching as practiced from the Creation by God's servants.

To teach millions, you must have a core of multi-thousands of trained and qualified teachers. God prepared instructors in the Old Covenant era, but it speeds up with Christ, the Apostles, and the establishment of His Church. That group of priest-teachers is growing; It must reach an optimum number of people who've shown God, by their belief and actions, they will be faithful to His Gospel message throughout eternity. This is the growing group with Christ at the summit as Top Teacher.

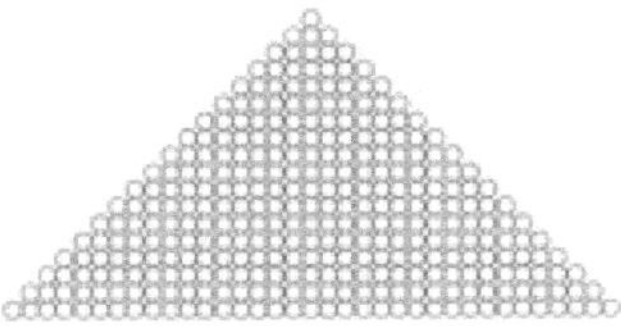

If you don't have a core of teachers ready and equipped, you'll have nothing but confusion, which is exactly the state we're in today. Then, it will be a different and wonderfully exciting story. Let the prophet Isaiah give you a glimpse.

Isaiah 30:18-21

18 And therefore will the LORD wait (Sam: during this waiting time, teacher training is ongoing), that he may be gracious to you, and therefore will he be exalted, that he may have mercy on you: for the LORD is a God of judgment: blessed are all they that wait for him.

19 For the people shall dwell in Zion at Jerusalem: you shall weep no more: he will be very gracious to you at the voice of your cry; when he shall hear it, he will answer you.

> 20 And though the Lord give you the bread of adversity, and the water of affliction, **yet shall not your teachers be removed into a corner any more**, but your eyes shall see your teachers:
>
> 21 And your ears shall hear a word behind you, saying, This is the way, walk you in it, when you turn to the right hand, and when you turn to the left.

God could raise teachers from stones, but He will not. He is preparing a body of Godly trained teachers. That's one reason for the present dispensation; you can join His team, under His conditions.

The words of Elihu are a fitting conclusion. "That which I see not teach you (God) me: if I have done iniquity, I will do no more" (Job 34:32). An appropriate definition of education.

Hygiene Preserves Health

Hygiene is not a word we hear often in the Covid-19 crisis. Authorities and the public look at measures as restrictive. Hygiene is preventive.

Hygiene is precautionary measures to avoid sickness and disease. Practical Bible wisdom is the precursor of preventive medicine. Here's a definition and its historical origin[1].

> **Hygiene**: The science of preventive medicine and the preservation of health. Also commonly used as a euphemism for cleanliness and proper sanitation.
>
> **Preventive medicine**: Medical practices designed to avert and avoid disease. For example, screening for hypertension and treating it before it causes disease is

1. https://www.medicinenet.com/script/main/art.asp?articlekey=7324

> good preventive medicine. Preventive medicine takes a proactive approach to patient care.

I'll ask you for a critical analysis of the example of screening for hypertension. Is it really preventive medicine? Not exactly, it's checking to see if you're sick or not. Don't get me wrong, it's a good practice, but not hygiene which is PRO-active; taking action before a problem arises. Preemptive is foreseeing the eventual problem of hypertension and adopting measures well ahead of an outbreak.

Read the history of hygiene[2].

> The word hygiene comes from Hygeia, the Greek goddess of health, who was the daughter of Aesculapius, the god of medicine. Since the arrival of the Industrial Revolution (c.1750-1850) and the discovery of the germ theory of disease in the second half of the nineteenth century, hygiene and sanitation have been at the forefront of the struggle against illness and disease.

The *invention* of hygiene is often attributed to Ignace Semmelweis[3] around 1850. He related germ-control to hand-washing to avoid

2. https://www.historylearningsite.co.uk/a-history-of-medicine/history-hygiene-timeline/
3. https://theconversation.com/ignaz-semmelweis-the-doctor-who-discovered-the-disease-fighting-power-of-hand-washing-in-1847-135528#_853ae90f0351324bd73ea615e6487517__4c761f170e016836ff84498202b99827__853ae90f0351324bd73ea615e6487517_text_43ec3e5dee6e706af7766fffea512721_In_0bcef9c45bd8a48eda1b26eb0c61c869_20fact_0bcef9c45bd8a48eda1b26eb0c61c869_2C_0bcef9c45bd8a48eda1b26eb0c61c869_20it_0bcef9c45bd8a48eda1b26eb0c61c869_20was_0bcef9c45bd8a48eda1b26eb0c61c869_2019th_c0cb5f0fcf239ab3d9c1fcd31fff1efc_prevent_0bcef9c45bd8a48eda1b26eb0c61c869_20the_0bcef9c45bd8a48eda1b26eb0c61c869_20spread_0bcef9c45bd8a48eda1b26eb0c61c869_20of_0bcef9c45bd8a48eda1b26eb0c61c869_20germs.

transmitting disease; there's a brief history of hygiene and the first reference is the Old Testament.

> The history of hand-washing extends back to ancient times when it was largely a faith-based practice. The Old Testament, the Talmud, and the Quran all mention hand-washing in the context of ritual cleanliness.

The Pentateuch, or five books of Moses, predate the Talmud and Quran by about 2000 years. They are not in the same league! I find the description of hand-washing extremely important, a faith-based practice. Maybe the author is referring to a religious practice, also needing spiritual faith.

Faith because it purportedly came from a supernatural power named God or Yahveh, transmitted by Moses. Many people question (lack of faith) God, Moses, and the veracity of the Old Testament. The Bible doesn't talk about germs or bacteria per se. That's medical jargon, interesting to know, but the essential is to perform practices to block pathogens from you.

> The primary work for hygiene and preventive medicine is still the Bible.

It's written in layperson's language for every single human being on this planet, at all times, but you had to take it on faith. Today, with modern technology and research, we understand health instructions in the Old Testament are based on verifiable scientific evidence. Covid-19[4] could've been avoided or drastically reduced in proportions had we respected Bible recommendations. It still can.

The Explanation devoted extensive space to the state of our planet's physical[5] and mental health[6]. They are two of the major battles we

4. https://theexplanation.com/covid-19-and-bible-quarantine-practical-advice/

fight, maybe even more so in the supposedly developed countries. We're long on sugar, salt, and supplements and short on exercise and wholesome nourishing food.

Practical Bible wisdom in the 21st century for hygiene, preventive medicine, and health reveals some advice we sorely need. We limit hygiene to body cleanliness, but it is much more. The header image alludes to additional preventive measures included in health; mental hygiene, emotional hygiene, and spiritual hygiene. The whole person or soul, from a Biblical perspective.

Full Health

The Hebrew word *shalom* is probably the best-known greeting. Lesser known is the more complete meaning it embodies. Full health; body, mental, emotional, spiritual. In this verse, Jacob invites Joseph to inquire about his brothers' *well-being,* their *state of health.*

> **Genesis 37:14**
>
> And he (Jacob) said to him (Joseph), Go, I pray you, see whether it *be well* (H7965) with your brethren, and well with the flocks; and bring me word again...

Here's the Biblical Hebrew meaning.

> **H7965**
>
> שָׁלוֹם shâlôwm shaw-lome'; or שָׁלֹם; from H7999 (שָׁלַם); safe, i.e. (figuratively) well, happy, friendly; also (abstractly) welfare, i.e. health, prosperity, peace:

5. https://theexplanation.com/a-healthy-body-is-the-quest-of-all-humans-how-are-we-doing/
6. https://theexplanation.com/mental-health-you-will-be-surprised-to-know-what-the-state-of-the-world-is/

> KJV - × do, familiar, × fare, favour, + friend, × great, (good) health, ([idiom] perfect, such as be at) peace(-able, -ably), prosper(-ity, -ous), rest, safe(-ty), salute, welfare, ([idiom] all is, be) well, × wholly.

Note the translations of shalom, *health* and *wholly*. We know this term means *peace*. The concept encompasses everything associated with an individual. Today's modern Hebrew greeting is: How are you? Ma shlomcha? מה שלומך. You see the three identical root letters (the sixth Key to master Biblical Hebrew[7]) of H7965 שלם (shin, lamed, mem (written differently when it's the last letter of a word)).

"How are you?" is a global question enquiring about the health of an individual's body, mind, emotions, and spirit.

Health worldwide

God's nation was to serve as an example. He is not only interested in their preventive hygiene but all nations.

> **Psalm 67:2**
>
> That your (God) way may be known on earth, your saving health among all nations.
>
> **3 John 1:2**
>
> Beloved, I wish above all things that you may prosper and be in health, even as your soul prospers.

God's desire for all people to be healthy is not simply a wand He waves. It's a two-way street. God doesn't clean our teeth and cut our

7. https://theexplanation.com/key-6-biblical-hebrew-word-roots-unlock-bible-meaning/

hair! We have to watch the sugary and salty diet, use a toothbrush, and go to a barber. Hygiene is part of serving God. He gives us directives but we have a vital part to play in hygiene.

Proverbs 3:6-8

6 In all your ways acknowledge him, and he shall direct your paths.

7 Be not wise in your own eyes: fear the LORD, and depart from evil.

8 It shall be health to your navel, and marrow to your bones.

The wisdom of Proverbs[8] is the application of God's ways for everyone. We're all equal human beings with bodies having the same biological processes worldwide. When we all do our part, we all benefit from good general health, no matter who you are or where you are.

Physical Health

The intention in this chapter is not to give scientific evidence or justifications for God's instruction; it points to God's wisdom about hygiene. Remember, belief involves faith, although nowadays, science backs up this instruction, even if it doesn't refer to Bible teaching.

Leviticus 11:27-28

27 And whatsoever goes upon his paws, among all manner of beasts that go on all four, those are unclean to

8. https://theexplanation.com/rules-for-life-wisdom-for-living-abundantly-in-the-world/

you: whoso touches their carcase shall be unclean until the even.

28 And he that bears the carcase of them shall wash his clothes, and be unclean until the even: they are unclean to you.

Don't just look at this as some antiquated ceremonial parade. This is practical hygiene for everyone in the nation and by extension all humans. Today we recognize how well-founded this instruction is. We know certain animals, dead bodies, and contaminated water transmit infections. This is fundamental wisdom, revealed 3000 years ago. Covid-19, animal and human conditions are a reminder of failed hygiene. This image does not relate to Covid, but it illustrates the lack of hygiene.

A chicken vendor sleeps on top of chicken cages at the Hau Wong road wet market in Kowloon City, China, in 2004. Dickson Lee/South China Morning Post/Getty

Here's a verse that throws a curveball at physical exercise. It recognizes it isn't the ultimate life now, but has some profit.

> **1 Timothy 4:8**
>
> For bodily exercise profits little: but godliness is profitable to all things, having promise of the life that now is, and of that which is to come.

In France, we have the hashtag #bougermanger. It means *move-eat*, and encourages people not to lead a sedentary life of eating, but to add some exercise. We're seeing the results of not enough *bouger* in the form of obesity. Here's a World Bank document regarding the worldwide overweight plague.

> Obesity has emerged as a global challenge[9], affecting developed and developing countries alike. Globally, overweight and obesity cost an estimated US$2 trillion per year, and 68 percent of all deaths are caused by noncommunicable diseases (NCDs), of which three of the four most common are diet related (namely cardiovascular diseases, cancers, and diabetes). Moreover, two-thirds of deaths from NCDs take place in developing countries, where also two-thirds of overweight or obese people live, casting obesity no longer as only a developed country challenge.

The anti-hygiene practices of over-eating and lack of exercise cause health complications. We also have the opposite, too much sport; 100 thousand seat sports stadiums[10] where professionals fight to win

---

9. http://documents1.worldbank.org/curated/en/221014994372768773/pdf/117200-REVISED-WP-Obesity-Overview-Web-PUBLIC-002.pdf

10. https://www.travelandsports.com.au/news/biggest-stadiums-in-the-world

like modern gladiators. These athletes torture their anatomy to reach and stay number one. The violence to their bodies often hampers them for the rest of their lives. Extremes are not healthy hygiene.

Sexual diseases

Much is debated, disputed, accepted, and prohibited in this area. This chapter is not an expose on what the Bible permits or forbids; we're discussing hygiene and health. For sex, the best hygienic and healthy practices are in a long-term faithful marriage relationship. This is the couple's union established by God and the one into which children can be born and nurtured.

All other sexual relationships open the way to spreading venereal disease as this article states[11].

> Regardless of how a person is exposed to a sexually transmitted disease, once infected, he or she can spread the infection to other people through oral, vaginal, or anal sex, even if he or she has no symptoms.

It all starts with one sick person having multiple partners regardless of gender. Pre-marital sex can be a nightmare for women; unfortunately, they endure contraception and abortion. There's lots of talk about the physical effects in both these domains, but the mental turmoil before and after such acts can be devastating.

Such practices or malpractices affect all men and women worldwide equally. Read Exodus 20, 22, Leviticus 18, 20, and Deuteronomy 23, 27 for explicit instructions. Bible wisdom is ahead of its time, this is pro-active hygiene.

Dietary laws

11. https://www.nichd.nih.gov/health/topics/stds/conditioninfo/causes

Once again, the question comes up, are they valid for the New Testament era? That's the wrong question, we're talking about hygiene and health. God didn't give these laws to forbid people from eating something *good* for them. All animals do not have the same purpose; some are specifically designed as scavengers to clean up the environment. They eat dead mice and rats. The question is, has the human digestive process changed between the Old and New Testament eras?

Do we, in the 21st century, have the same human body as they did a few thousand years before Christ when these laws were given? The answer is yes. Read about the prevalence of digestive disorders here[12]. *The Explanation* is not saying if Bible dietary rules were followed, there wouldn't be any stomach issues.

What we are saying is many of the Old Testament dietary restrictions now have a proven scientific and biological basis. Doctors know these injunctions are beneficial to our general health. Here's a dissertation emphasizing the viewpoint the Old Testament measures are primarily preventive[13]. In other words, they are not restrictive, not designed to deprive you of something good for you; the goal is to keep you in optimal health.

God gave dietary wisdom right from the start for the welfare of all His Creation. "Every plant yielding seed that is on the surface of all the earth, and every tree which has fruit yielding seed" (Gen. 1:29).

Daniel, when taken into captivity, requested a vegetarian diet because he knew it was beneficial for him (Daniel 1:10-12). It

12. https://www.worldgastroenterology.org/UserFiles/file/wdhd-2008-map-of-digestive-disorders.pdf

13. https://www.andrews.edu/library/car/cardigital/Periodicals/AUSS/1983-3/1983-3-01.pdf

doesn't mean he abstained from meat; he took care of his health with preventive measures.

There's a lot of scoffing about clean and unclean meats; many think this is part of the Old Covenant. Not so, it goes back to at least the time of Noah and the flood in Genesis 7:2. Recall, he took seven pairs of clean animals and only 1 pair of unclean animals into the ark. Why? it doesn't say. He and his family, eight people, were in the ark for just over one year. They obviously ate during that time and offered a sacrifice when they left the ark; all with clean animals and birds. From Creation, God gives dietary laws for the benefit of proper human hygiene.

Clothing

Regarding physical health and clothing, the Bible refers to mixed fabrics (Deuteronomy 22:11). The reason for not associating different fibers is they have distinct qualities not combining adequately. A similar, more readily understandable example is not plowing with an ox and donkey yoked together (Deut. 22:10), an agricultural measure. Beyond the consideration God wants His people to be pure and appreciate quality, hygiene also comes into play. Let's *modernize* this injunction by mentioning synthetic fabrics, often derivatives of petroleum by-products.

Watch this video about the science of grounding[14]. Synthetic soles on our shoes isolate us from the negative ions in the ground, ions our body needs to balance internal electric pulses energizing our organs. The result is poor hygiene. We can equate this with the principle of Adam and Eve putting on fig leaves[15]; they applied a short-term solution detrimental to them. Insulating ourselves from the earth can

14. https://youtu.be/H2YIafrkQy8

15. https://theexplanation.com/fig-leaves-or-clothing-tinker-or-build-practical-bible-wisdom/

cause inflammation and other unsuspected ills. Again, the principles revealed by a short but powerful law of hygiene should encourage us to realize the validity of preventive measures expounded in the Old Testament.

Mental Health

Mental health is a worldwide predicament today[16]. One reason is mischief and incompetence surround us. Not knowingly or willingly, but people are at a loss for wise counsel nowadays. Preventive health includes mental hygiene. The Bible gives cutting-edge wisdom to encourage mental balance, especially in trying times. This first passage reveals how hope in God puts calmness on your face; sounds poetic, but it's very real.

When it involves health, it gets very personal. Who can we turn to when science and often medicine don't provide solutions? Hope in a Divine Source won't bring the immediate answer you want, but in God, there's His long-term plan, including you and all humankind. The outcome is extremely positive.

Psalm 42:11

Why are you cast down, O my soul? and why are you disquieted within me? hope you in God: for I shall yet praise him, who is the **health of my countenance**, and my God.

Proverbs 4:19-23

19 The LORD by wisdom has founded the earth; by understanding has he established the heavens.

16. https://theexplanation.com/mental-health-you-will-be-surprised-to-know-what-the-state-of-the-world-is/

20 By his knowledge the depths are broken up, and the clouds drop down the dew.

21 My son, let not them depart from your eyes: keep sound wisdom and discretion:

22 So shall they be **life to your soul, and grace to your neck**.

23 Then shall you walk in your way safely, and your foot shall not stumble.

Proverbs 12:17-18

17 He that speaks truth shows forth righteousness: but a false witness deceit.

18 There is that speaks like the piercings of a sword: but the **tongue of the wise is health**.

Proverbs 13:17

A wicked messenger falls into mischief: but a **faithful ambassador is health**.

Proverbs 16:22-25

22 **Understanding is a wellspring of life** to him that has it: but the instruction of fools is folly.

23 The heart of the wise teaches his mouth, and adds learning to his lips.

24 **Pleasant words** are as an honeycomb, sweet to the soul, and **health to the bones**.

Proverbs 17:22

> **A merry heart does good like a medicine**: but a broken spirit dries the bones.

Various passages give us clues and insight into shoring up our mental stamina. How to look beyond physical circumstances; instruction in the above verses is not pie-in-the-sky fantasy. Yes, they take faith, but think about it; preventive medicine takes faith. You believe doing something (exercise, healthy eating) will generate a benefit in the future. *Doing* builds faith, and when it involves hygiene, leads to health as the next principle displays.

Behavior and Health

Above, we saw our actions affect our health. This is physical and spiritual hygiene. If we guide our behavior through Biblical ethics, the result is *shalom*, worthwhile physical and spiritual health.

Exodus 15:26

> And said, If you will diligently hearken to the voice of the LORD your God, and will do that which is right in his sight, and will give ear to his commandments, and keep all his statutes, I will put none of these diseases upon you, which I have brought upon the Egyptians: for I am the LORD that heals you.

Exodus 23:25

> And you shall serve the LORD your God, and he shall bless your bread, and your water; and I will take sickness away from the midst of you.

Future Health

Some fundamental Biblical hygiene is sadly lacking nowadays. Medical technology is there but is not the complete solution. Health must also include the application of God's rules of hygiene. There is coming a time when the general population will revert to this key understanding.

Jeremiah 30:17

For I will restore health to you, and I will heal you of your wounds, says the LORD; because they called you an Outcast, saying, This is Zion, whom no man seeks after.

Jeremiah 33:6

Behold, I will bring it health and cure, and I will cure them, and will reveal to them the abundance of peace and truth.

Ezekiel 47:12

And by the river upon the bank thereof, on this side and on that side, shall grow all trees for meat, whose leaf shall not fade, neither shall the fruit thereof be consumed: it shall bring forth new fruit according to his months, because their waters they issued out of the sanctuary: and the fruit thereof shall be for meat, and the leaf thereof for medicine.

There will be healing coupled with hygiene to maintain good health. Practical Bible wisdom is not time-sensitive, nation-sensitive, culture-sensitive, testament or covenant-sensitive. God's hygiene laws are for all peoples, past, present, and future. They assure and maintain stable physical, mental, emotional, and spiritual health.

Covid-19 and Bible Quarantine–Practical Advice

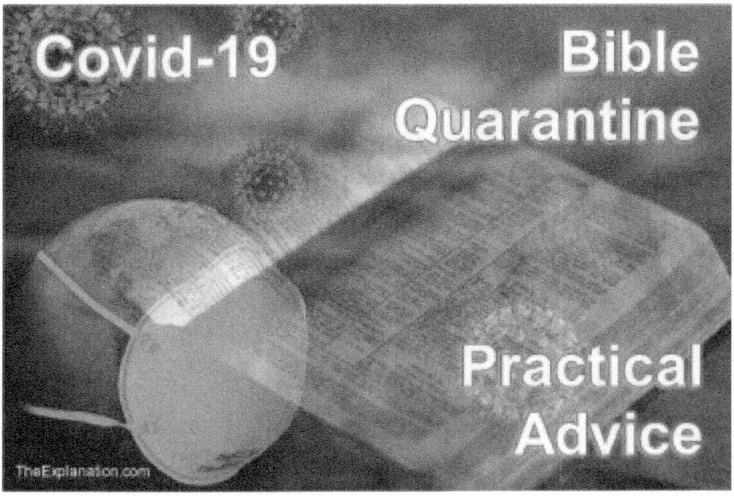

Covid-19 is a worldwide killer pandemic. The Bible is a worldwide instruction manual. Here's practical advice, revealed 3000 years ago.

Covid-19 and Bible quarantine. What a daunting subject. *The Explanation* hesitated to approach this subject because Covid-19 is a real vicious killer disease, if not a plague from God, as the Bible would refer to it. Since it's human-caused, what's the human remedy? Yes, there's the ultimate vaccination, but what about an intermediary solution? How can we stop, or at least slow down, the pandemic?

Covid-19 has reached such worldwide proportions and widespread impact; it is probably the biggest threat to humankind at the moment. Not only from a health point-of-view, but economically and socially, it has plunged many people into poverty and strife.

This is a very serious matter, you can't open up a publication, or look on social media, or listen to radio without someone offering advice about Covid-19. Be it scientific, medical, political, rumor, speculation, or grandmother's remedy. In the end, we have confusion with neither authoritative advice nor reliable solutions.

To prepare for this article, I searched on Google for *Covid-19 Bible* and *Covid-19 Bible quarantine*. Do that exercise for yourself. The results reflect the shallowness of religion and spiritual organizations to rise to the occasion and support people, even beyond their congregation. Although *The Explanation* does not put a stamp of approval on anything, that's not its role, I found one article with some sound advice[1]. Terris King, a pastor in Baltimore with many years of experience in the health field.

On the other hand, religion has received a lot of bad press because of blatant decisions made by their leaders regarding negligence of Covid-19. One major gathering in France[2] resulted in 2500 positive cases, 17 deaths and infection around the world, Burkina Faso, Corsica, Guyana, and Switzerland, the result of just one group.

The New York Times reported Covid-19 virus infiltration of services throughout the USA[3]. Hundreds of Covid-19 cases resulted from religious meetings respecting no rules.

---

1. https://www.statnews.com/2020/08/31/with-science-and-scripture-a-baltimore-pastor-is-fighting-covid-19-vaccine-skepticism/
2. https://www.reuters.com/article/us-health-coronavirus-france-church-spec-idUSKBN21H0Q2
3. https://www.nytimes.com/2020/07/08/us/coronavirus-churches-outbreaks.html

> The virus has infiltrated Sunday sermons, meetings of ministers and Christian youth camps in Colorado and Missouri. It has struck churches that reopened cautiously with face masks and social distancing in the pews, as well as some that defied lockdowns and refused to heed new limits on numbers of worshipers.
>
> Pastors and their families have tested positive, as have church ushers, front-door greeters and hundreds of churchgoers. In Texas, about 50 people contracted the virus after a pastor told congregants they could once again hug one another. In Florida, a teenage girl died last month after attending a youth party at her church.

Here's a report about how an ultra-orthodox religious community in Jerusalem[4] is handling, or rather, mishandling Covid-19.

> More than a way of life, prayer and study are the means for protecting life itself. According to Jewish sages, "One who engages in Torah study also protects the entire world." Indeed, "without Torah the world falls."
>
> The importance of engaging with the Torah explains why one prominent rabbi in Israel insisted even in March that "canceling Torah study is more dangerous than the coronavirus."
>
> Ultimately, the Israeli government intervened to enforce its coronavirus restrictions. On March 22, police were sent into Me'a She'arim, a Haredi neighborhood in

4. https://theconversation.com/jewish-history-explains-why-some-ultra-orthodox-communities-defy-coronavirus-restrictions-135292

> Jerusalem, to end public gatherings, close synagogues and shutter schools.
>
> They were met with curses, slurs and thrown stones. Some Haredim even called the Israeli police "Nazis."

With all due respect, one point I don't understand is the ultra-orthodox are very attached to the 613 mitzvot (commandments) in the Torah, the Law of Moses, the first five books of the Bible. These laws include Leviticus 13, which recommends, if not, commands distancing or isolation, applicable to Covid-19.

Whichever way you slice it regarding contagion, mixing healthy and unhealthy is harmful.

The Principle of Separation

To understand the Bible's approach to quarantine, health safety, and hence how to deal with epidemics and Covid-19, we must grasp a fundamental principle underlying God's entire approach to human beings. This might sound drastic, but there's no *middle ground*. It's yes or no, do or don't, in or out, up or down.

In the 21st century, when the keyword is *compromise*, God's outlook appears fundamentalist or extremist. You can't help that feeling, you can only explain why God is not adept at straddling the fence. Please, please keep in mind *The Explanation* is discussing this *no middle ground* concerning quarantine and Covid-19. I don't want to expand this subject but you know God also says, "love your enemy." Now, that's opposition and God favors it. Understand The Old and New Testament concepts, they are not contradictory but complementary; another subject.

Back to Covid-19 quarantine and the basic principle of separating two entities, not mixing them. God addresses this vital key on the first day of Creation in Genesis 1. Understand the figurative meaning of night and day[5] and the gigantic gulf between them. Read this article[6] from the book *Origin of the Universe*. You know the term *it was good*, pronounced by God at the end of each day of Creation, including the first day when He separated *light* from *darkness*. We could say it was in contrast to another statement, *it was bad,* before God's creative intervention.

God cuts through the Gordian Knot and calls a spade a spade.

The meaning of *quarantine*

The definition of quarantine comes from forty days[7] and dates back to the mid-14th century Bubonic plague in Europe. States established a cordon sanitaire, a restricted sanitary area, to restrain the movement of people. The area of Dubrovnik in Croatia was the first to do this on an island for 30 days. Later the Venetians extended it to 40 days because, for that plague, from infection to death was 37 days. They isolated ships, arriving from around the world, particularly China, for 40 (*quarante*) days, which gave rise to *quarantine*.

The scientific and medical concept of isolating people with infectious diseases is a common, if not a widespread phenomenon. The Bible story of Lazarus, covered with sores (Luke 16:20) lends his name to Lazarettos, [8]which were houses, ships, or islands reserved

5. https://theexplanation.com/it-was-good-is-a-translation-fiasco-of-gods-actual-creation-statement/

6. https://theexplanation.com/it-was-good-is-a-translation-fiasco-of-gods-actual-creation-statement/

7. https://en.wikipedia.org/wiki/Quarantine

for incurably sick people. One such is Lazaretto island near Corfu, Greece. In the 16th century, it had a monastery taking care of the lepers confined there. These colonies were not just people lying around on beds; some had communities with their own currency for internal commerce, something like a closed village. Among the earliest records of the establishment of a hospital for lepers is the Order of Saint Lazarus[9] of Jerusalem, founded by Catholic crusaders around 1119.

Isolation and seclusion are not recent phenomena. Probably the oldest document to reveal this practice is the Bible. Leviticus 13 details what to do in case of contagion. This is a very exhaustive, descriptive account.

> **Leviticus 13** the whole chapter.
>
> 45 And the leper in whom the plague is, his clothes shall be rent, and his head bare, and he shall put a covering upon his upper lip, and shall cry, Unclean, unclean.
>
> 46 All the days wherein the plague shall be in him he shall be defiled; he is unclean: he shall **dwell alone; without the camp shall his habitation be**.
>
> 47 The garment also that the plague of leprosy is in, whether it be a woollen garment, or a linen garment;

Read the entire chapter at UnlockBibleMeaning.com[10]. The Priests, descendants of the first Priest, Aaron, had the responsibility to oversee the proper functioning of this confinement. They had scientific and medical know-how, sufficient to identify boils, as well

---

8. https://en.wikipedia.org/wiki/Lazaretto

9. https://en.wikipedia.org/wiki/Order_of_Saint_Lazarus

10. https://unlockbiblemeaning.com

as decisional discretion to isolate people and houses; even order the destruction of a dwelling based on visible evidence (Lev. 14).

The events of the book of Leviticus take place in the Sinai desert where the Israelites camped for 40 years. Hence the reference to INside and OUTside the camp. Two distinct locations. Contagious people had to go OUT of the normal area into a specially reserved place for the contagious period of the disease. They were not outcasts left in a pitiful state with no sustenance. This place *outside* the camp was equipped and livable. Not necessarily 5-star, as we'd say today, but sufficiently equipped and supplied to continue an appropriate existence. There would've been all the facilities to take care of the sick, in whatever state they were.

Do a study at UnlockBibleMeaning.com[11] on the phrase *without the camp*. You'll also find this term in the New Testament, in Hebrews 11, regarding an aspect of Christ's ultimate sacrifice.

Contagious people are not necessarily bedridden. They can be just as active as any healthy individual. In which case, they take part in the life and animation of their camp. This includes all the trades, professions, and services needed for the village to function. These people were not lazy lie around worthless individuals. According to their health, they could contribute their skills and know-how to the contagious community. They took part diligently until the Priest, upon examination, found they were no longer contagious, in which case, they went back IN the camp to continue their regular functions.

God cares for the healthy and the sick.

When the Israelites crossed the Jordan and settled in the land now called Israel, there was sickness and other reasons to separate certain

11. https://unlockbiblemeaning.com

people from the main dwelling centers. This teaching included the construction and reservation of three cities set apart to receive special justice cases.

The point is, criminals live *separated* from the general population. Removal from normal citizenship and life, *putting out of the camp*, took place promptly after an infraction. There are practical ways of taking care of wrong-doers. These three cities were within the boundaries of the country, but *separate* in their administration and contact with the rest of society. This is another type of quarantine, not for health.

Swift Separation

Quarantine is only efficient if acted on *swiftly*; nip the problem in the bud. This is where communication from the street level, so to speak, must filter its way to top government officials who have both the know-how to evaluate the situation and the authority to make rapid decisions to solve national problems. Only a global system brings results.

Read this article about Duke University in the USA. It understands everyone, from top to bottom and bottom to top, must get involved. Testing, tracing, quarantine: How Duke will fight the coronavirus on campus this fall[12].

> From daily symptom monitoring to isolation procedures, Duke is implementing testing, tracing and quarantining to combat the spread of the coronavirus on campus this fall.

12. https://www.dukechronicle.com/article/2020/07/duke-university-testing-tracing-quarantine-fight-coronavirus-campus-fall

> All students living in the Durham area and faculty and staff (Sam: everyone) who regularly visit campus will also be required to complete a daily symptom-monitoring survey on an app.
>
> Michael Schoenfeld, vice president for public affairs and government relations, wrote that students will receive a daily text message at noon if they have not yet submitted the survey and will then have two hours to complete it before their DukeCard access is turned off (Sam: it's *on* or *off*, no middle-ground). Once the survey is completed, their DukeCard will automatically turn back on or trigger clinical outreach depending on their survey answers.

Schoenfeld wrote, in a message to The Chronicle, students who live in Duke housing and need to be quarantined will be transported and housed in East House and Jarvis residence halls on East Campus.

The last paragraph reveals Duke has allocated two *separate* dorms to quarantine positively tested students. Total isolation, no ifs, buts, or maybes. They remain in this confined space, where they continue their studies and follow all lectures remotely. Food and medical care, along with all other amenities, take place within those confines.

- Competent management and organization.
- Swift massive testing and results.
- Swift separation into adequately prepared quarters.
- Swift quarantine under proper circumstances and supervision.

These are the practical ways to contain the Covid-19 pandemic.

This takes organization from top-level to ground-level. It is difficult, especially if you don't have the proper organizational skills and authority in place and the ability to enforce the rules. But, as they say, that's the cost of doing business.

You're in or you're out

In the study of Genesis 3, in *Agony of Humankind*[13], I pointed out how God put the man and woman out of the Garden of Eden. Sounds very negative, but God is planning long-term, not short-term, and this expulsion, under the right circumstances, is necessary. It's a positive step to help them reclaim their spiritual health.

> **Genesis 3:24**
>
> So he drove out the man; and he placed at the east of the garden of Eden Cherubims, and a flaming sword which turned every way, to keep the way of the tree of life.

Let's look at the deeper meaning of the Biblical Hebrew for *drove out.*

> **H1644**
>
> גָּרַשׁ gârash gaw-rash'; a primitive root; to *drive out* (H1644) from a possession; especially to expatriate or divorce:
>
> KJV - cast up (out), divorced (woman), drive away (forth, out), expel, × surely put away, trouble, thrust out.

Adam and Eve became spiritually unhealthy; their behavior altered their minds[14]. They were no longer in harmony with the Garden's

13. *https://theexplanation.com/read-all-the-content-of-agony-of-humankind-online/*

14. https://theexplanation.com/get-out-of-my-garden-god-told-adam-and-eve-why/

proper spiritual attitude characterizing God and His Garden. He expelled them, cast them out; you might think it's severe coming from God, but the Biblical Hebrew is unequivocal. If you're not in conformity with the ethics, environment, behavior, health of a particular place, you don't belong there. God quarantined, so-to-speak, Adam and Eve to Eden, still a beautiful location; He continued to care for them, but they were separated from the Garden.

Later we find the same expulsion of Cain from Eden. "Behold, you (God) have *driven* me (Cain) *out* (H1944) this day from the face of the earth" (Genesis 4:14).

Be it physical or spiritual, the result is the same; a separation takes place. We find exactly the same principle in the New Testament, "But they that are without God judges. Therefore put away from among yourselves that wicked person" (1 Corinthians 5:13).

God put out Adam, Eve, and Cain; identical for the *wicked person* in the Corinthian church. But the goal is always to bring people back into the fold, INto the camp. Maybe you have never thought or received instruction about it, but Adam, Eve, and Cain are not on the OUTside forever. If God put them out *definitively* for eating one fruit from the forbidden tree then, where's His mercy. The Bible story shows they will come out of spiritual quarantine just like billions of others. The point here is not spiritual but physical health, Covid-19 quarantine.

The goal is to find who is contagious and to isolate and treat them as quickly as possible. Once the period finished, remove them from quarantine as the Priests did in Leviticus 13. They see evidence for putting people in quarantine, just as they see evidence for removing those same people from quarantine and re-immersing them in full life with their family and loved ones.

Practicality of the Bible for the 21st century

We recognize the sensibility of this delicate but oh so important timely and global subject. Not only does the Bible address this issue, but it is the first book to do so. There have been leper colonies historically, but it is not until the 14th century, over 2000 years since Leviticus was written, that we see quarantine mentioned in literature.

In Leviticus, you have a leader governing a full-fledged nation. There is a group of designated and trained leaders who oversee this nation and receive down-to-earth guidelines to follow and apply in the specific case of contagious diseases. This is just one aspect of the *Health Ministry* (if I may call it such to help you realize how up-to-date this instruction is) for taking care of this nation.

It's not just a description of quarantine. Leviticus and elsewhere are all about a governmental system with procedures to follow. Old Testament Israel was a nation of hundreds of thousands of people, men, women, and children. They were just like all other nations, hard-headed, stiff-necked, and difficult to govern. Their advantage was they received all the practical laws and regulations to run the nation efficiently and successfully.

One of the most important and overlooked passages of scripture is about national government.

Deuteronomy 4:4-8

4 But you that did cleave to the LORD your God are alive every one of you this day (Sam: Just before entering the Promised Land).

> 5 Behold, I (Moses) have taught you statutes and judgments, even as the LORD my God commanded me, that you should do so in the land where you go to possess it.
>
> 6 Keep therefore and do them; for this is your wisdom and your understanding in the sight of the nations, which shall hear all these statutes, and say, Surely this great nation is a wise and understanding people.
>
> 7 For what nation is there so great, who has God so near to them, as the LORD our God is in all things that we call upon him for?
>
> 8 And what nation is there so great, that has statutes and judgments so righteous as all this law, which I set before you this day?

This is the *common sense* of scripture. Read those verses again. God, through Moses, about 3,500 years ago, gave His nation laws valid for ALL nations at ALL times. God never abandoned His people, ALL the people in the world. It is the people worldwide who abandoned God. He clothed Adam and Eve[15], gave Moses all the procedures for running a nation, gave Solomon Proverbs so all people know how to run their lives[16]. Yes, there's certain adaptability over time, but ALL the practical basics are there. Quarantine in the Covid-19 crisis is just one of them. These Bible laws are *valid* in today's society.

During the Covid-19 crisis, more and more people are turning to the Bible[17] for answers. One goal of *The Explanation* is to show you

15. https://theexplanation.com/critical-thinking-antidote-to-the-agony-of-humankind/

16. https://theexplanation.com/rules-for-life-wisdom-for-living-abundantly-in-the-world/

17. https://medium.com/what-if-ventures/covid-19-is-driving-more-americans-to-the-bible-than-therapy-109aef31fc91

the Bible is relevant for the 21st century. It's a manual with practical solutions to current problems. The answers are present; it reveals how to combat Covid-19; we need to learn how to dig out the gems of wisdom.

Ecology: Home, Country, Land Ethics

The ecology equation is simple. Air, water, and land must be sustainable and accessible to provide sufficient resources for all living beings.

Ecology is the right balance between the environment and living beings. People and fauna live and survive off the land, air, and water; there must be sufficient quantity and quality. What is the most balanced way to maintain this equilibrium?

The word from which we derive *ecology* comes from the Greek *oikos*, meaning *household, home*, or *place to live*. Ecology[1] is the relationship between living organisms and their environment, meaning other organisms and their physical surroundings.

There are a couple of conclusions from this.

1. https://www.britannica.com/science/ecology

1. Physical health is relative to the quality of air, water, and land.
2. Mental health depends on:
    a. Their physical health.
    b. Their self-realization and satisfaction.
    c. Their social interactions.

When we analyze today's industrial society, do we have a sustained healthy environment? Do we have healthy, self-realized, socially interactive people?

The quick answer might be *yes*, outwardly, but *not* inwardly regarding people, and *not* regarding the environment. Why yes outwardly? Some positive scientists argue life is longer, healthier, more prosperous, with more opportunities than at any other time in history. And there is some substance to this affirmation.

Others would argue the biggest challenge facing humankind is depression[2], a state of mind, the result of the physical (air, water, land) and social (people's relationships) being out of alignment. Whether you look at the present status as a glass half full or half empty, I think we'd all agree there is room for improvement and some basic elements need serious thought and action.

A people-oriented, sustainable environment is possible

Here's *The Explanation's* approach we've discussed at length elsewhere. God is Creator[3], the Bible is His Word[4]; He created the *physical* (air, water, land) and the *human* (body and mind). He gave goals and instruction[5]: Genesis rulership and relationships. He lays

2. https://theexplanation.com/mental-health-you-will-be-surprised-to-know-what-the-state-of-the-world-is/

3. https://theexplanation.com/i-am-gods-name-or-deep-human-spirituality-which/

4. https://theexplanation.com/foolishness-gods-word-true-theology/

out the plans for individual well-being and collective well-being. Since He's the God of ALL humankind, He did so for the vast majority who do not believe in Him and the minority of believers. God provides the physical needs and the know-how instructions for ALL His Creation.

This chapter is practical Bible advice curated from examples and instructions in the Bible. It also includes cases of people who are applying Biblical principles without realizing their origin; trial and error can lead to the discovery of God's Old Testament way of life.

Immediately at Creation, the Bible reveals ecology. Each day adds to the environment so Earth becomes a home, an *oikos*, for humankind. The third day of Creation[6] specifically refers to the value of land covered with grass and trees, meadows, and forests.

Genesis 1:10-13

10 And God called the dry land Earth; and the gathering together of the waters called he Seas: and God saw that it was good.

11 And God said, Let the earth bring forth grass, the herb yielding seed, and the fruit tree yielding fruit after his kind, whose seed is in itself, upon the earth: and it was so.

12 And the earth brought forth grass, and herb yielding seed after his kind, and the tree yielding fruit, whose seed was in itself, after his kind: and God saw that it was good.

5. https://theexplanation.com/genesis-1-reveals-basics-social-relations-rulership/

6. https://theexplanation.com/dry-land-seas-and-flora-why-this-combination-on-day-3-of-creation/

Seas, lakes, land, and flora set in motion the air (oxygen), the water (drink, wash), and land (food) systems. The home has pure air, clean water, and fertile land. Humankind breathes, drinks, and feeds itself. This combination inaugurates the recycling of air, the water cycle, and the regeneration of ground fertility. The next day (four) God establishes the four seasons; for thousands of years, the system worked automatically.

Rain on time, harvests, fruit

The Garden of Eden with the outflowing river assured a source of life-giving water to everything bordering it. It's gone for now, although there are prophecies of its return with healing trees on its banks (Ezek. 34). Later on, God gave rain (Genesis 2:5) to all nations, and through Israel made a promise which is subject to a specific condition.

> **Leviticus 26:3-5**
>
> 3 If you walk in my statutes, and keep my commandments, and do them;
>
> 4 Then I will give you rain in due season, and the land shall yield her increase, and the trees of the field shall yield their fruit.
>
> 5 And your threshing shall reach to the vintage, and the vintage shall reach to the sowing time: and you shall eat your bread to the full, and dwell in your land safely.

The Explanation does not wield God's Word and prophecy as a stick to hit people over the head. There is the ecology of rain, seasons, land, harvests, trees, fruit, and the threshing of grain-yielding bread. Safety and prosperity reign, but this is a conditional promise according to verse 3. These statutes are the ethics God gave His nation, and through it, to *all* nations[7] (Deuteronomy 4) around the world.

Ecology lasts so long as we do our part. When we waver and fall, we can no longer count on all the circumstances and benefits necessary for balanced sustainability. We're living in unprecedented times; think about cause and effect. We've been aware of global warming for about 100 years[8]; it's been headline news for only 3 decades. What's going on?

Biodiversity

The *days* (events) of Creation are a series of divine imperatives empowering Earth with vitality.

And God said, "Let there be light" (Gen. 1:2-3). Humankind has continually tried to force food growth, to get higher yields or faster production. We've tried continuous light with mixed results[9]. Yes, you can increase certain aspects of nature, but they tend to boomerang with some letdown in reproduction, health, vitality, or quality.

God said, "Let the earth bring forth grass, the herb yielding seed, and the fruit tree yielding fruit after his kind, whose seed is in itself... And God created great whales, and *every* living creature that moves, which the waters brought forth abundantly, after their kind, and every winged fowl after his kind: and God saw that it was good" (Gen. 1:11, 21).

7. https://theexplanation.com/how-to-govern-a-country-responsibly-practical-bible-advice/

8. https://www.nationalgeographic.com/magazine/2018/07/embark-essay-climate-change-pollution-revkin/

9. https://link.springer.com/article/10.1134/S1021443715030176

We might read *every* in this context with quantity in mind. I suggest we also think of it in terms of biodiversity. Here's a quote from The Guardian revealing the value of biodiversity[10]. At the same time, it takes an audit affirming the sixth mass extinction is underway.

> Others appear bizarre—tropical tortoises and spider monkeys seemingly have little to do with maintaining a stable climate. But the dense, hardwood trees that are most effective in removing carbon dioxide from the atmosphere rely on their seeds being dispersed by these large fruit-eaters.
>
> When scientists explore each ecosystem, they find countless such interactions, all honed by millions of years of evolution. If undamaged, this produces a finely balanced, healthy system which contributes to a healthy sustainable planet.

Here's the biodiversity in the word *every* at Creation.

> **Genesis 1:28-31**
>
> 28 And God blessed them (Adam and Eve), and God said to them, Be fruitful, and multiply, and replenish the earth, and subdue it: and have dominion over the fish of the sea, and over the fowl of the air, and over *every* living thing that moves upon the earth.
>
> 29 And God said, Behold, I have given you *every* herb bearing seed, which is upon the face of all the earth, and *every* tree, in the which is the fruit of a tree yielding seed; to you it shall be for meat.

10. https://www.theguardian.com/news/2018/mar/12/what-is-biodiversity-and-why-does-it-matter-to-us

30 And to *every* beast of the earth, and to *every* fowl of the air, and to *every* thing that creeps upon the earth, wherein there is life, I have given *every* green herb for meat: and it was so.

31 And God saw *every* thing that he had made, and, behold, it was very good. And the evening and the morning were the sixth day.

Some readers might want to argue over the reference to *evolution* in The Guardian article compared to *Creation* in the Bible. That's another subject relating directly to belief or non-belief in a powerful God. Right now, such a debate is *not* the point. The issue is *all* parties agree with the need for biodiversity and ecology. Bible wisdom promotes both necessities for the sustainability of Earth's ecosystems and it gives all humanity dominion in this field.

Farming, Meadows, Feasts, Seasons

Some might look down on agriculture, and farming as manual compared to financial and technical opportunities. Our 21st century is further advanced than 2000 years B.C., but you can't eat money and computers. Many of God's servants were directly involved in agricultural, not to say ecological activities. The following scenario includes the awareness of ecology and a practical solution to maintain sustainability.

Genesis 13:2-9

2 And Abram was very rich in cattle, in silver, and in gold.

3 And he went on his journeys from the south even to Bethel, to the place where his tent had been at the beginning, between Bethel and Hai;

> 5 And Lot also, which went with Abram, had flocks, and herds, and tents.
>
> 6 And the land was not able to bear them, that they might dwell together: for their substance was great, so that they could not dwell together.
>
> 9 Is not the whole land before you? separate yourself, I pray you, from me: if you will take the left hand, then I will go to the right; or if you depart to the right hand, then I will go to the left.
>
> 10 And Lot lifted up his eyes, and beheld all the plain of Jordan, that it was well watered every where, before the LORD destroyed Sodom and Gomorrah, even as the garden of the LORD, like the land of Egypt, as you come to Zoar.
>
> 11 Then Lot chose him all the plain of Jordan; and Lot journeyed east: and they separated themselves the one from the other.

Nobody got the short end of the stick. The fertility and availability of land existed in both places. Over-grazing is not ecological. The policy was spread out, use the available resources, don't cram together. Ecology means home, everybody should have space, some land, and eventually the ability to cultivate. I'm not suggesting we all become farmers, but the Bible emphasizes an agrarian society clarified in the next chapter. We'll discuss the sabbatical resting of the land, another key ecological practice we'd do well to heed in the 21st century.

One of the well-known terms appearing about 20 times in the Bible is *a land of milk and honey*. For this to be the case, definite conditions need to be met, and they must include ecology.

Exodus 3:8

> And I am come down to deliver them out of the hand of the Egyptians, and to bring them up out of that land to a good land and a large, to a land flowing with milk and honey;

The tribes of Israel having spent forty years in the desert had a total change of scenery. A land of milk means grazing cows, fertile pastures, healthy bulls. A land of honey relays images of meadows and wildflowers; today we're aware of the dying-off of bees. As usual, there's debate about why, whatever the cause, there's upset ecology with the land, air, and water. All those elements were in coordination in Canaan for it to be a land of milk and honey.

Trees play a vital role in ecology by drawing rain clouds, birds, and other fauna, as windbreaks, and for regenerating the soil. There's an essential place for them.

Psalm 148:9-10

> 3 Praise you him (God), sun and moon: praise him, all you stars of light.
>
> 9 Mountains, and all hills; fruitful trees, and all cedars:
>
> 10 Beasts, and all cattle; creeping things, and flying fowl:

Trees, cedars, and other biodiverse essences are marvels of nature we are to preserve and manage wisely. Throughout the Bible, we find verses with ecological overtones.

Deuteronomy 20:19

> 19 When you shall besiege a city a long time, in making war against it to take it, you shall not destroy the trees thereof by forcing an axe against them: for you may eat of them, and you shall not cut them down (for the tree of the field is man's life) to employ them in the siege:
>
> 20 Only the trees which you know that they be not trees for meat, you shall destroy and cut them down; and you shall build bulwarks against the city that makes war with you, until it be subdued.

No cutting down fruit trees, with the others, if in doubt, abstain. Obviously, better to avoid war and sieges, this is another subject.

Another ecological principle regards polluted wells that God's priests could cure. This is not practical advice today, but under the right circumstances, it could happen.

Humans plague ecology

Here is a 26-minute video by Daniel Christian Wahl[11] who catalyzes transformative innovation, cultural co-creation, whole systems design, and bioregional regeneration. The first few minutes are vital viewing during which he clearly states how unacceptable the present situation is.

He gives a lot of excellent resources on regeneration of ecology, how to restore sustainability. There are several organizations and many projects worldwide, but it may be too little, too late.

At the conclusion, he quotes Joanna Macy, "The key thing we need to change starts in the human heart." She is not the only one who

11. http://www.facebook.com/100014615418677/videos/486122621884914/

knows the root of this problem, in fact, most problems, the *human heart*. That is a euphemism; it refers to the human mind, the seat of our emotions, motivations, imaginations, thinking, and reasoning.

The Explanation asserts the key to understanding humankind is the mind[12]. All the regenerative solutions revolve around projects to plant trees, dig wells, permaculture, etc. Those are solutions, but very local answers to a global problem that is out of hand. We're putting band-aids on a patient with a terminal disease; not realizing it's going to take a massive change of heart.

The role of *The Explanation* is to show how this change of heart is going to occur.

Solutions on the human level

Books have and are being written on this subject. So it would be silly to try to cover all bases here. There's just one issue I'd like to develop, urbanization. The development of megacities to the detriment of countryside and towns. The 21st century industry, technology, communication ages have led to globalization. This has pulled people out of the countryside into mega-centers of 10+ million population specialized megalopolises. Concentration and desertification. Both metropolises and towns have emerged impoverished financially, socially, and otherwise. Rubbish and fumes accumulate in a cluster while *all* the foodstuff has to be shipped in to feed this concentration. Life is sucked out of the countryside to the mobbed centers.

Metropolis vs Town

We've moved viable, meaningful, profitable employment out of the towns into cities. We cannot say, countryside living is better and

12. https://theexplanation.com/understanding-the-human-mind-key-to-gods-plan/

healthier. Some aspects are, but others not. In France, surprisingly, rural life expectancy rates are dropping below city rates. Why? Because close medical help is no longer available. Doctors, like other professionals, concentrate in major areas.

If we want to recapture fuller lives, we need the best of both worlds. Join primary and secondary industries: wool and woolen clothes, family chicken farm, and feed. Local land producing resources + local transformation industry. Fulfilling work with nature to produce raw materials + creative work with raw materials to produce quality finished products. Grains, greenery, livestock, minerals to produce bread, conserves, meat dishes, wooden, stone, etc. utility products.

Here are a few examples from Auvergne, a rural region in the South of France. I drew them from a TV program called *Faut Pas Rêver* (Don't Dream), in Auvergne, Land of Volcanos[13]. Salers cows > Salers cheese. Thierry Courtadon, a sculptor[14] of volcanic rock. Thiers[15] transformation of metal into world-renowned knives and cutlery. Brewer des Estives[16] barley malt with Gentian > specialized beer > Serge Vieira[17] 2 star Michelin Guide Chef. The protein-rich, residual cereal becomes cow feed, a closed-circuit within a few kilometers with no waste.

Psalm 65:9-13

---

13. https://www.france.tv/france-3/faut-pas-rever/2110213-en-auvergne-au-pays-des-volcans.html

14. http://ateliercourtadon.com/

15. https://ville-thiers.fr/le-couteau-le-thiers/

16. https://brasseriedesestives.com/

17. https://sergevieira.com/

9 You visit the earth, and water it: you greatly enrich it with the river of God, which is full of water: you prepare them corn, when you have so provided for it.

10 You water the ridges thereof abundantly: you settle the furrows thereof: you make it soft with showers: you bless the springing thereof.

11 You crown the year with your goodness; and your paths drop fatness.

12 They drop upon the pastures of the wilderness: and the little hills rejoice on every side.

13 The pastures are clothed with flocks; the valleys also are covered over with corn; they shout for joy, they also sing.

We will not be farmers! These verses give a vibrant picture of the role nature plays in human life. The respect of nature is ecology, land ethics. We find this practical Bible wisdom throughout God's Word.

Agriculture–Wisdom for the 21st century

Agriculture, essential for food, but endangered because of soil, salary, and sustainability issues. Practical Bible wisdom to the rescue.

Agriculture is the world's biggest employer, with over 40% of the world's population directly or indirectly involved. Yet, it is fraught with dreams and nightmares. Who wouldn't want a country house with a plot of fertile soil for homegrown nutritious produce? But village life for city dwellers is not readily workable in the 21st century.

At first sight, agriculture in the Bible doesn't seem to be a preoccupation. However, when we take a closer look, it occupies a place of honor. It's the first accomplishment of God following

Creation of the man as well as including the first directive given to humans.

Genesis 2:8-10

8 And the LORD God planted a garden eastward in Eden; and there he put the man whom he had formed.

9 And out of the ground made the LORD God to grow every tree that is pleasant to the sight, and good for food; the tree of life also in the midst of the garden, and the tree of knowledge of good and evil.

10 And a river went out of Eden to water the garden;

15 And the LORD God took the man, and put him into the garden of Eden to dress it and to keep it.

16 And the LORD God commanded the man, saying, Of every tree of the garden you may freely eat:

Those verses summarize both the functional work[1] and diet of humankind. *The Explanation* showed this surface translation hides the primary understanding of a deeper spiritual meaning[2]. Refresh your knowledge with the links; this chapter focuses on the agricultural aspect.

There are vital verses in Genesis leading into the above environmental context. They give important clues about land, land

---

1. https://theexplanation.com/dress-keep-garden-of-eden-man-destined-to-be-a-gardener/

2. https://theexplanation.com/river-of-living-water-profound-spiritual-meaning/

cover, water, and growing seasons. The third[3] and fourth[4] days of Creation are enlightening in this field (pun intended).

Genesis 1:9-13

> 9 And God said, Let the waters under the heaven be gathered together to one place, and let the dry land appear: and it was so.
>
> 10 And God called the dry land Earth; and the gathering together of the waters called he Seas: and God saw that it was good.
>
> 11 And God said, Let the earth bring forth grass, the herb yielding seed, and the fruit tree yielding fruit after his kind, whose seed is in itself, upon the earth: and it was so.
>
> 12 And the earth brought forth grass, and herb yielding seed after his kind, and the tree yielding fruit, whose seed was in itself, after his kind: and God saw that it was good.
>
> 13 And the evening and the morning were the third day.

Read about the emphasis on dry land[5], and the same day God covers it with grass, herbs, and trees. The inference is to cover the land to protect it, keep the humidity *in* the ground. The second principle is biodiversity. A third point to retain is the presence of trees. This description flies in the face of monoculture with its vast treeless fields planted with one crop and left uncovered after the harvest. The

---

3. https://theexplanation.com/dry-land-seas-and-flora-why-this-combination-on-day-3-of-creation/
4. https://theexplanation.com/day-4-of-creation-sun-and-moon-establish-calendar/
5. https://theexplanation.com/dry-land-seas-and-flora-why-this-combination-on-day-3-of-creation/

result is infertile soil and billowing dust, leading to depletion of the all-important topsoil. The principles of the third day of Creation are the basis for sane agriculture.

Creation days 4, 5, and 6 add further bricks to the edifice. Fertile soil depends on humus, a combination of legumes, earthworms, and microorganisms in a symbiotic relationship. Humus[6] is the end product of totally decomposed compost which takes years, hence the need for a protective covering over time to maintain and build the soil. We can't ask land to give, give, give without returning *everything* it gives. Artificial fertilizer only restitutes a minimum in wrong conditions, it's a short-term solution. Remember Adam's and Eve's fig leaves[7]; the key is humus, which retains water against drought, and minerals that roots capture for plant vitality.

Land cover and trees play a key role in the nitrogen cycle[8]. There's 71% nitrogen in the atmosphere and 3.3% in the human body. Some say nitrogen is the basis of life, why? Because it's the composition of amino acids, building blocks of human cells. There is *no* way the human body captures atmospheric nitrogen directly. Plant roots acquire the nitrogen which we recuperate when we eat vegetables, fruit, and meat. Animals digest plants, also transforming the nitrogen into amino acids consumable by humans, a lesson from Creation Day 3, the need for soil and soil cover.

Creation Days 5 and 6[9] bring birds to disseminate seed and grazing animals to produce manure. It is a holistic system we call sustainability, ecology, or conservation. The principles of agriculture

6. https://www.gardeningknowhow.com/composting/basics/compost-vs-humus-in-garden.htm

7. https://theexplanation.com/fig-leaves-or-clothing-tinker-or-build-practical-bible-wisdom/

8. https://theexplanation.com/hydrogen-helium-nitrogen-oxygen-mystery/

9. https://theexplanation.com/creation-day-5-and-6-god-created-fish-fowl-and-fauna/

have been available for thousands of years in God's Word. Let's move on with Creation week, looking at it from our agricultural perspective.

Genesis 1:14

And God said, Let there be lights in the firmament of the heaven to divide the day from the night; and let them be for signs, and for seasons, and for days, and years:

This verse warrants a forthcoming book. Detractors who talk about a contradiction of creating the sun on the first and fourth days neither understand the Biblical Hebrew nor the overall plan behind the Creation narrative. There's a chronological story here; once you've planted, you need to harvest the produce. Verse 14 is about seasons[10] (the Biblical Hebrew reveals this), spring, summer, fall, and winter, not creation. The reference to the sun and moon is their usage, in short, the establishment of a calendar.

Not only planting and harvesting for agriculture, but all the Godly festival seasons revolve around this calendar[11]. Those Feast Days show the steps of God's plan for the salvation of humankind. We've swept God's calendar under the rug for both planting and harvesting the physical fruits of the Earth, and the spiritual fruits of salvation.

Ecclesiastes 3:1-2

1 To every thing there is a season, and a time to every purpose under the heaven:

2 A time to be born, and a time to die; a time to plant, and a time to pluck up that which is planted;

---

10. https://theexplanation.com/spring-wheat-harvest-how-seasons-schedule-growth/

11. https://theexplanation.com/day-4-of-creation-sun-and-moon-establish-calendar/

Today, the climate crisis has changed the planting and harvesting seasons. Did you know the biggest producer of tomatoes in Europe is Holland[12] with *no* land, using hydroponics? They're grown in oversized greenhouses. Did you know the biggest worldwide exporter of roses is Kenya[13]? Globalization gives us roses year-round. No seasonal produce, we supply and consume what we want when we want. No more seasons. Such vegetables and flowers are genetically modified for power growth and to support both travel and long conservation, at the expense of nutrition and health.

Sabbatical Year

Regarding specific laws related to agriculture, there aren't many. The existing ones involve details rather than overall guidance. There's one short, but imposing law with vast implications. Not only for agriculture but for the lifestyle of the entire nation and its citizens. The Sabbatical year for agricultural land.

---

12. https://www.nationalgeographic.com/magazine/2017/09/holland-agriculture-sustainable-farming/#_853ae90f0351324bd73ea615e6487517__4c761f170e016836ff84498202b99827__853ae90f0351324bd73ea615e6487517_text_43ec3e5dee6e706af7766fffea512721_The_0bcef9c45bd8a48eda1b26eb0c61c869_20Netherlands_0bcef9c45bd8a48eda1b26eb0c61c869_20enjoys_0bcef9c45bd8a48eda1b26eb0c61c869_20high_0bcef9c45bd8a48eda1b26eb0c61c869_20yields_c0cb5f0fcf239ab3d9c1fcd31fff1efc_crops_0bcef9c45bd8a48eda1b26eb0c61c869_20in_0bcef9c45bd8a48eda1b26eb0c61c869_20addition_0bcef9c45bd8a48eda1b26eb0c61c869_20to_0bcef9c45bd8a48eda1b26eb0c61c869_20tomatoes._6cff047854f19ac2aa52aac51bf3af4a_text_43ec3e5dee6e706af7766fffea512721_Over_0bcef9c45bd8a48eda1b26eb0c61c869_20the_0bcef9c45bd8a48eda1b26eb0c61c869_20past_0bcef9c45bd8a48eda1b26eb0c61c869_20three_0bcef9c45bd8a48eda1b26eb0c61c869_20decades_c0cb5f0fcf239ab3d9c1fcd31fff1efc_anywhere_0bcef9c45bd8a48eda1b26eb0c61c869_20else_0bcef9c45bd8a48eda1b26eb0c61c869_20in_0bcef9c45bd8a48eda1b26eb0c61c869_20the_0bcef9c45bd8a48eda1b26eb0c61c869_20world.
13. https://en.wikipedia.org/wiki/Floral_industry

Leviticus 25:2-7

2 Speak to the children of Israel, and say to them, When you come into the land which I give you, then shall the land keep a sabbath to the LORD.

3 Six years you shall sow your field, and six years you shall prune your vineyard, and gather in the fruit thereof;

4 But in the seventh year shall be a sabbath of rest to the land, a sabbath for the LORD: you shall neither sow your field, nor prune your vineyard.

5 That which grows of its own accord of your harvest you shall not reap, neither gather the grapes of your vine undressed: for it is a year of rest to the land.

6 And the sabbath of the land shall be meat for you; for you, and for your servant, and for your maid, and for your hired servant, and for your stranger that sojourns with you.

7 And for your cattle, and for the beast that are in your land, shall all the increase thereof be meat.

The fundamental point to retain is this occurs every seventh year, like the weekly Sabbath, the seventh day of rest for people. The Sabbatical year is a year of land rest. To produce nourishing food for six years you must maintain and build fertility. The first thought is deprivation, "what are we going to eat?!" Hint, remember, during the 40 years in the desert, with the manna on the sixth day, a double portion.

Verse 22 adds a dimension to our understanding. "And you shall sow the eighth year, and eat yet of old fruit until the ninth year; until her fruits come in you shall eat of the old store." Quite amazing, in the 8th year there will still be stock from the *old store*. This can *not* be from the 7th year because you're not allowed to harvest and keep anything. So, it must be from the *sixth* year. God blessed that crop so there was extra, and like Joseph in Egypt, they stored it for the years in which there is less food.

1. No sowing, no harvesting of crops.

Remember Day 3 of Creation, land, and land cover. We do not leave the land UNcovered and untended. Just like the Sabbath is a day of spiritual rejuvenation, likewise the seventh year for the land. In modern talk, we'd say leaving the land fallow[14]. To some, this means plowing and nothing else. Not so, plowing can be detrimental, disturbing microorganisms and fungi growth in the soil. We can't get into the details and I'm not a specialist. Read up on agricultural practices at the included links. We plant a cover crop like clover or lupin to fix nitrogen, it becomes green manure[15], which decomposes and forms the basis of humus.

The consequences of no sowing are no harvesting, and therefore no selling of produce during the seventh year until the harvest of the eighth year.

Note verse 6, "the land shall be meat for you." All those in your home for whom you're responsible, your hired hands and those who help you *can eat* from the spontaneously grown produce. The household can eat any perennials[16], berries like strawberries, raspberries, fruit,

---

14. https://en.wikipedia.org/wiki/Fallow

15. https://en.wikipedia.org/wiki/Green_manure

16. https://www.thespruce.com/perennial-foods-1388677

vegetables (rhubarb), herbs, and nuts. This variety of volunteer growth would encourage diversification of production, which comes to fruition at different times during the year. We discussed this in *Origin of the Universe*, the availability of year-round produce[17].

2. Animals are plenteous and unaffected by the Sabbatical year.

Leviticus 25:7 says, "And for your cattle, and for the beast that are in your land, shall all the increase thereof be meat." Animals are beneficial for the land. They eat the grass and return dung; the seven-year cycle enhances fertility because animals graze on the cropland. Going back to Creation week we see the integration of Days 3, 5, and 6, land, land cover, insects, birds, and animals.

The meat produced is local, fresh, and wholesome for the household.

Conclusion: The professionals in agriculture had sufficient during the Sabbatical year. They had more time for other occupations: reading, studying, occupational advancement, professional diversification, maybe remunerative hobbies.

However, think about those *not* involved with agriculture. It becomes very difficult, if not impossible, to survive. Under 21st century living conditions, the application of this law would be a catastrophe. We know it won't happen, so we don't need to go there. This law applied to the entire nation, it's the same year for everyone.

Every seventh year there'd be a shortage of some basic commodities. On the other hand, the presence of animals, meat, eggs, and milk would be plentiful. The land Sabbath would even encourage this, as sales of these products would rise for the benefit of those in agronomy.

---

17. https://theexplanation.com/day-4-of-creation-sun-and-moon-establish-calendar/

Producers easily store grains, but farmers who solely depend on cereals for their income had no new products for sale. You store vegetables and fruit by drying, freezing, or bottling.

Under God's system, there would be *no* local fresh fruit and vegetable markets operating anywhere in the nation during the year of rest. The Land Sabbath is simply one of self-sufficiency in fruit and vegetables via homegrown production! The ramifications delve into households and extended families working together, as well as the availability of land. The whole notion of city and country living needs revisiting.

For the 21st century

How practical are Biblical principles for agriculture in today's society? On a national scale, probably not a lot. On an individual scale, adaptation is the key. Just because we can't do everything doesn't mean we do nothing. Each situation is unique, so it's impossible to be specific. But there are principles we can apply from agriculture and the Land Sabbath.

Vegetable gardens[18] at home, in schools, and communities are a key initiative anyone can take. Detroit[19] is a prime example in this field, but many other cities around the world are encouraging such programs.

Urban Agriculture[20] involves introducing greenery to the city. On rooftops, in parks and squares. Bringing people together is another aspect of gardening.

18. https://www.gardeningknowhow.com/edible/vegetables/vgen/family-vegetable-garden-size.htm

19. http://detroitagriculture.net/

20. https://en.wikipedia.org/wiki/Urban_agriculture

Regenerative Agriculture[21], unfortunately, we sorely need this. Fortunately, there are more and more people getting involved, saving what used to be fertile land, returning it to healthy production. Major programs of reforestation[22] are taking place, especially in Africa.

Organic Farming. Very specialized, not for everyone, it is much appreciated with the term *bio*. This type of farming is essential, but along with vegetable gardens, urban and regenerative agriculture, they are not the solution today[23] on a large scale basis. It would not feed the mega-cities around the world.

The implications for the occupational orientation of the nation are manifold. This leans heavily toward a society based on agriculture and not industry. It greatly affects the layout and architecture of our cities. Don't get me wrong, I'm not saying we're going back to the Middle Ages. On the contrary, we have to find the right balance between the two. In the West, we've swung too far, too much to industrial farming and industry in general, which is one cause of the state of our land and ill-health (Deuteronomy 28).

God created humankind from the dust of the ground. We are agricultural beings! We need to walk barefoot on real grass, plant flowers, get our hands dirty in fertile soil, see the results of growing our own vegetables, savor the taste of fruit picked from the trees in our yard. It's where we came from, what we are; that part of life helps maintain a sane mind in a sane body.

---

21. https://en.wikipedia.org/wiki/Regenerative_agriculture

22. http://www.fao.org/3/T0115E0m.htm

23. https://www.washingtonpost.com/lifestyle/food/why-small-local-organic-farms-arent-the-key-to-fixing-our-food-system/2017/09/21/146f72b2-9e4d-11e7-8ea1-ed975285475e_story.html

Homesteading[24] is a return to a balance of agriculture in modern society. Again, it's not for everyone by any means. But, along with smallholding[25], it gives a glimpse and a glimmer of hope into how appropriate agriculture serves a population. Here's an article about Biblical agronomy[26] from a hands-on, successful farmer who shares his experience.

The land Sabbath and its emphasis on agriculture and countryside living are utopic in today's society, but in a future Biblical scenario, it becomes the norm. The following description is a new tomorrow, a new Godly order where the fruits of land Sabbath agricultural practices will be apparent.

Micah 4:1-4

1 But in the last days it shall come to pass, that the mountain of the house of the LORD shall be established in the top of the mountains, and it shall be exalted above the hills; and people shall flow to it.

2 And many nations shall come, and say, Come, and let us go up to the mountain of the LORD, and to the house of the God of Jacob; and he will teach us of his ways, and we will walk in his paths: for the law shall go forth of Zion, and the word of the LORD from Jerusalem.

3 And he shall judge among many people, and rebuke strong nations afar off; and they shall beat their swords into plowshares, and their spears into pruninghooks: nation shall not lift up a sword against nation, neither shall they learn war any more.

24. https://en.wikipedia.org/wiki/Homesteading

25. https://en.wikipedia.org/wiki/Smallholding

26. https://worldagriculturesolutions.com/2019/10/10/biblical-agronomy/

> 4 But they shall sit every man under his vine and under his fig tree; and none shall make them afraid: for the mouth of the LORD of hosts has spoken it

Every family with a vine and fig tree. Difficult to imagine if you live in LA, NY, New Delhi, Shanghai, Buenos Aires, or Tokyo. We've turned things upside down. But practical Bible wisdom lays out the pattern for improving our agriculture and consequently our way of life in today's society. It shows us the potential in a new society where the fruits will become reality.

Economy. Managing Your House

Economy. Is it the stock market or a household? Is the goal to accumulate money or decent living conditions?

News screams economy at us from every angle. We criticize the Covid-19 lockdowns because they put such a damper on the economy. We've closed stores, hotels, restaurants, stopped travel and tourism, throwing millions out of work. We're pitting quarantine against the economy to see which we damage the least.

The 2008 economic crisis, sparked by the subprime fiasco, made us rethink how the economy works. The Covid-19 crisis has hit the global economy with such impact it should cause us to think about our priorities. What is an economy? How should we look at the economy?

We are discussing this from a practical Biblical point of view. Why? Because most believe the Bible is not written for the 21st century modern technology era with computers and stock markets. The posit of *The Explanation* is the Bible reveals practical wisdom about matters of economy. There are enough principles and details to show us what we should emphasize in the economy.

Read about the four major economic systems here[1]. I suggest you read it because it is an excellent summary of the key points of view.

1. Traditional.
2. Government control.
3. Supply and demand or no government control.
4. Mixed market. A mixture of 2 & 3, government and private sectors.

Let's highlight the economy from two angles. First, a family must have a regular income to live. Second, to have the national infrastructure, roads, bridges, communication, health, water supply, etc., you need financial and material resources to build and maintain such a complex network.

Note what the above article says about the traditional economy system, "the traditional system, unlike the other three, lacks the potential to generate a surplus. Nevertheless, precisely because of its primitive nature, the traditional economic system is highly sustainable. In addition, because of its small output, there is very little wastage compared to the other three systems."

Interestingly, the article uses a 21st century buzzword, *sustainable*, to describe the traditional economic system. It also states the problem;

---

1. https://corporatefinanceinstitute.com/resources/knowledge/economics/economic-system

not generating a surplus to build and maintain the infrastructure. What if there's a way for the traditional system to generate a surplus?

Traditional Economy

Modern 21st century citizens of a sprawling metropolis might tend to look down on the *primitive nature* of a traditional economy. In *Audit of the Universe*, describing body care, I wrote this.

> Consider a medieval farmer in Europe or in Asia. He woke up near dawn to tend his fields and livestock, working until sunset made it too dark to see. Besides farming and shepherding, each day required him to chop wood, carry water and walk for miles. Each calorie he took in by eating required hard physical labor to produce and earn. Those calories were fresh and largely unprocessed and included many fruits, vegetables, and whole grains. Excellent for body care. Our bodies are designed for movement and work[2].
>
> Compare this to a modern executive's relationship with food. He wakes before dawn and returns home after dark, but his workday comprises sitting in his car or sitting at a desk. His calories—often, of which he consumes more than he expends—are commonly prepackaged and preprocessed. His diet contains fewer whole grains, fruits or vegetables, and more fat, sugar, and salt.
>
> Our relationship with food has changed significantly over the centuries. What used to require a thousand calories to produce now takes fifty calories to buy. Whole grain loaves from grain we grew have given way to soft, sugary

2. https://theexplanation.com/skeleton-perfect-support-for-body/

> bread we buy from a rack at the store, or a "Happy Meal" bought and consumed in the car. This imbalance, like the other imbalances we've examined in our audit, causes problems — in this case, illnesses like obesity, diabetes, and heart disease. In developed nations worldwide, the cost of medical problems related to overeating far exceeds the costs of malnutrition.

The traditional way affects far more than the economy. Please understand, I'm *not* suggesting we all become Asian farmers. The Bible, however, places the economic emphasis on production from the land.

Bible economy

We find the origin of the word *economy* in the Bible. In Greek, *oikonomie*, about ten times in the New Testament.

> **Luke 12:42**
>
> And the Lord said, Who then is that faithful and wise *steward* (G3623), whom his lord shall make ruler over his household, to give them their portion of meat in due season?

The steward is the economist. In this scenario, he is a servant given the responsibility of ruling over a household. This example contains the major elements of the *economy*.

> **G3623**
>
> οἰκονόμος oikonomos oy-kon-om'-os; From G3624 and the base of G3551; a house distributor (that is manager) or overseer that is an employee in that capacity; by

extension a fiscal agent(treasurer); figuratively a preacher (of the Gospel):

KJV - chamberlain, governor, steward.

Money and Resources

Our economy today is based on *money* and *consumer goods*. Money in the form of stock markets, dividends, savings, interest, gold... and cars, telephones, electronic gadgets... To boost the economy we watch the government, banks, in particular, the monetary policymakers. We increase or lower interest rates, discounts, and incentives to *push people to consume;* it's money-oriented. We draw people into cities and put them behind computers to push buttons and print paper.

The *oikonomos* relies on stewardship to operate a house. This means providing food, shelter, and clothing, the essentials. Those are the basics. True wealth is the capacity to produce what we need from the raw materials we possess.

The basis of the economy is land and the human mind. Land because it alone supplies food, shelter, and clothing. Mind, because it alone allows us to transform the produce of the land into sustainable and durable products.

In the 21st century, we have removed our economy from the land. We've ruined our arable food-producing fertile soil and we're exhausting essential raw materials via industrial extraction methods. These principles include the oceans, which provide 40% of the world population with sustenance. We are squandering the wealth on which the economy lies.

Basic concepts of economy

This is practical Bible wisdom. The following writings assume you believe God, as Creator, has a plan for humankind whom He placed on this Earth. It further assumes you believe the Bible is His Word and instruction to live our lives. Please review these points.

Psalm 24:1

> The earth is the LORD's and the fulness thereof; the world, and they that dwell therein.

All the land and resources belong to God, not to you and me. We may buy a plot of land to build a house or a farm, but we are not the ultimate owner. Here is what God states.

Leviticus 25:23

> The land shall not be sold for ever: for the land is mine; for you are strangers and sojourners with me.

God instructed the Israelites as they entered Canaan. The land and resources were divided up and distributed to the tribes, but ultimately nothing belonged to them. Each one of them, like us, is an *oikonomos*, a steward of the land and its resources.

Go back to Genesis 1:26 to see the fundamental law governing the economy. "And God said, Let us make man in our image, after our likeness: and let them have dominion over the fish of the sea, and over the fowl of the air, and over the cattle, and over all the earth, and over every creeping thing that creeps upon the earth." We are caretakers of the land and all it produces.

This is where appropriate agriculture practices come fully into play. We discussed agriculture in the last chapter, how we treat the land and the oceans is the basis of the economy. Today, unfortunately, we are swiftly moving in the opposite direction. There is a wake-up counter-swing with the realization we've gone too far. Whether we've passed the point of no return is another question; we are a long way from God's economic guidelines.

Not anti-material, but anti-materialism

God placed all things, the material world, into the hands of humankind for good use. It is not His intention we adopt a philosophy of abstinence or hedonism. We should avoid both extremes of minimalism and maximalism. We have to wonder whether capitalism and stock markets have gone too far in the latter direction.

1 Timothy 4:7-11

7 For we brought nothing into this world, and it is certain we can carry nothing out.

8 And having food and raiment let us be therewith content.

9 But they that will be rich fall into temptation and a snare, and into many foolish and hurtful lusts, which drown men in destruction and perdition.

10 For the love of money is the root of all evil: which while some coveted after, they have erred from the faith, and pierced themselves through with many sorrows.

11 But you, O man of God, flee these things; and follow after righteousness, godliness, faith, love, patience, meekness.

Note it does *not* say money is the root of evil. Money is necessary and useful as a currency and means of exchange. There is absolutely nothing inherently wrong with money. It is its abuse, the love of it that sparks dilemmas. This leads to questions of ownership and wealth.

Private enterprise and property

Some of God's most faithful servants possessed and acquired property and animals. To build the ark, Noah must've had access to tremendous resources. Abraham, Isaac, and Jacob were land and cattle owners. God blessed Solomon with abundant riches. The key places of worship, like the Tabernacle and Temple, were sumptuous constructions.

God is not against any of this richness. Remember, however, it went to Solomon's head and eventually got the better of him spiritually. One cannot put their desires and hope in the material, as 1 Tim. 4:11 aptly puts it.

Labor

There are many verses about the value of labor. We have forgotten the value of manual labor relegating it to a lower level, particularly when associated with agriculture. It's messy and arduous, appropriate means should be taken to make all manual labor as rational and safe as possible.

Keep in mind the achievement and positivity issuing from creating something with your hands, witnessing the results of your vigorous efforts. Harvesting the crops with the sweat of one's brow generates gratifying benefits for both body and mind.

The fourth commandment is the Sabbath rest, but also six days shall you labor and do all your work (Exodus 20:9).

> **Proverbs 23:4** Labour not to be rich: cease from your own wisdom.
>
> **Proverbs 10:16** The labour of the righteous tends to life: the fruit of the wicked to sin.
>
> **Proverbs 13:11** Wealth gotten by vanity shall be diminished: but he that gathers by labour shall increase.
>
> **Proverbs 14:23** In all labour there is profit: but the talk of the lips tends only to penury.
>
> **Proverbs 21:25** The desire of the slothful kills him; for his hands refuse to labour.
>
> **Eccl. 2:17-26** (to read) 24 There is nothing better for a man, than that he should eat and drink, and that he should make his soul enjoy good in his labour. This also I saw, that it was from the hand of God.

Labor represents about one-third of our working day, it is not a negligible quality and has many benefits beyond remuneration. When accomplished under the right conditions, it keeps the body and mind sparkling with creative ideas rendering fulfillment and contentment, the best benefits of all.

Salary

Without laborers, many things would never get accomplished. Some people aspire only to labor and they love it. We just had a patio waterproofed by an artisan, a true professional; his keen know-how and precise gestures were music to my ears and eyes. He's worked for his boss for over 12 years and was just happy to continue doing the type of work he does. It's a pleasure to watch a craftworker doing what they love best.

> **Luke 10:7** And in the same house remain, eating and drinking such things as they give: for the labourer is worthy of his hire. Go not from house to house.

> **1 Timothy 5:18** For the scripture says, You shall not muzzle the ox that treads out the corn. And, the labourer is worthy of his reward.

I remember working as a technical writer and finishing a project for a mobile phone. Then having to write my employer umpteen times and wait for three months before he finally paid my due.

> **Leviticus 19:13**
>
> You shall not defraud your neighbour, neither rob him: the wages of him that is hired shall not abide with you all night until the morning.

Unfortunately, sole proprietors and businesses close, not because they're unviable rather they lose solvency, buyers wait forever to pay their bills, putting suppliers and manufacturers in jeopardy. These are the basic rules of the economy.

Levites

God reserved one tribe specifically to serve Him and accomplish God's tasks in favor of the Israelites.

When Joshua led the Israelites into the land of Canaan (Joshua 13:33), the sons of Levi were the only Israelite tribe granted cities but not land ownership, "because the Lord the God of Israel Himself is their inheritance" (Deuteronomy 18:2). The priests were to minister at the altar, burn the sacrifices, and teach the law.

Deuteronomy 33:8-10

> 8 And of Levi he said, ...
>
> 10 They shall teach Jacob your judgments, and Israel your law: they shall put incense before you, and whole burnt sacrifice upon your altar.

Teaching Jacob your judgments is not just teaching *religion, things pertaining to God and the sacred*, as some might express it. Teaching God's judgments is far-reaching. For instance, this book about various subjects, including economy, is teaching God's principles, His judgments on these matters. The bottom line of this statement is the Levites were the Ministry of Education.

They administered the cities of refuge which housed people who had committed misdoings, like killing someone inadvertently. We broached some very interesting details of justice some six chapters ago. Suffice to say, they had the key role in applying justice in the nation of Israel. They were the impartial enquirers and judges; we'd say they assumed the role of the Ministry of Justice.

Education and justice are major segments for the welfare of a nation. In modern terms, Levites were public servants, totally independent from a financial point of view. Nobody paid them directly. They lived from the tithes, the 10% people contributed, and offerings for the functioning of the Levitical Priesthood.

The Sabbatical year and land

In agriculture, we discussed the seventh year of land rest and the benefits to rejuvenate the land and people. Every seventh cycle of Sabbatical years, there's a Jubilee year. I don't know of anywhere but the Bible, such a disposition is laid out. It has widespread repercussions for the inhabitants of the entire nation. Once every 50 years means you'd take part once, maybe twice, in your lifetime, so it was a very special event.

Debt is possibly the biggest enemy of an economy. Why? Because you devote more and more of your revenue to pay it off. You dispose of less and less revenue to feed your family and purchase necessities. Debt causes a spiral into poverty, leading to being out of house and home. We discussed Biblical principles of aid for the poor but the Jubilee is the ultimate answer to debt and property loss.

Leviticus 25:8-13

8 And you shall number seven sabbaths of years to you, seven times seven years; and the space of the seven sabbaths of years shall be to you forty and nine years.

9 Then shall you cause the trumpet of the jubile to sound on the tenth day of the seventh month, in the day of atonement shall you make the trumpet sound throughout all your land.

10 And you shall hallow the fiftieth year, and proclaim liberty throughout all the land to all the inhabitants thereof: it shall be a jubile to you; and you shall return every man to his possession, and you shall return every man to his family.

> 11 A jubile shall that fiftieth year be to you: you shall not sow, neither reap that which grows of itself in it, nor gather the grapes in it of your vine undressed.
>
> 12 For it is the jubile; it shall be holy to you: you shall eat the increase thereof out of the field.
>
> 13 In the year of this jubile you shall return every man to his possession.

Every fifty years there is a moratorium on debt. *All* liabilities are wiped off the books, and *all* land is restored to the original family owner. The implications are far-reaching, families are reunited, it is a fresh start in life. Imagine if you were born into a poor family, your father could've been killed in an accident or died from ill-health or had a business setback for whatever reason. The property was sold and your family went from homestead ownership to salaried employee.

There's nothing wrong with the latter scenario, but it is much better to be self-sufficient in your own home with your own fertile land and animals. Every fifty years, the property reverted to its original homesteader. Remember, *all* the land belongs to God, we're stewards for a time... up to 50 years. We can work that land and earn profits; in the end, it becomes a level field, everyone has the same departure. We might want to call this a second chance.

Some people who lost out because they mismanaged or simply couldn't handle the load need time to learn. Working as an employee on someone else's property not only gives you a stable salary but especially a learning opportunity. It's an apprenticeship in stewardship. Exactly the qualities you need when you return to your property.

Some might consider this unjust because you have to relinquish something you own. How much wealth do you need to live decently? In this area, of the rich getting richer, and the poor getting poorer, capitalism has much to be desired. Would it be impossible to apply today? Well, certain authorities have proposed setting aside the debt of some Third World countries they can never pay.

Could it be done on a private level? I doubt it could be imposed on a national level. But consider, the countryside is becoming deserted and houses are falling into ruin with villages being abandoned. In Europe, some mayors have offered homes for 1 Euro[3] in an effort to revitalize their environment. It takes a big heart to take selfless measures, but it might be the only way to bring some sanity back to an economy gone wild. Bible wisdom offers practical solutions to the most material problems.

---

3. https://dispatcheseurope.com/expat-essentials-1-euro-deals-on-homes-are-attracting-people-back-to-europes-abandoned-villages/

What are God's Religious Practices? Why?

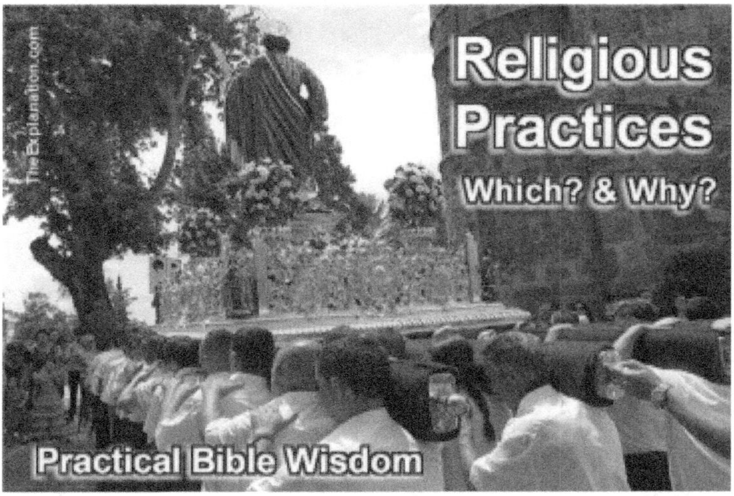

Religious practices are varied and common to all religions. You'd be surprised about their origins.

Religious practices conjure up pictures of fasting, abstinence, vows, prayers, sacrifices, offerings, and pilgrimages like the image above. Practical Bible wisdom both promotes and prohibits certain practices. We'll delve into some of the multicolored religious ceremonies.

This final chapter goes full circle back to Chapter 1.1. Let's step back and consider the raison d'être of religious practices and why they retain their importance. To understand them in the Old Testament, grasp the Godview of the commandments in His plan.

Matthew 22:36-40

36 Master, which is the great commandment in the law?

37 Jesus said to him, You shall love the Lord your God with all your heart, and with all your soul, and with all your mind. This is the first and great commandment.

39 And the second is like to it, Thou shall love your neighbour as yourself.

40 On these two commandments hang all the law and the prophets.

First question: What is *all the law* and the *prophets*? Second question: Why does Christ immediately follow with the following question?

41 While the Pharisees were gathered together, Jesus asked them,

42 Saying, What think you of Christ? whose son is he? They say to him, The Son of David.

43 He said to them, How then does David in spirit call him Lord, saying,

44 The LORD said to my Lord, Sit you on my right hand, till I make your enemies your footstool?

45 If David then call him Lord, how is he his son?

46 And no man was able to answer him a word, neither dared any man from that day forth ask him any more questions.

This is an example and quote from Psalm 110. In these eight verses, Christ cites the entire Old Testament through its three parts: Law, Prophets (verse 40), and Writings (Psalms). He is showing the religious leaders He is the Lord of the Bible. Here's the relationship to religious practices: The two great commandments sum up *all* the law, in the three parts of the Bible.

IF you apply the two, they incorporate ALL the others. For the 10 Commandments, the first four are the love of God while the last six are the love of neighbor. ALL the practices and law in the Bible fall into one of the two great commandments; meaning the laws in Exodus, Leviticus, Deuteronomy and all the ethics found in the book of Proverbs are twigs and branches of the trunk of the tree, represented by the two commandments.

Here's another vital difference between religious practices in the Old and New Testaments. Under the Old Covenant, laws were spelled out. You shall... You shall not... There are more *shall nots* than *shalls.* Why? Because God is talking to *babes, children.* In the New era, there are only two Commandments and they are *you shall.* You don't tell a mature spiritual person NOT to do this and that. Furthermore, you don't spell out all the details to a wise person. They need the principles: coupled with the wisdom of God; they know how to apply the details.

Here's a specific religious practice in the Old Testament regarding meat offered to idols.

Exodus 34:12-15

12 Take heed to yourself, lest you make a covenant with the inhabitants of the land where you go, lest it be for a snare in the midst of you:

> 13 But you shall destroy their altars, break their images, and cut down their groves:
>
> 14 For you shall worship no other god: for the LORD, whose name is Jealous, is a jealous God:
>
> 15 Lest you make a covenant with the inhabitants of the land, and they go a whoring after their gods, and do sacrifice to their gods, and one call you, and you eat of his sacrifice;

The above context indicates several religious practices we are to avoid. Practices to do with pagan altars, images, and forests or edifices built to resemble groves. Wisdom says don't get caught up (snared) where you're stuck and can't withdraw. In verse 15 there's a precise religious practice to avoid, *eat of his sacrifice*. Numbers 25:1-2 corroborates this principle when God condemns Israel for eating sacrifices made to the gods of Moab.

Now, review and meditate on the principle Paul gave the Corinthian Church. This is an excellent example of mature New Covenant Christianity compared to a list of specific *shall nots* of Old Testament religious practices.

> **1 Corinthians 8:1-13**
>
> 1 Now as touching things offered to idols, we know that we all have knowledge. Knowledge puffs up, but charity edifies.
>
> 4 As concerning therefore the eating of those things that are offered in sacrifice to idols, we know that an idol is nothing in the world, and that there is none other God but one.

5 For though there be that are called gods, whether in heaven or in earth, (as there be gods many, and lords many,)

6 But to us there is but one God, the Father, of whom are all things, and we in him; and one Lord Jesus Christ, by whom are all things, and we by him.

7 Howbeit there is not in every man that knowledge: for some with conscience of the idol to this hour eat it as a thing offered to an idol; and their conscience being weak is defiled.

8 But meat commends us not to God: for neither, if we eat, are we the better; neither, if we eat not, are we the worse.

9 But take heed lest by any means this liberty of yours become a stumblingblock to them that are weak.

10 For if any man see you which has knowledge sit at meat in the idol's temple, shall not the conscience of him which is weak be emboldened to eat those things which are offered to idols;

11 And through your knowledge shall the weak brother perish, for whom Christ died?

12 But when you sin so against the brethren, and wound their weak conscience, you sin against Christ.

13 Wherefore, if meat make my brother to offend, I will eat no flesh while the world stands, lest I make my brother to offend.

Question: Is Paul telling members of the Church of God they can disobey the Old Testament religious practice of not eating meat offered to idols? No, he is doing no such thing. He is explaining how to love God and love their neighbor according to the spirit of the law. A mature Christian evaluates a religious practice simply by asking; is what I'm doing pleasing to God and showing spiritual respect to my neighbor? (the two commandments) It takes the Holy Spirit to guide us to the correct answers. Paul gave them and us the tools, so to speak, to evaluate our religious practices in the 21st century.

Religious Practices abound worldwide

This book has a theme, practical Bible wisdom. It's written to help readers appreciate the relevance of this 2000-year-old book for us today. The principles, if followed in the 21st century, would procure peace and prosperity. I'm not saying spiritual salvation because that is New Testament theology to which God calls His people.

There are books, TV programs, and websites about all types of religious practice. From sitting atop a pillar[1] to walking on burning coals, from rolling around on the ground to living your life without clothes.

I already intended to include this topic of religious practices when I received an email regarding the intriguing title of a book. *Divination in the Bible, A Practical Guide to Talking to God.* Find it if you like; the word *divination* made me curious. We know what the Bible says, so what does this author mean? You decide, but people are coming up with supposedly new practices all the time. Beware, some are dangerous.

---

1. https://listverse.com/2017/08/09/top-10-challenging-religious-practices-from-across-the-globe/

As Wikipedia points out, religious practices come in many areas and forms[2]:

> They may include rituals, sermons, commemoration or veneration (of deities and/or saints), sacrifices, festivals, feasts, trances, initiations, funerary services, matrimonial services, meditation, prayer, music, art, dance, public service, or other aspects of human culture.

To prepare for writing this chapter, I studied the 613 mitzvot in the Torah[3], which are direct dos and don'ts taken from the five first books of the Bible, the Law. Religious Jewish people try to apply these precepts in their daily lives. These are the details of the two great commandments as mentioned above. It must be kept in mind certain conditions present 3000 years ago are not so today. We don't have a country, twelve tribes, the Kohanim (the Priests, direct descendants of Aaron, brother of Moses), the Levites who occupied positions of leadership in Temple affairs (no Temple either), and administrative positions like educators and judges.

With all those points and others in mind, the principles of those books are still practical Bible wisdom. Consider the Temple as the Church of God and the leaders as the leadership of God's Church today. As you study these precepts, ask yourself the question, how can I apply this in the 21st century?

As I did this, I categorized them for more relevance; here they are in alphabetical order. Your study might reveal other categories, some overlap.

---

2. https://en.wikipedia.org/wiki/Religion

3. https://en.wikipedia.org/wiki/613_commandments

> 10 Commandments, agriculture, animals, assembly-church, behavior, body, calendar, city, dead, destroy, diet, false prophets, family, feasts, government, health, idolatry, impure, monetary, justice, king, Kohen, labor-slavery, Levite, money-increase-tithe-restitution, Nazarite, neighbor, offering, peace, physical injury, poor, prophesying, purification, religion, sabbath, sacrifice, self-reproach, servant, sex, sin, study-teach, war, washing, woman, word, work, worship.

I would say, the first overriding precept regarding religious practices and anything else, for that matter, is to avoid following what is not practical Bible wisdom. Pagan practices are explicitly forbidden. We are not to mix them with practical Bible wisdom. It does not enhance proper Bible practices, in fact, it is just the opposite.

Listening to false religion

With the globalization of cultures and the implantation of Eastern religious practices as a way of life for many, warnings like those below carry little weight nowadays, yet they are clear and essential.

> **Deuteronomy 12:30-32**
>
> 30 Take heed to yourself that you be not snared by following them, after that they be destroyed from before you; and that you inquire not after their gods, saying, How did these nations serve their gods? even so will I do likewise.
>
> 31 You shall not do so to the LORD your God: for every abomination to the LORD, which he hates, have they done to their gods; for even their sons and their daughters they have burnt in the fire to their gods.

> 32 What thing soever I command you, observe to do it: you shall not add thereto, nor diminish from it.

It's our choice of what religious practices we want to follow.

Profane His Name

There is a *sacred names* movement as well as many individuals who focus on the pronunciation of God's name. For them, it must be Yahweh (Hebrew: יַהְוֶה), the proper name of the God. They insist on using the original Hebrew name of Jesus, transliterated as Yeshua, Yahshua, or Yehoshua.

> **Lev. 22:32**
>
> Neither shall you profane my holy name; but I will be hallowed among the children of Israel: I am the LORD which hallow you,

Each of these religious practices is a piece in the puzzle and has its role to play. But overemphasizing one or another is not a balanced approach. Profaning God's holy name is not referring to pronunciation. We find various names of God in Greek throughout the New Testament. Practical wisdom tells us this is a reference to HOW to use God's name. It's not an exclamation to throw around loosely when something goes wrong. Or an epithet to line our sentences without even thinking what we're saying, that's profanity and blasphemy.

Mediums

Certain countries, notably in Africa, have populations leading their lives based on the word of gurus. We have more and more of them in Western countries. Fortunetelling, card-reading, tarot, consulting the dead are professions and lucrative for practitioners. Advertisements in newspapers abound, and we're even harassed by solicitors on street corners. At certain metro stops in Paris, someone will hand you a business card inviting you to a session. Religious practices of this nature have always been rampant. There are direct warnings.

Deuteronomy 18:10

> There shall not be found among you any one that makes his son or his daughter to pass through the fire, or that uses *divination* (H7081), or an observer of *times* (H6049), or an *enchanter* (H5172 nachash-hiss), or a *witch* (H3784),

As crazy as it sounds, child sacrifices[4] still take place in the 21st century in some countries in Africa. Fire continues to be a part of many human religions[5] and cultures. Candles are used in various religious ceremonies; bonfires, eternal flames are reminders of notable occasions. Halloween is a pagan fire festival on October 31. The Olympic Flame is ceremonially lit and extinguished while burning throughout the games.

Look at the meaning of these Hebrew words, namely *nachash* (H5172) for *enchanter*, the same name as the Bible Serpent[6], otherwise known as the devil.

H7081

---

4. https://humanists.international/2010/11/ritual-killing-and-human-sacrifice-africa/

5. https://en.wikipedia.org/wiki/Fire_worship

6. https://theexplanation.com/fallen-from-heaven-the-fate-of-lucifer/

קֶסֶם qeçem keh'-sem; from H7080 (קָסַם); a lot; also divination (including its fee), oracle:

KJV - (reward of) divination, divine sentence, witchcraft.

H7080

קָסַם qâçam kaw-sam'; a primitive root: properly to distribute, i.e. determine by lot or magical scroll; by implication, to divine:

KJV - divine(-r, -cation), prudent, soothsayer, use (divination).

H6049

עָנַן 'ânan aw-nan'; a primitive root; to cover; used only as a denominative from H6051 (עָנָן), to cloud over; figuratively, to act covertly, i.e. practise magic:

KJV - × bring, enchanter, Meonemin, observe(-r of) times, soothsayer, sorcerer.

H5172

נָחַשׁ nâchash naw-khash'; a primitive root; properly to hiss; i.e. whisper a (magic) spell; generally, to prognosticate:

KJV - × certainly, divine, enchanter, (use) × enchantment, learn by experience, × indeed, diligently observe.

H3784

> כָּשַׁף kâshaph kaw-shaf'; a primitive root; properly to whisper a spell, i.e. to inchant or practise magic:
>
> KJV - sorcerer, (use) witch(-craft).

Some religious practices above are rampant in the 21st century. Biblically, this is not a healthy situation. Do a study of each of the categories of the arbitrary number of 613 precepts in the books of the Law. You'll see the religious practices God said to avoid and to follow.

Why have any rituals and practices at all? The key attributes of humans are their minds and their hands[7]; thoughts and actions. Religious practices are for the mutual strengthening of the spiritual mind and accomplishing Godly works. Religious practices express all the ways we love God and love our neighbor. The spiritual mind manifesting itself through our physical works.

With practical Bible wisdom in mind and religious practices, we've listed some of them, like the Feasts and the Rest Day in this book. These practices are ongoing as long as there are humans on Earth serving God. They continue even after Christ returns, as witnessed by festive events in the last chapters of Ezekiel. The religious practices reinforce our spiritual understanding.

---

7. https://theexplanation.com/consciousness-and-human-mind-you-cant-have-one-without-the-other/

Epilogue

Is there Evidence for Bible Wisdom? I believe so. I hope the subjects in this book have opened and deepened your mind to the gems in the Bible. It's been a smorgasbord of hard-to-deal-with issues many readers grapple with. However, one of the overriding themes I've emphasized is the Bible as an instruction manual for all of humankind. These are universal principles for the correct functioning of the unique human race we are.

Let's go one step further together. If you believe in a Powerful God as Creator of humankind and Author of a guide for life, then realize this same God has a very good reason for setting humans on Earth and allowing us to perform, with both the good and bad, the uplifting and downgrading conditions we find abundantly around us in the 21st century.

What's happening on our planet? How did the Universe come about, and where is it headed? Especially why did God place humanity here and what's God's goal? These are, at the same time, fundamental but profound questions. It goes far beyond a statement of beliefs or Church Creed. We're talking about God's Creed, what He declares. That has been the approach of *Evidence for Bible Wisdom*. Let God do the telling.

The Explanation applies this approach to all its writing. To continue your quest and understand God's plan for humankind, you need to delve into the first five minutes, the plot, or the goal of the Bible story. *The Explanation* series does just that, with an eye-opening approach. The basis is Biblical Hebrew. No, it's not complicated, you don't have to learn any alphabet, grammar, or vocabulary. The same method to unlock Bible meaning with the 7 steps to master Biblical

Hebrew employed in this book is the basis. So you're already up and running.

Here's a brief summary.

1. Inventory of the Universe

There are too many pieces in the universal puzzle for even one of them to have an independent role. ALL must work harmoniously assembled together. Remove *one* piece and the Universe is in for trouble. *Inventory of the Universe* establishes a *worldview* including *every* aspect of space, atmosphere, water, land, flora, fauna, life, body, and mind. It ends with a comparison of animal and human life to reveal the insurmountable gap.

This book renders invisible things clearly visible. Neither the word *God* nor *Bible* is mentioned in the book. However, it should cause a reader to *think*. *Inventory* is *evidence* (not proof) that there must be something *superior* to chaos and hazard for the highly complex but minutely assembled Universe to exist.

5* Review - verified purchase: Amazing! Reviewed in the United States on May 19, 2021.

This book is amazing! First of all, as an evangelist who delves deeply into the Word of God (the Bible?), I had already surmised what Sam is saying in this book. Second, as a scientist, it makes so much sense that our universe could only have been created out of intelligent design, no other way. The detail that he writes is phenomenal; I understand every bit of it. I only wish that I had this book back in the 70s when I was teaching general science to 9th graders; they would have latched on to it with far more enthusiasm than those boring textbooks that we had that many of them could not even read. But I would have used this book instead to teach them a well-rounded science course from it. And they would be so much better for it because they would have appreciated and embraced science. Fantastic!

2. Audit of the Universe

Our Universe, an interwoven marvel of *systems in systems,* functions to provide humans on Earth everything needed for an abundant life. We know of nowhere else in the Universe where all these conditions (not just water and fertile soil) even begin to exist. What are humans doing with their habitat? In the 21st century, ecology and climate control are the buzzwords. They reveal the extent of the damage we humans have caused to our own home. There are very few signs of a reversal of tendency.

Audit of the Universe asks, "is the glass of peace and prosperity getting fuller or emptier?" A thinking person should know the answer to this query simply via the time displayed by the Doomsday Clock[1]. This method is calculated by humans themselves. It has nothing to do with God, Who, again, is not mentioned in *Audit.*

Humankind knows where it stands. It's got its hand in the fire and doesn't feel the hurt. Humanity isn't waking up to the dire situation in which it has placed itself. That too is a mystery. Think, why?

3. Audit of Humankind

Humanity causes its own demise. We've got to find out why. What makes humans tick? Who are we? What makes a human, human? Humans are unique and much more capable than the smartest of animals, whichever one that might be. Specifically, what characterizes humans, all humans, worldwide?

1. https://thebulletin.org/doomsday-clock/current-time/

The singularity of humans is not their upright stance or language capacity. It is their qualities based on their endowment with a MIND. We all possess singularities like creativity[2], imagination[3], learning[4], decision-making[5], challenges[6], and ruling life[7]. That's what makes humans human. That's the insurmountable gap with animals.

Then comes how humans FUNCTION, human nature[8], free will[9], human behavior[10], ethics[11], justice[12], self-reproach[13], forgiveness[14], and love[15]. These functions of humankind are present solely because humans possess consciousness and mind.

Humanity socializes[16], rules[17], and reasons[18]. Today, in our enlightened age of information, science, and artificial intelligence,

---

2. http://theexplanation.com/creativity-sets-humankind-apart-from-and-above-all-other-life-on-earth/
3. http://theexplanation.com/imagination-another-singularity-of-humankind-in-your-mind/
4. http://theexplanation.com/bears-dont-learn-to-ride-bicycles-humans-learn-that-and-much-more/
5. http://theexplanation.com/your-choices-tell-us-who-you-are-in-fact-they-identify-you/
6. http://theexplanation.com/challenge-accompanied-courage-needed-face-new-struggles-another-human-singularity/
7. http://theexplanation.com/rule-life-responsibly-the-key-human-singularity/
8. http://theexplanation.com/human-nature-and-consciousness-the-definition/
9. http://theexplanation.com/free-will-we-all-possess-it-but-we-cant-always-utilize-it/
10. http://theexplanation.com/human-behavior-is-the-expression-of-human-nature-and-free-will/
11. http://theexplanation.com/ethics-are-the-blueprint-for-behavior-how-humanity-should-function/
12. http://theexplanation.com/justice-goes-hand-in-hand-with-ethics-to-obtain-peace/
13. http://theexplanation.com/self-reproach-the-essential-beginning-step-toward-real-peace/
14. https://theexplanation.com/forgiveness-the-healing-bond-for-humans-to-function-peacefully/
15. https://theexplanation.com/love-is-the-most-distorted-english-word-heres-why/

there's no consensus in any of these fields; they're all fractured into umpteen directions.

We have a pile of studies that show all these characteristics of humankind. Yet, we are incapable, or unwilling, to assemble this information into a coherent, complete picture. The reasoning of the world's best minds is at loggerheads. We debate endlessly, never coming to any valid conclusions. True for all the above fields. True of the one underlying key factor that motors all humans, the mind. ALL the research, studies, billions of dollars invested in the endeavor have rendered nothing. We are still ignorant. This book to pull back the curtain.

4. Origin of the Universe

If the reasoning of humans cannot establish coherent completeness, maybe we need to look elsewhere for some wisdom. How about the Sacred Books[19], purportedly inspired by *outside* of this world intelligence and wisdom. Okay, but how do we decide which book is the Book[20], if there is one?

The Sacred Book must answer all the why questions[21] that have been raised In *Inventory* and *Audit* and it must display coherent completeness. *only* the Bible fills these requirements[22].

16. https://theexplanation.com/read-all-the-content-of-audit-of-humankind-online/

17. https://theexplanation.com/read-all-the-content-of-audit-of-humankind-online/

18. https://theexplanation.com/read-all-the-content-of-audit-of-humankind-online/

19. https://theexplanation.com/sacred-books-can-point-us-direction-peace-prosperity/

20. https://theexplanation.com/sacred-books/

21. https://theexplanation.com/why-questions-are-the-first-questions-to-ask-about-the-universe/

22. https://theexplanation.com/the-sacred-book-if-it-exists-could-it-possibly-be-the-bible/

As we begin Genesis 1, it explains the ins and outs of *Inventory of the Universe* including planet Earth, resources, ecology, and *why* God put humanity here. The very first chapter of the Bible immediately answers that *primary why* questions. The answers are to establish proper relationships and rulership[23]. Those two goals are the crux of all the problems, the heart of the mystery, we face in the world. Genesis 1 is a contemporary instruction manual[24].

It reveals how to have satisfying relations and rulership in the 21st century. Furthermore, from the start, Genesis explains the relationship of humankind to God kind[25] and the reason we need training in relationships and rulership.

5. Origin of Humankind

Where do humans come from? What is their composition? Why the *wisdom gap* between animals and humans? Three basic questions where science, philosophy, and religion are not in agreement, both withIN their own disciplines as well as among them.

A few Bible verses, particularly Genesis 2:7 answer all three of those questions, and many more. This epilogue is not the place for answers, but you need to understand the role of *neshama*.

By the time you finish *Origin of Humankind*, you'll begin to have a Godview regarding *Inventory* and *Audit of the Universe* and *Humankind*. Humans, psychology, consciousness, mind, and the spiritual world will all come into focus. The mystery of what a human being is, a body and a mind working in coordinated harmony, will underline the relevance of the Bible narrative.

23. https://theexplanation.com/genesis-1-reveals-basics-social-relations-rulership/

24. https://theexplanation.com/genesis-1-science-with-big-bang-and-the-bible-with-creation-in-accord/

25. https://theexplanation.com/made-in-the-image-of-god-the-definition/

6. Origin of Woman

In the 21st enlightened century, it is a paradox that we don't know what a woman's role is. We have many movements about women's rights, and they certainly have rights, but there's no agreement on what they are. And more importantly, why there are women, equal but different from men[26]. How can you have something *equal* and *different*, at the same time, mystery? Sociology hasn't figured that one out.

The end of Genesis 2 answers that question and related queries. Some laugh at a term like helpmeet[27] or the dumb myth about coming from a rib[28]. Once you get into the Hebrew, the vista changes and the mystery unravels. You come away with solid solutions.

7. Agony of Humankind and the Antidote

The Bible is one coherent Word of God, the Logos of God[29]. Genesis 1-2 are the first five minutes of revealing the main characters. But there's one essential point missing.

Why is the world in such a state?[30] The title of the seventh book includes the descriptive *agony* to summarize this state of affairs. It *answers* that question. It goes to the heart of the issue, *human self-wisdom*[31]. Humankind thinks it can solve its problems, like stitching together fig leaves[32] to cover their nakedness. A rather

26. https://theexplanation.com/gender-equality-gender-inequality-or-gender-compatibility/

27. https://theexplanation.com/helpmeet-the-surprising-god-given-role-of-woman/

28. https://theexplanation.com/god-created-woman-and-reveals-humankinds-future/

29. https://theexplanation.com/what-has-the-lego-construction-set-got-to-do-with-the-truth-if-anything/

30. https://theexplanation.com/state-of-the-world-in-2020-agony-of-humankind/

31. https://theexplanation.com/wisdom-of-god-or-the-serpent-which-one-roused-eve/

ludicrous solution, I think we'd all agree. Yet, humanity turns around and patches up its predicaments with fig leaves that fall off and wither away!

Thankfully the Bible doesn't just underline the quandaries humans find themselves in; it also freely gives the antidote. The ethics for living abundant lives in the 21st century. Instead of paying attention and searching out the Bible's wisdom, we write *how to* book after *how to* book. *Personal experience* book after *personal experience* book. Oh yes, they can be helpful, but these are the fig leaves. We need substantial and reliable clothing[33]. That's the wisdom of the Bible.

The Bible is the record of the ups and mainly downs of the free will decisions of humankind. Human history over the past couple of thousand years follows on in the wake of the Old and New Testaments corroborating the upheavals that plague humankind. The end is amazingly encouraging.

Seekers will find Bible wisdom continues in *The Explanation* series.

32. https://theexplanation.com/critical-thinking-antidote-to-the-agony-of-humankind/

33. https://theexplanation.com/rules-for-life-wisdom-for-living-abundantly-in-the-world/

Annex

Biblical Hebrew—What a Language

Limited vocabulary, but so expressive

Compared to Biblical Hebrew with about eight thousand words, the 20 volume Oxford Dictionary exposes 171,000 English words in current use. Quite a difference. One might think that with an infinitely smaller vocabulary, Biblical Hebrew would be easier to understand. On the contrary, there's much less controversy with the millions and millions of words in the Oxford Dictionary than the entire 419,687 words of the Old Testament, mainly in Biblical Hebrew.

We are going to make a brief incursion into an exciting aspect and complexity (or simplicity) of Biblical Hebrew. I expound this significantly in *Origin of the Universe*, the third book of *The Explanation* series, and the online course *7 Keys to Master Biblical Hebrew*.

It's these complexities/simplicities which open the way for the multitude of *interpretations* of the biblical texts–the cacophonic confusion that surrounds the most printed, and probably the least understood book of all times.

As one of my Hebrew teachers said, "every translation is an interpretation." Simple and profound, each language has its vocabulary that rarely has an identical counterpart in another language. So, how do you decode it? A translator's sensitivity, culture, education, and even belief or non-belief come markedly into play.

Keep in mind that I'm not asking you to believe or accept any of this, what I'm saying, what you might think the Bible says or doesn't say, whether the Bible is true or false. All of that is neither here nor there. We're dealing with the literary best-seller of all times that was originally written in Hebrew. All we're doing is analyzing some vocabulary.

Let's jump into the deep end of Biblical Hebrew

Here are four biblical texts from the King James Bible. Notice the highlighted, *italicized words*.

Exodus 21:19

If he rise again, and walk abroad upon his staff, then shall he that smote him be quit: only he shall pay for the *loss* of *his time*, and shall cause him to be thoroughly healed.

Proverbs 20:3

It is an honour for a man *to cease* from strife: but every fool will be meddling.

Isaiah 30:7

For the Egyptians shall help in vain, and to no purpose: therefore have I cried concerning this, Their strength is to *sit still*.

Obadiah 3

The pride of your heart has deceived you, you that dwell in the clefts of the rock, whose *habitation* is high; that says in his heart, Who shall bring me down to the ground?

In the image below, even if you do not know Biblical Hebrew, it is easy to see that the 4 Hebrew words from excerpts of the four verses above have three identical letters: *shin*, *beth*, *taf*. (We write Hebrew from right to left that's why the English is *jumbled* and also needs to be read, in blocks, from right to left).

What I submit to you is this: From reading these four verses in English–or in any and other translations–you'd never guess or know in 1000 years that these four phrases come from ONE ORIGINAL Hebrew word *shevet*. And you'd be hard-pressed to find the relationship between these phrases if any.

What do these four English words, from the single Hebrew word *shevet* have in common?

- Loss of time
- Ceasing
- Sitting still

- Habitation / cease

This short expose is not intended to give answers. It is simply to explain that the four options: Observation, Philosophy, Science, and Religion, exposed in the final chapter of *Audit of Humankind*, are not the only ways humans can use their minds to reason. There's a fifth option: Theology. That possibly hasn't been properly explored to find out about what makes our world tick.

If I go to the crux of the matter and give you a challenge, ask a well-known political or another experienced leader, question a philosopher, quiz a scientist, query a religious representative about those four verses above. Ask them what relationship there is between the four different translations of the unique Hebrew word.

Can they enlighten us? I wonder, maybe. Well, proper theology can and will inform us.

In conclusion, this is just a hint, an inkling of what Biblical Hebrew is all about. You don't have to read Biblical Hebrew; you don't have to memorize it; you don't have to learn its vocabulary to deepen your comprehension of theology.

I will not give you the answer now to the above puzzle, but I will provide you with the tools and show you the METHOD so you can Unlock Bible Meaning for yourself, and find the answer to this enigma, and many others. Help and more in-depth understanding of Biblical Hebrew and ultimately, the sacred book–the Bible–is not far away.

Your Language Can't Translate Biblical Hebrew

Languages fall short of the Bible text's richness

Let's start at the beginning. You might have little or no knowledge of the Bible, that's fine. You might consider the Bible to be a bunch of fables of no particular interest other than tales to tell kids. Frankly, that's fine too. You might even believe that the Bible is full of lies and is a *negative book*. Well, you're entitled to your viewpoint.

All of that said, one point remains. The Bible is the best-seller of all times and one way or another; it is *a piece of literature*. If not for any other reason, but general knowledge, it behooves you to have even a cursory understanding of its contents. Let's take a closer look, I guarantee you it's going to be very revealing.

Bible Translations

The vast majority read the Bible in their native language. That's normal. Because the Bible has such a broad audience, it has been translated into 636 languages. The New Testament into 1442 tongues and portions of the Bible into yet another 1145 dialects, making it the most translated book of all times with new translations still appearing.

In a nutshell, Bible translations (which have taken a lot of effort and scholarship) are constructive, but they are incomplete for one excellent reason. The original words, mainly in Hebrew and Greek, have more meaning than what can be rendered in any translated word or phrase. How can I affirm this? Simply because if you take any translation, you'll see that a SINGLE original word–let's say in Hebrew–has been translated with MULTIPLE words in the translation, no matter what the language.

If it were so simple, every single Hebrew word would have just one translated word. But each Hebrew word has more than one–some have fifty different translations. Yes, you read that correctly–50 different renderings for the same Hebrew word as we'll shortly see.

You need to ask the fundamental question: How can ONE Hebrew word have FIFTY different translations? These are expert linguists and Bible scholars who are doing their utmost to stay faithful to the original text.

The answer to that question is why I wrote this e-book and developed a free video course:

> 7 Keys to Master Biblical Hebrew–A Study Method to Unlock Bible Meaning, with no fuss.

Biblical Hebrew is the original language of the Bible. You need to understand why a single Biblical Hebrew word can be rendered *correctly* with up to 50 words in your native language. The vast majority of the original language words have multiple translations. With that understanding in mind, I think you can easily and quickly realize that when you read ONE word or ONE short phrase in your native language you are getting understanding, but your understanding is INcomplete.

Don't misunderstand what I'm saying here. Your native language translation in 99.99% of cases is correct. You can understand what the a/Author of those words is saying even if sometimes it is difficult. What I'm saying is that understanding of the Bible in any of the 636 or thousands of translations is only PARTIAL understanding.

And partial understanding can lead to erroneous comprehension of the text. Just like incomplete understanding of any subject, be it, science, history, geography, or mathematics, can lead to error. Especially when we think we are drawing conclusions based on complete comprehension–because that's what we believe or have been given to understand.

Following is just a brief answer to the above fundamental question regarding multiple native language translations for one Biblical Hebrew word. It is a preview of the online course with the same title where you'll discover several unspoken characteristics of Biblical Hebrew. If you want to understand the Bible, you need to be aware of these principles.

You may not be aware of some examples I evoke here–all the more reason to join the course and increase your general knowledge. A friend of mine told me recently that he was playing a quiz game with some friends and a Bible-related question came up which he answered to the surprise of everyone there! He told me he knew the answer because of one of our conversations. You never know when this information is going to come in handy. Not that it's your primary motivation.

I'll even say that most people with some knowledge and interest in the Bible are not aware of these seven keys and indeed not of this study method to unlock Bible meaning.

Here's an overview of the seven keys:

1. Biblical Hebrew words have Various Meanings

I've already mentioned this one. Here's an example that I think everyone is aware of because of *The Ten Commandments*. Again, remember, I'm not asking you to believe that this story ever took place or even that Moses existed and received the Ten Commandments from God. Just consider this as literature, written originally in Biblical Hebrew. The Hebrew word used in this context for *commandment* (Exodus 24:38) is *davar*. It's used about 1400 times in the Hebrew Bible. Here is a simple list of over 50 words and phrases used as translations in the English language King James Bible:

Act, advice, affair, answer, because of, book, business, care, case, cause, certain rate, commandment, counsel, decree, deed, due, duty, effect, errand, evil favored, hurt, language, manner, matter, message, thing, oracle, portion, promise, provision, purpose, question, rate, reason, report, request, sake, saying, sentence, some (uncleanness), somewhat to say, speech, talk, task, thing (concerning), thought, tidings, what(-soever), which, word, work.

Why can *a straightforward word* have so many translations? What is the implication of this?

It means that sometimes when you read the KJV and come across one of these 50 words, in fact, it is the same word as *commandment* like in the Ten Commandments; this is only one example of how translation affects comprehension. Think about this: practically EVERY SINGLE word in Biblical Hebrew has MULTIPLE translations in your native language. This Biblical Hebrew course will explain why this is so.

Each Biblical Hebrew Word is a Precious Jewel

Biblical Hebrew words are thrilling discoveries

Each Biblical Hebrew word is like a rough stone to be dug up, cleaned off, and viewed under a magnifying glass to reveal its glitter and perfection. Let's continue with four more principles to master Biblical Hebrew: Keys 2-5.

2. Words can have Opposite Meanings

Here's a word most people are aware of: elohim. If you asked someone for its translation, I think 100% of the time you'd hear *God,* and that is correct. But it can also refer to angels, judges, gods, and goddesses.

In Genesis 31:30, the translation *gods* refers to idols. Exodus 12:12 talks about the *gods* of Egypt using the word elohim; this has nothing to do with *God* (whether you believe in idols or God). Even the context shows that the *gods of Egypt* are the opposite, as the verse says the *Lord* will smite their *gods-elohim*.

In Psalms 82.6, human beings are called elohim. How do you explain that? As an added interesting biblical fact, in the New Testament we see the term *god of this world* (2 Corinthians 4:4) with the Greek *theos*, which refers to god but in this verse, *god* opposes *God*. Do you know who this god of this world is (even from a literary point of view)?

Thinking that *elohim* is *God* is correct, but that comprehension is not complete. Not understanding the total opposition of the meaning of Hebrew words can lead to significant misunderstandings; this is just one point in what I refer to as coherent completeness[1]. Elohim = God is correct but INcomplete.

These *oppositions* go further, in that they teach us lessons about life. Here's another translation example among dozens that I'll show you how to spot in the Bible course. The biblical Hebrew word for *eat* and *war* is *lacham*, the common word used in modern Hebrew today for *bread* derives from this: lechem. We all eat, basically every day, even multiple times in a day. It is one of the most common human activities. Why is the same Hebrew word also used for *war*?

Why did the author leave such ambiguity? What is the implication of this?

3. Words can have Concrete & Abstract meanings

How would you express *hand* on a piece of paper or stone? You'd draw its outline: ? A *hand* is very concrete you can see and touch it, you can easily picture it and envision its shape. Now, how would you represent the concept of *success* or the idea, *you did it*. Well,

1. http://theexplanation.com/coherent-completeness-is-the-logical-reasoning-of-the-ssource/

you could use a variation of something concrete to denote a notion, sentiment, or feeling, like this: ✌ *victory*. Just like the sentiment of love is expressed with a concrete and tangible heart ♥. We're even using the word *concrete* (cement and gravel) here abstractly.

Today we use many pictograms, icons, and smileys thinking this is a *modern* form of expression. It goes back to the origins of written language itself when the formation of alphabets began.

Biblical Hebrew goes back to those origins when letters and root words represented concrete, tangible, visible items like a: hand, house or a head ☺ Biblical Hebrew is replete with the concrete expressing the abstract. Here are just a few examples:

- Breath represents spirit.
- Head designates the beginning.
- Eyes point to understanding.
- A lion pictures strength.
- Sleep suggests torpor.

Like today we use a light bulb to depict a bright idea or that Eureka, eye-opening, aha moment. The real and visible representing the conscious and invisible.

The English word *head* translates from the Hebrew *rosh*. Here's how rosh is rendered in various places in the King James Version of the Bible: band, beginning, captain, chapiter, chief(-est place, man, things), company, end, excellent, first, forefront, (be-)head, height, (on) high(-est part, (priest)), principal, ruler, sum, top. No less than seventeen different English words.

Did you know that the first word of the Bible, in the book of Genesis, is this word *head, beraisheet,* with a slightly different pronunciation which I'll explain later? In Genesis 1:1 it is translated by probably the best known Bible quotation: *in the beginning*.

Understanding some of the 17 translated words above in your native language helps comprehend that this *beginning* is somehow related to the notion *excellent*, another rendering of this same Hebrew word. I won't get into the association of these two variant translations for the same Hebrew word now. Suffice to say, there's a relationship.

But this is important considering the very next verse in Gen 1:2, which states: the earth was *without form and void*. If the beginning is associated with *excellent,* how do we explain this chaos? Do you see what I mean by grasping partial meaning from a translation, but not full comprehension? As a result, Genesis 1:1 has more interpretations than ever. If you get the first sentence in a story wrong, how can you understand the rest? You've missed a critical point.

For now, retain this third key: That the concrete, tangible, physical words that your hands can reach out and touch like *head* represent abstract conceptual ideas that emanate from the mind like *excellent*. We shall see the relevance of this key shortly when I get into Genesis 1:1.

4. Words can have Literal and Figurative meanings

Dual meanings are not unique to Hebrew; we find them in English and other languages too. For example, *night* literally is the twelve hours of darkness, but figuratively we use it in expressions like *a long night for the survivors*. *Night* can also refer metaphorically to *dark, evil,* or *confusion*. Translations only render one of those meanings, generally the most obvious, and without getting into it here, but I do in due course, it is mainly only the literal meaning.

Case in point: Genesis 1:2 where we read: *darkness was upon the face of the deep*. I will show you, and you can check it for yourself, but not only was there an *absence of light* but darkness figuratively means to *destroy*, and *make a noise*.

If all you grasp from this verse is the literal darkness, you've missed at least half the meaning which is not transmitted by the translation. And the figurative comprehension might be equally, if not more important than the literal translation. What have *destruction* and *noise* got to do with creation? What is the implication of this? What does it do for comprehension when we miss fifty percent of the author's meaning?

5. Names of men and women have significance

Just one example. *Noah*, as you know, was instrumental in the story of the worldwide flood that covered even the mountains. I'm just repeating what the book of Genesis says. Whether you believe it's true, a legend, a lie, or if you've never read it or can't decide, don't matter. There are many statements in the Bible that say there was a flood.

What I want to draw your attention to is the word *noah*, with a small *n,* is first and foremost a derivative of a Biblical Hebrew word *nooach*–not just a name. This word *nooach*, and its other derivatives, are used over 70 times, and they have been translated, among others, by *cease, be confederate, lay, let down, (be) quiet, remain, (cause to, be at, give, have, make to) rest, set down*.

When you understand just this one point, you can realize that a recent blockbuster film that depicts God and Noah as putting a definitive end to all of humankind is incorrect. Yes, God destroyed humanity according to the Bible story (it doesn't matter now whether you believe this piece of literature) but, if you understand the meaning of Noah's name you realize that somewhere in this story, there is *quiet* and *rest*.

Maybe you don't understand how and where the *quiet* and *rest* fit in (that's where *Unlock Bible Meaning* comes into play) but, if you know the meaning of Noah's name, the central figure in this account, that should give us some comfort. It also should make us wonder why a man named *quiet* and *rest* was the key figure in massive destruction.

Two major questions that are misunderstood, about the flood episode, are:

> How can a righteous and peaceful God put people to death?
>
> The whole question of death and the afterlife is a concern for all of us.

Coupled with this is the concept from point 3 that these names can have both literal and figurative aspects to them. The point is one name, identity, descriptive for a man or woman can have multiple meanings.

Translations *capitalize* the word identifying an individual (Noah), and we tend to take it solely as a name. Well, in Biblical Hebrew, there is no capitalization! It's just another word like all the others, including all the nuances that these 7 Keys to Master Biblical Hebrew will unlock for better Bible understanding.

For now, incredible as it might sound, whether or not you believe it, the meaning of *noah*–referring to *comfort*, and that entire episode, as gruesome as you might consider it, has some incredibly comforting lessons.

But you'll have to be a little patient until we reach Genesis 6. There is so much to unlock before then to put the Bible story in context and give its theological perspective.

Biblical Hebrew Roots Anchor Comprehension

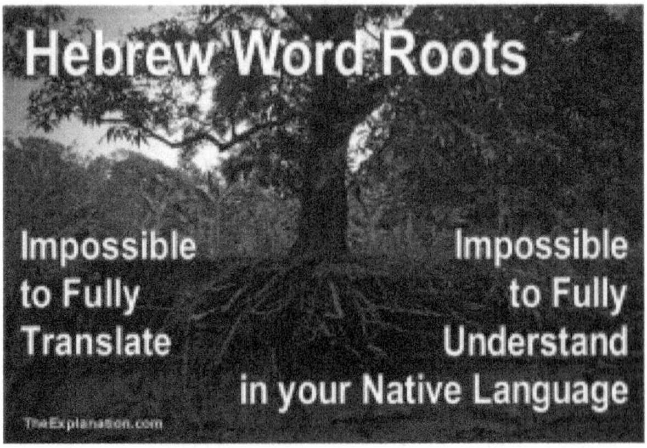

Roots are the writing base of the Bible.

Biblical Hebrew roots and Hebrew word stories are the final two keys of our series to master Biblical Hebrew. Both principles are basic, especially the latter. Most Bible readers are not aware of them. Even religious and theological (as differentiated from *intellectual*) Bible scholars are unaware of the most crucial seventh key.

6. Biblical Hebrew construction is based on Roots

Each biblical Hebrew word builds upon a *base*, a common denominator. Here's an English example of a family of words with a common thread: ocular, utrocular (I hadn't heard of that one either), monocle, monocular, binoculars, oculus, oculist. You might not know the meaning of all these words, but you can spot the common denominator: oculus–about the *eye*.

In English we practically never refer to the *common root* of words but, in Biblical Hebrew (and in modern Hebrew) we do. Roots are a fundamental key to understanding meanings and relationships.

The Hebrew Bible only contains about 8600 different words repeated over and over to compose the text. These 8600 words develop from approximately 2000 roots or fundamental building blocks like *oculus*. There's a root, a single trunk, from which other words branch out. Understanding this helps us grasp the relationships between words, some, even most, of which are not clear at first sight.

We've already seen examples of this with *rosh* (head, beginning) and *noah* (quiet, rest) as well as with *lechem* (eat, war). Every word in Biblical Hebrew is a root or the derivative of a root. It is impossible to see this in your native language where different unrelated translated words, like the three examples above: head/beginning, quiet/rest, and eat/war, cannot render full meaning when taken separately.

Another factor to do with the 2000 roots is that some of them are interrelated, further enhancing the relationships and meanings. I can't get into it here but, for those who know a little Hebrew, here's the transliteration of three words: *yashav*, *shevet*, *shoov*. Their underlying meanings include *sit*, *Sabbath,* and *return*. I say underlying meanings because, as we saw with *noah,* there are multiple native language translations for each of these three roots.

When you read any of these three words in your native language, there's absolutely no way of even knowing they have a common root, let alone realizing there's a definite relationship between those three concepts. I'll even say that for most scholars who read and study Biblical Hebrew, this relationship is unknown or not apparent.

For those not aware of this, the common denominator of *yashav*, *shevet*, and *shoov* comprises the two letters *shin* and *beth* (pronounced here as *vav*). It is impossible to see these roots and hence, these intricate and revealing relationships in any translation. I repeat, the native language translations of these words are correct. But they reveal a very limited amount of information. It is impossible to have a complete understanding.

If you reread the above points, you'll now realize that each Biblical Hebrew word: elohim, rosh, and noah is a root (rosh is the only one here) or a derivative of a root. The point is, you're seeing fundamental concepts in Biblical Hebrew that open up a complete understanding of this best-seller, the Bible. Whether or not you believe the Bible, it's full of words that will open up this literary marvel as never before.

I'll show you how to easily and quickly identify Biblical Hebrew word roots and find all the derivatives and their meanings. We'll be discussing this in the Hebrew course, and soon you'll be able to get a much more complete understanding of full Biblical Hebrew word meanings.

7. Biblical Hebrew Words tell Stories

Stories take us full circle back to point 1. The King James translators (and other translators for all different translated versions in all languages) ended up using MULTIPLE words in English to render ONE Biblical Hebrew word. The result is that sometimes we end up with a jumble of *foreign language* words that don't seem to make sense.

Somewhere, somehow, there's a relationship between them. I call that association of words a *story*. Yes, practically every word, and especially the roots, has a tale to tell. It is these accounts that unlock

Bible meaning. There's an exciting story behind shevet, noah, rosh, lechem, and hundreds of other words and roots.

Understand that we're not talking about *counting letters* or *hidden code* or *deciphering symbols* or anything of that nature. While I'm on the subject, when I refer to Hebrew roots, I am not referring to the *Hebrew Roots movement* which proposes a return to first-century Hebrew Roots Christianity. What I'm talking about here has nothing to do with these organizations and concepts with which I am not associated, in any way, shape, or form.

We're talking about Biblical Hebrew vocabulary and the dictionary meaning of words. Just like in your native language, if you don't understand a word, you take a dictionary and look it up. That's what we'll be doing. Looking at the meaning, the FULL meaning of Biblical Hebrew roots and words. It's this full meaning that is the word story.

I will say bluntly, you've never heard these stories before. Without these word stories, it is impossible to grasp a full understanding of what the A/author of what we call the Old Testament has in mind.

I'll conclude this section by bringing us back to another fundamental principle. As mentioned in point six, there's a relationship between the three roots *yashav, shevet, shoov;* they are interconnected, each telling its own story and each being a part of a larger story; this is what I call *coherent completeness.*

Well, coherent completeness goes much further than that: The 2000 roots are interconnected, not grammatically but figuratively. The 8600 Biblical Hebrew words are interconnected. In the end, I believe, they all tell ONE story. *Each Biblical Hebrew word is a puzzle piece.*

In *Inventory of the Universe* and *Audit of the Universe*, I turned over all the pieces that make up our physical and non-physical Universe. Turning them right-side-up, giving you an overview of what this Universe is all about and what state it's in right now. In *Origin of the Universe*, we're going to turn the Biblical Hebrew words of Genesis over, one by one. We're going to see their relationship with each other as well as their relationship with our Universe.

We're going to turn Biblical Hebrew words right-side-up and make *coherent completeness* out of all this information. The combined and interrelated stories of the Biblical Hebrew roots will tell us the story of our Universe. They will reveal to us the *Origin of the Universe*.

Bonus–The 8th Key: Active–Passive Verbs

Here's a quick example to illustrate this point: In English, we could say, "the teacher taught a course to the students or learners."

Think about what's happening here: a teacher is tutoring a subject, let's say math.

One person is *giving* the math, and the others are *receiving* the math. The first, the teacher, is the active element. The others, the learners, are the passive elements. In English, we use two separate words: *teach/learn* for the *active/passive*. In Hebrew we can use the same root with interspersed modifications, like vowels, to express this: *melamad* and *talmid*. The root being the three letters: *lamed*, *mem*, and *daled* (lmd).

One Biblical Hebrew root expresses both the active and the passive.

Once again, translations are a great introduction to begin to understand the Bible. But it is impossible to see the word roots and hence the various concrete and abstract, literal and figurative meanings as well as the word relationships and therefore their stories.

Translations are limited in their scope; this is something that Bible readers are not aware of and is one point that leads to incomplete comprehension.

In the course *7 keys to master Biblical Hebrew, a study method to Unlock Bible Meaning* I'll expand each one of these keys that I've evoked in this annex, by using real Biblical Hebrew word examples.

There'll be Biblical Hebrew word mysteries that you'll solve; I'll help you, using the freely accessible online Bible tools[1]. But, the goal of this course is for YOU to ACQUIRE a STUDY METHOD so you can unlock Bible meaning yourself. All I want to do is help you study your Bible better.

Here's the challenge

Here's the first mystery you'll crack it's the first puzzle that I ran across in Biblical Hebrew some 30 years ago that helped me develop this master course to Unlock Bible Meaning applying Biblical Hebrew. Remember that we're not focusing on Biblical Hebrew per se, Biblical Hebrew is only a means to understand what the Bible is telling us.

In the book of Genesis, the Bible states that Adam and Eve were *naked* (Genesis 2:25, 3:1), in the following verse it shows the serpent was *subtil* (old King James English spelling where we'd put *subtle*). The *mystery* is that in Biblical Hebrew, both these words are practically identical (I'd even say identical and I'll explain why during the course) and come from the same root (aram). You can use the Interlinear Bible at UnlockBibleMeaning.com[2] to verify this.

---

1. http://www.unlockbiblemeaning.com/

2. https://unlockbiblemeaning.com/

The question is, what's the full story being told by this word and its use in this context in Genesis immediately after the Creation story. Again, I repeat, whether or not you believe the Creation story, it doesn't change the way this story was recorded; however, long ago it was written.

When you solve this mystery, which we'll do during the first lessons of the course, you'll have an answer to one of the most asked worldwide questions about today's society. I guarantee you'll be amazed. But at least as important as the answer is the Bible study method you'll begin to incorporate for your ongoing studies.

Enroll in this course here and solve the mystery of naked and subtil[3]. Very revealing.

3. https://theexplanation.com/course/unlock-bible-meaning-with-7-keys-to-master-biblical-hebrew/

www.TheExplanation.com

Join The Explanation Newsletter[4] ... no spam, total privacy

Sam's latest blog post notifications and information about

The Explanation.

4. https://mailchi.mp/theexplanation.com/7keystomasterbiblicalhebrew

Don't miss out!

Visit the website below and you can sign up to receive emails whenever Sam Kneller publishes a new book. There's no charge and no obligation.

https://books2read.com/r/B-A-GZZJ-GFANB

BOOKS 2 READ

Connecting independent readers to independent writers.

Also by Sam Kneller

The Explanation
Inventory of the Universe
Audit of the Universe
Audit of Humankind
Origin of the Universe
Origin of Humankind
Origin of Woman
Agony of Humankind and the Antidote

Standalone
Evidence for Bible Wisdom

Watch for more at https://www.TheExplanation.com.

About the Author

SAM KNELLER was born in London and has lived in the United Kingdom, South Africa, Spain, Canada, Israel, Belgium, and for the past forty years in France. After spending twenty-five years in the Christian ministry, Sam taught website creation at the American University in Paris.

He also worked as a technical writer and founded BonjourLaFrance.com, a successful site for travel and tourism in France. All the while delving into Biblical Hebrew and the Bible in preparation for this series of books about Genesis and God's Plan.

He is currently occupied with webmastering, studying, teaching, and writing his weekly blog TheExplanation.com

Read more at https://www.TheExplanation.com.

Printed in France by Amazon
Brétigny-sur-Orge, FR

32413141R00238